Signifying Woman

CONTESTATIONS

A series edited by

WILLIAM E. CONNOLLY

The Other Heidegger
by Fred Dallmayr

Political Theory and the Displacement of Politics
by Bonnie Honig

The Inner Ocean: Individualism and Democratic Culture
by George Kateb

The Anxiety of Freedom: Imagination and Individualist in Locke's Political Thought
by Uday Singh Mehta

Signifying Woman: Culture and Chaos in Rousseau, Burke, and Mill
by Linda M. G. Zerilli

Signifying Woman

Culture and Chaos in
Rousseau, Burke, and Mill

Linda M. G. Zerilli

Cornell University Press

Ithaca and London

First published 1994 by Cornell University Press.

Library of Congress Cataloging-in-Publication Data

Zerilli, Linda M. G. (Linda Marie-Gelsomina), 1956–
  Signifying woman : culture and chaos in Rousseau, Burke, and Mill / Linda M. G. Zerilli.
    p.   cm. — (Contestations)
  Includes bibliographical references and index.
  ISBN 0-8014-2958-7 (alk. paper). — ISBN 0-8014-8177-5 (pbk. : alk. paper)
  1. Feminist theory.   2. Feminist theory—Political aspects.   3. Political science—History.   4. Women in public life.   5. Rousseau, Jean-Jacques, 1712–1778.   6. Burke, Edmund, 1729–1797.   7. Mill, John Stuart, 1806–1873.
I. Title.   II. Series.
HQ1190.Z47   1994
305.42'.o1—dc20   93-31618

Printed in the United States of America

⊗ The paper in this book meets the minimum requirements of the American National Standard for Information Sciences— Permanence of Paper for Printed Library Materials, ANSI Z39.48-1984.

To my parents
Marie A. Zerilli and Armand F. Zerilli

Woman is field and pasture, but she is also Babylon.

—Simone de Beauvoir

. . . the outline of the signified thing vanishes.

—Julia Kristeva

Contents

Acknowledgments

Like all discursive productions, this book emerged through a dialogic interplay of multiple voices. I am deeply indebted to several people. To begin, I thank Zillah Eisenstein, from whom I learned about the fascinating world of feminist theory, and whose work has been an inspiration to me. I also express my gratitude to Paul Thomas and Michael Rogin, both of whom encouraged me to pursue nontraditional lines of argument and to take intellectual risks. They made graduate school the experience it ought to be—emotionally exhilarating and intellectually intoxicating. Hanna Pitkin's work on Machiavelli and gender served as my model for the kinds of readings that are possible in political theory.

To my colleagues at Rutgers University I owe a large measure of thanks. Stephen Bronner has been the kind of friend one needs when undertaking the seemingly endless task of rewriting a book manuscript. Benjamin Barber offered encouragement and valuable advice on various matters. And lively conversations with Gordon Schochet and Gerry Pomper have helped me to clarify some conceptual matters. To Susan Carroll and Cynthia Daniels I owe my sanity.

Several graduate students at Rutgers are dear to me as both friends and colleagues. Patrick Moloney read the entire manuscript and offered detailed comments. His help, support, and advice were invaluable. Wendy Gunther-Canada provided me with insights into Rousseau, and her work on Mary Wollstonecraft has helped me to think through eighteenth-century debates on gender. The students who participated in my seminars on French feminist theory and political theory—in particular, Deirdre Condit, Samantha Frost, Anne Manuel, Ed Angelina, Laurie Naranch, Loretta Serenekos, and Karen Zivi—generated a provocative debate about language and gender that helped me to refine the central theses in this book.

Special thanks to George Shulman, Sonia Kruks, and Mary Dietz, who read and commented on the manuscript. Amanda Zerilli gave advice on translation and comprehension matters in Rousseau. Kirstie McClure did the kind of close reading one associates with the ideal editor. She also spent many hours debating book titles, clarifying concepts, and keeping me entertained. Marcia Ian also provided intellectual support and comic relief. Bonnie Honig put an enormous amount of time and effort into this project, reading and rereading the entire manuscript. Her editorial advice pushed me to refine my line of argument, and her own work in this series inspired me to complicate my interpretive approach to political theory. William E. Connolly also deepened my understanding of political theory. His advice greatly enabled me to improve the manuscript, and his interest helped me to finish it.

I presented early versions of Chapters 2 and 3 at the American Political Science Association Conventions in 1987 and 1989. An earlier version of part of Chapter 3 was published in *The Eighteenth Century* 33, no. 1 (1992), copyright 1992 Texas Tech University Press. I am grateful for permission to use this material here. I am indebted to the Center for the Critical Analysis of Contemporary Culture at Rutgers University for providing me with a 1988–89 fellowship that enabled me to begin work on the manuscript. The Rutgers Research Council and The Walt Whitman Center for the Culture and the Politics of Democracy at Rutgers provided research funds to complete revision of the book.

Roger Haydon at Cornell University Press contributed his enthusiasm and was extremely helpful and cooperative. Thanks too to Kay Scheuer and Joanne Hindman at the Press, and to John Thomas for his excellent copyediting. I also thank Christine Di Stefano, who was kind enough to share her work on Mill before the publication of her book *Configurations of Masculinity*.

Connie Cowart Murray, Laurie Naranch, and Rebecca (Claire) Snyder worked tirelessly as research assistants. They tracked down documents, checked references, and offered valuable editorial advice. Thanks to Paul Babbitt and especially B. Kiki Jamieson for their help with the index.

Finally I thank my friend, Katherine Grayson, and family—Marie Zerilli and Armand Zerilli, Amanda Zerilli and William Skipper, Jeffrey Zerilli and Stephanie Zerilli—for putting up with me over the years and for loving me. Thanks also to my family in Germany—Hilda, Wilfried, Mauritia, and Alexandra Gnädig—for their love and understanding. To Gregor Gnädig I owe the most. He discussed, debated, supported, and survived "the book"; he also reminded me that there is a world beyond it.

L.M.G.Z.

Princeton, New Jersey

Signifying Woman

CHAPTER ONE

Political Theory as
a Signifying Practice

Political theory has been a heroic business, snatching us from the abyss a vocation worthy of giants.

—Norman Jacobson

Woman, the other-from-man . . . is the term that designates at once the vanishing point of our culture's fictions of itself and the condition of the discourses in which the fictions are represented.

—Teresa de Lauretis

For some time now feminists have been rereading the canonical texts of political theory with an eye to mapping the connections between representations of gender and representations of the political.[1] Citizen man, many have argued, is not a generic but a gendered category to which woman cannot be added because it is constructed precisely through her exclusion.[2] Notwithstanding significant differences among political theorists, it appears that most have cast woman as a perennial outsider to public life, and as a disruptive outsider at that—one whose disorderly nature places her at odds with the civic community. Indeed woman—and I use that term here in accordance with its usage in the Western tradition and in distinction to the social beings called women—occupies a place in the historical discourse of political theory akin to that of the foreigner. She is the radical social other against whom theorists define men as citizens; she is also the radical sexual other against whom they define men as men.[3] Woman is the term, at once familiar and alien, known and unknown, that I consider anew in this book.

In traditional political theory, woman has been virtually syn-
onymous with the social disorder that calls for masculinist strategies
of containment such as the domestication of women and their banish-
ment from public life. My own approach to the concept takes as a
departure point feminist analyses of the cultural constitution of
woman as the ground of representation and as a signifier of the logic
of difference, sexual and political. I ponder the extent to which
woman is both the condition and the vanishing point of canonical
political theory. To put it somewhat differently and more specifically, I complicate feminist readings of woman as the perennial
outsider by showing that, in the modern texts of Jean-Jacques Rousseau, Edmund Burke, and John Stuart Mill, woman is neither outside the margins nor at the margins of the political; instead, she
constitutes and unsettles those margins. A frontier figure that is
neither wholly inside nor wholly outside political space, woman is
elusive, sometimes reassuring, yet also quite dangerous. She signifies
both culture and chaos—one can never be sure which. In the ambiguity, however, lie her symbolic power for the political theorist and
the possibility of a feminist criticism.

Indeed, like every other term of political discourse, woman is
fraught with ambiguity. Despite essentialist appearances to the contrary, woman is an "essentially contested concept,"[4] one that is
always subject to the interrogation of new generations of readers.
Woman is not an embodied social referent or extralinguistic entity to
be discovered or re-presented, whether truly or falsely; she is rather a
cipher, a series of absences to be filled, spaces to be organized,
protean energies to be harnessed. Political theory invests her with a
remarkable if threatening symbolic mobility. Woman is not a being
but a signification—wholly arbitrary and fundamentally unstable
because dependent for its meaning on the relational structure of
language. She is a complex, discursive site of sociosymbolic stabilization and destabilization, a site of cultural meanings that are constructed and contested across a wide range of signifying practices,
including that of political theory.

What does it mean to treat political theory as a signifying practice
and woman as a signification? How does this interpretive approach,
influenced by post-Saussurean linguistics, square with that of such

commentators as Norman Jacobson, Sheldon Wolin, and Judith Shklar, all of whom have long emphasized the rhetorical structures and figurative dimensions—in a word, the literariness—of political theory?[5] How does it square with feminist critiques of the Western tradition which hold the figure of woman to be a discursive construction, a masculinist one to be treated with extreme caution?

In posing these questions this way I map out a network of strategic alliances in order to put the referential model of language (i.e., language as re-presentation) into question and to reveal the workings and human costs of political theory's discursive mode of naturalization, especially its naturalization of sexual difference. I open a conceptual space for a feminist intervention into canonical political theory in which to explore the semiotics of gender and politics. In this space I invite the reader to consider these (among other, yet to be enumerated) interpretive possibilities: (1) to analyze a text is to ask not *what* does it signify but *how* does it signify, that is, to question the figuration rather than the re-presentation of objects, including woman and the political;[6] (2) the theorist employs the symbolic resources of language to generate rather than simply communicate political meanings; (3) these meanings are produced through the play of linguistic signs that are perfectly arbitrary and intrinsically unstable; (4) this instability of language is related to the fundamentally unsettled character of politics *as a realm of speech* and of the citizen *as a speaking being*; and (5) the theorist refuses this arbitrariness and dissonance in language and politics, figures it as the disorderly and disordering woman, and seeks to contain her, which is to say as well language and politics, with proper femininity.[7]

Following Ferdinand de Saussure's account of language, I treat the political theory text as composed of "differences with no positive terms."[8] To think about language in this way—as articulation rather than representation, as defined by the principle of difference rather than identity[9]—is to recognize, for example, that the term "woman" has no meaning apart from the term "man," that both derive their meaning from the differences between them and, what is more, those between them and all other terms.[10] Man and woman emerge through the process of signification, as the effect of the play of innumerable differences. They are unstable since, to paraphrase

Saussure, the most precise characteristic of each resides in being what all other terms are not.

Although most feminist political theorists neither adopt the parlance of post-Saussurean linguistics nor emphasize the fundamental instability of the sign, they do intimate their understanding of the differential relations of language when they argue that woman cannot be added to the political theory category of the citizen.[11] Although feminists rightly call our attention to the constructed meanings of woman within the canonical texts, they do not challenge as forcefully as they might the notion that theorists do little more than ascribe political significance to a sexual difference that is assumed to be produced elsewhere, that is, wholly outside the signifying structures of political theory texts themselves. Political theorists do not invent, needless to say, the meaning of woman (any more than they invent that of any other concept, be it man, rights, power, or consent). Yet they do code the term "woman" in ways that not only contribute to (rather than simply mirror) the historical articulation of sexual difference but also, and at the same time, subtend or service more particularized theoretical interventions into highly charged discursive arenas of political contestation.

Rather than treat woman either as an embodied social referent or as a term whose meaning preexists its figuration, narrative invocation, and circulation in the political text, I examine woman as she is produced symbolically and deployed rhetorically in theoretical interventions in historical debates about the crisis in political meaning. It is this crisis, as Jacobson tells us, that provokes the theorist to write, to take up his pen in an effort to fashion political order out of what he deems to be political chaos.[12] But if the theorist responds to a critical state of human affairs, says Jacobson, he also names the problem and in naming attempts to define it and what his readers are to do about it. Political theory appears to describe "things as they are," but it actually constitutes meaning and is emphatically performative: it uses language to determine what shall count as a matter for political concern and debate; it uses tropes and figures to bring about certain effects in the reader. The theorist puts diegesis in the service of the illusion of mimesis. He weaves a story out of historical events that only appear to have an intrinsic meaning (tragic or comical, calamitous or propitious) in his account apart from the specific significance that his own rhetoric gives to them.[13] Constructing a narrative landscape loaded with all manner of perils and inflected with the urgency of his authorial voice, the theorist, as Jacobson so astutely observes, names (or thereby constitutes) our dread, then offers us solace.[14] In the texts I examine, anxiety and its resolution are indeed inscribed in rhetorical productions—the dread goes under the name of the disorderly woman, the solace under proper femininity.

Why should dread be figured as the disorderly woman, solace as proper femininity? Approaching this question in Rousseau, Burke, and Mill, I try to show, in each case, that the theorist's articulation of the crisis in political meaning is to a large extent an articulation of the crisis in the meaning of woman, and that the stabilization of the former turns on that of the latter. Femininity, in their texts, is no essence but a form of political artifice or "solace"—not unlike a Leviathan, a Prince, or a social contract. Each deploys woman to halt the play of signifiers that characterizes language and that the theorist associates with a vertiginous state of social and political affairs. The theorist's effort to fix the meaning of woman evinces his anxiety-ridden recognition that the term itself is wholly conventional, fundamentally unstable, and yet somehow the ground of political meanings; it evinces the extent to which the figuration of woman is bound up with that of the political.[15]

Fueling and mocking the political theorist's anxious attempt to stabilize the meaning of woman and thus of politics and even language itself are those women who revel in subverting the term that marks them as man's sexual other, those who take pleasure in "the abuse of words."[16] In the chapters that follow I take account of the historical context of representation and show that the theorist's concern about the inversion or confusion of social relations is in part a response to the social practices of women who defied dominant cultural notions of femininity or the particular theorist's ideal of woman. Central to my argument is a sustained analysis of woman in political theory as a signifier not only of sexual difference but also of class difference, not only gender disorder but also class disorder. The theorist never responds simply to women who step out of woman's proper place; he responds rather to women who, in doing so, throw into confusion the social relations of both gender and class. What appears as the recurring, timeless political theory refrain about the disorder of women, in other words, is always articulated on and through the theorist's intervention into specific historical debates about sexuality and class.

My primary objective in this study, then, is to focus on the symbolic dimension of a diverse group of modern political theory texts and to explore their figuration and discursive uses of woman. I do not think, however, that various versions of the disorderly and disordering woman can be contested adequately by pointing to their patent absurdity, by exposing their logical contradictions, or by highlighting their rhetorical function in justifying the exclusion of women— or, in the case of Mill, some women—from public life.[17] For one thing, the meaning of woman, like all other terms of political discourse, is produced by not only the power of logic or argument but also that of metaphor.[18] And, if such critics as Paul de Man and Michèle Le Doeuff are right in claiming that even the most logically rigorous of philosophical texts are permeated by metaphorical language, there can be no such thing as a substratum of argument in any discourse which escapes figuration.[19] Rather, every argument is constructed through and dependent on the very tropes it may eschew as an obstacle to truth.

But there is another reason why feminists do well not to dismiss competing figures of woman as so much illogic: textual contradictions do not necessarily diminish the power of tropes to generate the symbolic space of political meaning. If there are figurative aspects to the canonical texts which, according to Shklar, cannot be evaluated simply in terms of "their legitimacy or validity or their grammatical correctness," then we need a somewhat different critical strategy than that pursued by most feminist political theorists.[20] It is important but not enough to expose the logical flaws in, as well as the ideological character of, arguments about woman and to show how they foreclose the facile solution of adding women to the category of the citizen.[21] That the disorderly and disordering woman is cast in a symbolic role in a political theory that is all out of proportion to what historians have told us about women's actual political power, moreover, suggests that there is a significant linkage between what is socially peripheral and what is symbolically central.[22] We therefore need an interpretive approach that attends to those symbolic meanings of woman that may not reflect women's social status or cohere into anything like a sustained argument about politics.

Taking as my working hypothesis Shklar's claim that "what is said cannot be separated from how it is expressed," I examine woman in accordance with the study of rhetoric as a means of figuration and persuasion.[23] Because they attend to how texts signify as well as to what they signify, such commentators as Shklar, Jacobson, and Wolin help dispute, however unwittingly, the referential model of language and, in their best moments, even show the mutual imbrication of the what and the how of signification in the production of sociosymbolic meaning. They thus help open a space in which to expose political theory as a signifying practice that takes and passes itself off as a mode of representation, effaces the constitutive character of its own language, and thereby also occludes its own rhetorical production of woman as bearer of culture and chaos.

I depart from Shklar, Jacobson, and Wolin, however, by showing that language, as Mikhail Bakhtin holds, always means more than one wants it to mean, and that, therefore, the theorist is not its master.[24] The familiar scholarly image of the theorist as the heroic spokesman for the good society (or even Jacobson's image of him as a dangerous mythmaker) too often assumes that the theorist stands above the disorder he purports to describe and is a master of the signifying structures he employs. I take it as axiomatic that no writer has that kind of distance on social events and control over language. It is not only that the theorist has no final say over how his texts will be or ought to be interpreted but also that, to invert Shklar's point above, how something is expressed is not always in a direct relation of semantic coincidence to what is said.

What cannot be explained by the study of rhetoric is a recurring figure we find in the otherwise diverse political tracts of Rousseau, Burke, and Mill: the figure—if figure it can be called—of the abyss. The abyss cannot be adequately accounted for as one of many rhetorical devices employed consciously by the theorist to symbolize the perils of political conflict or to instill fear in his readers. Almost always associated with the disorderly qua sexualized woman, the abyss resists modes of interpretation that seek either to refer it back to some notion of authorial intention or, even less persuasive, to explain it as an expression of the theorist's "personal" anxiety about female sexuality. Something else is at work in such imagery, something that calls for an interpretive strategy that goes beyond the study of rhetoric as a means of persuasion, on the one hand, and beyond psychobiographical accounts of political theory, on the other.

In the texts of Rousseau, Burke, and Mill, the abyss marks the place where rhetoric, so to speak, collapses. It is the site of a failure of meaning, or rather of the moment when language can no longer signify a sociosymbolic crisis. There is a profound sense in the texts I examine that signification itself is out of control; a threatening but nevertheless symbolizable topsy-turvy world of class conflict and gender inversion gives way, in a kind of accelerating disintegration of social and sexual categories of difference, to a frightful mingling of classes and genders, and, with it, to a virtual collapse in the value of property or money. The abyss is most often associated with a semiotic chaos, and woman nearly always figures the abyss. Beyond the law, she beckons men into the void where political meaning, even symbolic meaning itself, vanishes. Woman becomes a marker and a scapegoat for the utter failure of meaning, for sociosymbolic bedlam.

To explain why that is so and why political theorists should attend to it, I draw on the insights of Julia Kristeva, a contemporary French feminist theorist who works on language from within the theoretical traditions of post-Saussurean linguistics and Freudian psychoanalysis. I invoke Kristeva not to argue for a psychobiographical reading of Rousseau, Burke, or Mill but rather to think through the complex act of writing a political theory, to reflect on the status of woman as the borderline generally of the symbolic order and specifically of political space, and to interpret the curious image of the abyss. I elaborate the different strands of Kristeva's theory of signification in the chapters that follow, but at this point it is useful to explicate the broad outlines of her argument and suggest why I find it useful for reading political theory texts. Advancing an approach to language that contests formalism, Kristeva invites a textured and, to some extent, historical consideration of political theory as a signifying practice.

Arguing that scapegoating is precipitated by the refusal to recognize the strangeness in the self or the fundamentally split character of subjectivity, Kristeva helps us to understand the social, linguistic, and psychic mechanisms that produce woman as a scapegoat in political texts.

Turning away from Saussure's focus on langue (universal rules of grammar and syntax) and toward what he called parole (the speech act in social context), Kristeva develops "a theory of meaning which must necessarily be a theory of the speaking subject."[25] She takes up Bakhtin's "dialogic" theory of language, which isolates the utterance and shows that it is oriented toward another, be it one's outer or inner addressee.[26] Bakhtin examined "the 'word',", writes Kristeva, "as a territory in which instances of discourse confront each other, 'I's' which speak. 'Dialogic' is the term which indicates that the discourse belongs doubly to an 'I' and to the other, that Spaltung of the speaker which psychoanalysis was to establish with scientific caution."[27] Refuting the idea of a single unitary language and emphasizing the polysemous, multivoiced character of languages, Bakhtin thus showed that the subject does not conform its speech to an abstract, universal set of grammatical rules, and that it splits in two—entering into a dialogue with an other that may be none other than itself.

Bakhtin revealed language to be the heterogeneous site of multiple meanings in, among other things, his account of the carnival—a topsy-turvy world characterized by hybridization and intermixture, defilement and degradation, excess and play.[28] The speech of the carnival is tied for Bakhtin to the body, and specifically to its grotesque and transgressive features. The language of the body, as Kristeva puts it, is also that of "the poetic word, polyvalent and multi-determined, [which] adheres to a logic exceeding that of codified discourse and fully comes into being only in the margins of recognized culture."[29]

Kristeva takes up Bakhtin's accounts of the carnival and of dialogism to argue for a speaking subject that is split into two voices. On her account, though, language is dialogic in the psychoanalytic sense: in language unconscious drives make themselves felt. Kristeva wishes to explain those elements of poetic language that exceed communicative meaning by looking closely at that which is repressed on the subject's entry into language proper. She employs Freudian psychoanalysis, especially as it is elaborated by Jacques Lacan, to argue for "two modalities of . . . the same signifying process": the semiotic and the symbolic.[30] Whereas the latter refers to the rules of grammar and syntax to which the individual speaker must conform to speak and be understood, the former refers to the complex of infantile bodily drives and pregenital sexuality that push against rational discourse without dissolving it into nonsense. The symbolic is associated with the law and name of the father, that is, with the incest taboo and the general prohibition on the child's relation to the maternal body. The semiotic preserves the traces of this repression and introduces a "wandering or fuzziness into language," "that which escapes Bedeutung."[31]

Arguing that meaning is always composed of both symbolic and semiotic elements, Kristeva explores the unfinished character of the subjective experience of primal separation which structures and subverts the series of distinctions and oppositions (e.g., masculine/feminine, nature/culture) that organize language and society.[32] In *Powers of Horror*, Kristeva advances her theory of "abjection" to account for the instability of the speaking subject, for the scapegoating of women that characterizes Western culture, and for writing as a rite that works to maintain the boundaries between self and mother. Abjection, she argues, is a "demarcating imperative" that guards against whatever threatens the subject, especially the masculine subject, with maternal reengulfment; it is that which is cast off or rejected as "being opposed to I."[33] Although abjection is originally a preoedipal affair that establishes the very first difference between the infant and the mother, the abject continues to menace the speaking subject because the initial act of casting out or off the mother is never accomplished with any certainty or finality:

We may call it a border; abjection is above all ambiguity. Because, while releasing a hold, it does not radically cut off the subject from what threatens it—on the contrary, abjection acknowledges it to be in perpetual danger. But also because abjection itself is a composite of judgement and affect, of condemnation and yearning, of signs and drives. Abjection preserves what existed in the archaism of preobjectal relationship, in the immemorial violence with which a body becomes separated from another body in order to be—maintaining that night in which the outline of the signified thing vanishes and where only the imponderable affect is carried out.[34]

Confronted with the abject, the I is confronted with "a massive and sudden emergence of uncanniness," with something which, as Freud observed, is experienced as being at once familiar and alien, known and unknown—the archaic and unsignifiable relation to the maternal body.[35] "What is abject," writes Kristeva, draws the subject "toward the place where meaning collapses." It is "what disturbs identity, system, order. What does not respect borders, positions, rules." The subject tries to master or keep at bay the abject with linguistic signs which—like the defilement rites that keep the difference between the pure and the impure, the clean and the unclean, the sacred and the profane—"parcel out, demarcate, delineate an order, a framework, a sociality." Inasmuch as writing also "causes the subject who ventures into it to confront an archaic authority on the nether side of the proper Name," however, this subject finds itself—both despite and because of writing—on the brink of the abyss, where the signified thing vanishes.[36]

Kristeva's theory of abjection as a complex and recurring cultural process helps explain the association of woman with what exceeds meaning proper, with what menaces the political theorist as writing subject, and, not least, with the image of the abyss. Her work permits a contestation of the idea that woman's *nature* is disorderly inasmuch as it shows that woman, by being coded as maternal within a patriarchal culture, is coded as being that which at once upholds and threatens social, symbolic, and psychic borders. That coding, however, is itself unthinkable in the absence of some analysis of signification. And, as the recent work of Christine Di Stefano, Tamasin Lorraine, and Carole Pateman has shown, that coding cannot be (re)read without attending to the production of that ambiguous achievement that goes under the name of masculinity.[37]

Kristeva's work bears as well on the very act of writing a political text and has the advantage of theorizing a "writing subject" that is neither "a phenomenological transcendental ego nor the Cartesian ego but rather a subject in process/on trial [*sujet en proces*]." The text too is a work in process/on trial: "In the practice of the text, deep structures or at least transformational rules are disturbed and, with them, the possibility of semantic and/or grammatical categorial interpretation."[38] Departing from the traditional study of rhetoric, Kristeva seeks to locate the places in a text where meaning is revealed to be what all meaning is, namely, unstable because at bottom constructed negatively and produced by a split subject. In contrast to those who focus on the realization of author intentions in language, she takes into account both the consciousness and the unconsciousness of writing subjects as they constitute themselves and are constituted within and through the symbolic meanings of the text. Her focus on the writing subject, rather than on the author as a historical personage, avoids the mistake made by those critics who thought they could psychoanalyze the writer by studying his or her biography and by interpreting his or her texts through the lens of what they had learned about the writer's life.[39] Thus Kristeva's theoretical object is not the life but the text—only the text.

My main quarrel with Kristeva concerns what appears to be her steady move away from the initial insights of Bakhtin, who stressed the importance of attending to the social context in which a text is produced,[40] and toward those of Freud, who focused almost exclusively on the subject, which he conceptualized in terms that permit little historical variability. Although I am persuaded that abjection underwrites and undercuts the subject as it is constituted in modern Western societies, I am skeptical of Kristeva's claim that one can dig beneath the layers of cultural specificity to reveal a "deep psychosymbolic economy" with universal features.[41] I am rather more concerned to explore the question, barely broached in *Powers of Horror*, of the sociohistorical manifestations of the demarcating imperative that is subjectively experienced as abjection. Thus, although I find Kristeva useful for explaining some aspects of the political text, I also insist on the need to complicate her psycholinguistic approach with an analysis of historically variegated meanings, paying particular attention to shifting conceptions of gender and class. One ought to guard against the universalizing gesture not only of structuralism but also of psychoanalysis. To do otherwise is to risk re-producing the very term one wishes to critique—woman.

Finally, let me say a word about the theorists whose texts I examine here. Rousseau, Burke, and Mill articulate republican, conservative, and liberal political theories. These categories are somewhat imprecise and, in fact, have been contested in the scholarly literature, but I take them as adequate for marking a broad range of political theories from which to consider the symbolic meanings of woman. Spanning, as these theorists do, the historical period from the early eighteenth to the late nineteenth century, their texts can be evaluated as part of a larger effort to develop a narrative about shifts in the meaning of woman within the distinctively modern era that begins with the Enlightenment. It is not my intention, then, to advance an argument that conflates the differences among theorists so as to insist on their similarities when it comes to woman—an ahistorical project I consider to be as futile as it is misguided. My aim, rather, is to show how these diverse theorists define and make discursive use of woman as they respond to various forms of social conflict and advance their distinct political visions.

I have chosen these three theorists as well because each *produces* woman as transgressive to service his larger argument about the crisis in political meaning. Complicating Kristeva's psycholinguistic approach, I argue that the trope of the disorderly woman is used in the political theory text not only to tame the unnameable abject but also to encode, to make sense of, social, cultural, and political change. Woman as the bearer of chaos is the familiar and known (if also the uncanny and unknown) figure invoked to symbolize the larger social, economic, and political forces that appear to each theorist to be increasingly outside the realm of human control and to threaten specific configurations of gender and class: these are (for Rousseau) the forces of civilization, (for Burke) of revolution, and (for Mill) of capitalism.

Unlike Rousseau, whose fervent complaint about the disorder of women is infamous though perhaps not fully understood, Burke and Mill might appear at first to be unlikely candidates for this study. Burke does not devote volumes to the "woman question" as Rousseau does, and what he does say often takes the form of hyperbole. It is for that very reason that he suits my investigation into the symbolic dimensions of a political theory. Burke's "French Revolution," as I refer to his representation of the complex historical event, both works and unravels precisely at those points where his texts collapse into an unbounded sensibility (most famous, perhaps, is the point at which he reports shedding tears on behalf of poor Marie Antoinette). Mill is of special interest to me because he supports women's citizenship and appears likewise to be the antithesis of Burke and Rousseau in his mode of address. Mill's reputation as a committed feminist and paradigmatic rationalist, however, must be squared with the class distinctions he draws between different kinds of women, distinctions that emerge in the context of his impassioned and not always logical account of the dangers of overpopulation—that is, with his Malthusianism. Although Mill is intensely critical of male power, his writings, like those of Rousseau and Burke, depict the uncontrolled female or, rather, the maternal body as a threat to property, civic community, and class harmony. That body, Mill argues, must be contained by the proper femininity he otherwise so powerfully condemns. It is in light of his standing as a feminist and a rationalist that Mill presents a particular challenge for the kinds of reading I advance.

There is yet another reason for my choices, and this one relates to the broader project undertaken in the following pages: the reframing of the so-called woman question in political theory such that the feminine object of its sincere, manly, and quite hysterical concern is read as a signifier rather than a signified, sign rather than referent. When woman is understood to be constituted in and by the discourse of a political theory—when she is understood as a signification that is produced by a split subject trying to maintain its fragile hold on the symbolic order, make sense of social change, and delimit the scope and character of politics—woman cuts across traditional interpretive divides. Conventional questions about each theorist's attitude toward women (is Rousseau a sexist? is Burke a paternalist? is Mill a feminist?)—miss the fact that these thinkers never get to *women*; they are too captivated by their struggle with *woman*. They are far too haunted by those aspects of the self, language, and politics which refuse to be settled, logicized, unified—in a word, called to order. Policing the borderlands of their own identities, fascinated with the very frontier figure who draws them toward the abyss, Rousseau, Burke, and Mill will come face to face with an unnameable otherness, irreducible difference. They will try to name it, contain it; to repel it, expel it. They will not succeed. But they will code it *woman*.

CHAPTER TWO

"Une Maitresse Imperieuse":
Woman in Rousseau's Semiotic Republic

Nature's most charming object, the one most able to touch a sensitive heart and to lead it to the good, is, I admit, an agreeable and virtuous woman. But where is this celestial object hiding itself? Is it not cruel to contemplate it with so much pleasure in the theatre, only to find such a different sort in society?

—*Letter to D'Alembert*

To quest for the celestial object, to unmask its earthly referent, such was the task for the writer whose texts bear the manly signature "Jean-Jacques Rousseau, citizen of Geneva." The former he found in the imaginary world of reverie, the latter everywhere else, and above all in the theater—representational site of the unauthentic, performative site of female power. Indeed, for Rousseau the theater is a woman in masquerade, a cunning coquette who courts the look of a captive male audience bewitched by the spectacle of female self-display. Thus fixated on the simulacrum of womanly virtue, thus beguiled by a "counterfeited sweetness," men are lured away from their civic duties and toward that other sort of woman in society: the disorderly and disordering woman who is without modesty, utterly without shame, and whose illicit desire for mastery confounds the natural order of an active masculinity and a passive femininity.

The theater is a female space in which nothing is as it seems, a topsy-turvy world of disguise and deception presided over by "the sex that ought to obey."[1] And yet gender inversion on the stage, says Rousseau, is but a dramatic rendering of the everyday scene of the salon, where a similar overvaluation of the feminine object translates into a counter-spectacle in which it is the man who masquerades, the

man who plays to the female gaze, the man who loses his "constitution" by "amusing women."

> Every woman at Paris gathers in her apartment a harem of men
> more womanish than she. . . . But observe these same men, always
> constrained in these *voluntary prisons*, get up, sit down, pace con-
> tinually back and forth to the fireplace, to the window, pick up and
> set down a fan a hundred times, leaf through books, glance at pic-
> tures, turn and pirouette about the room, while the idol, stretched
> out motionlessly on her couch, has only her eyes and her tongue
> active.[2]

In the very next sentence, Rousseau contains this "perversion of
natural relations" by reading his own representation of counterfeit
masculinity as clear evidence of the gallant's "restlessness," of his
rustic virility in revolt against the "sedentary and homebound life"
that nature imposes on woman, and that woman then imposes on
man. The natural man is still discernable under the vile ornaments of
the courtier, says the Genevan, still visible under the feminine artifice of our vaunted urbanity. This is the citizen who refuses the
command of a female idol and heeds only the call of Mother Nature.
Not content to be passive and beautiful, he wants to be active and
useful. Perhaps. Then again—the phrase "voluntary prisons" suggests an alternative meaning: the male voyeur in the female space of
the theater shares with the exhibitionist in that of the salon a "feminine" passivity and even subservience all the more terrifying to the
extent that it is not in fact refused but rather desired.

That men might take no little pleasure in gender inversion and in
submission to a dominatrix was the remarkable psychological insight
of a theorist who confessed his own mixed delight in self-display, not
to mention his "strange taste" in erotic fantasy: "To fall on my knees
before a masterful mistress, to obey her commands, to have to beg
for her forgiveness, have been to me the most delicate of pleasures."
Could it be that, just as the autobiographer "was preserved by that
very perversity which," as he says, "might have been my undoing,"[3]
a crime against nature that gave rise to the godsend of his sexual
temerity with women and his overactive imagination, so too might

the man or the citizen be saved by keeping him on his knees before the one who gives the law in love? But saved from what? From women, it would seem. On his knees before whom? Not before women but before woman: that celestial object, that magnificent fetish, the imperious and mute woman of the male imaginary who protects man against that other sort of woman and all her sex, against the speaking woman of the theater and the salon, but also, indeed especially, against that uncanny other woman in himself.

Exploring the possibility that it is not fidelity to nature but a crime against nature, a perverse desire, that emerges as the central issue in Rousseau's political theory, I should at once highlight his challenge to the binarism of masculinity and femininity and his quick retreat into a rigid conception of sexual difference. What Rousseau teaches and fears is that natural man and woman are pedagogical constructions and highly unstable ones at that. There is a profound sense in his writings that gender boundaries must be carefully fabricated and maintained because they have no solid foundation in nature, because what announces "man" or "woman" is not anatomical difference but instead an arbitrary system of signs that stands in permanent danger of collapsing into a frightening ambiguity of meaning and a loss of manly constitution.[4] For what haunts the writer Rousseau above all else is the similitude of his sexual other, his dread of becoming woman—his own terrible recognition that, to borrow Shoshana Felman's words, "femininity inhabits masculinity, inhabits it as otherness, as its own disruption."[5]

Rousseau's repeated and familiar warnings against the "disorder of women" evince his fear that, if the code of gender difference is not strictly adhered to at each and every moment, all is lost.[6] There will not be any citizens because there will not be any men. Contesting the critical consensus that Rousseau presents us with the choice of making either a man or a citizen (since one cannot make both at once), I show that to be the latter one must, in the first place, be the former, and that to be a man is to be no more a product of nature than is to be a citizen to be a "denatured" man.[7] To represent themselves as members of the republic, men must first contract to represent themselves as members of their own sex. They must renounce the elegant discourse and elaborate dress of the demimonde, those signifiers of class privilege and counterfeit masculinity. The social contract, it turns out, is a linguistic and sartorial contract, an agreement about the proper symbolic forms of communication among citizens. Simple attire and direct speech are to function as outward signs of men's devotion to each other and to the universalistic principles of the patrie.

Excluded from the social contract, of course, is woman. But her absence is the foundation of the social pact. For woman is the "scapegoat," in Kristeva's words, "charged with the evil of which the community duly constituted can then purge itself."[8] Even as the trope of the disorderly woman carries powerful rhetorical effects that lend urgency to Rousseau's case for the contract, the figure who leads mankind into the abyss, I argue, is a scapegoat precipitated by the disorder in men: that feminine other within the citizen-subject who, despite his almost phobic avoidance of woman, "will always be marked by the uncertainty of his borders and of his affective valency as well."[9]

The Maternal Voice

There is something curious about the frontispiece to the *Discourse on the Origin and Foundations of Inequality among Men*. The image is of a Hottentot male, scantily dressed, carrying a large cutlass at his side and wearing a long V-shaped necklace. Beneath it stand the words "He goes back to his equals."[10] The Hottentot is departing, as Rousseau explains in a note to the reader, from the Dutch missionaries who had raised him at the Cape of Good Hope as a Christian and in the practice of European customs. "He was richly dressed, he was taught several languages." Then comes the day when, while visiting Hottentot relatives, he makes "the decision to divest himself of his European finery in order to clothe himself in a sheepskin." He returns to the mission, hands over to the governor of the Cape a bundle that contains the vile artifice of his past and makes this speech: "Be so kind, sir, as to understand that I renounce this paraphernalia forever. . . . The sole favor I ask of you is to *let me keep the necklace and cutlass* I am wearing; I shall keep them *for love of you*" (my emphasis). To which Rousseau adds, the civil-savage awaited no reply but immediately ran away and "was never seen again at the Cape" (225–226).

Why does the Hottentot, having seen the truth of his degenerate civil existence, nevertheless retain the necklace and the cutlass? Why does he not hand over the whole paraphernalia to those effeminate Europeans from whom it came? And why does this parable introduce the *Discourse on Inequality*? The answers to these queries may be found in the words, "I shall keep them for love of you." Before I elaborate further, we must wander a bit in the woods with the author Rousseau.

To enter the pure state of nature one must set "all the facts aside" (103). Evoking an Edenic space-time where man was "without speech" and "remained ever a child" (137), the *Discourse on Inequality* takes the reader on a fully imaginative journey in search of man's primordial condition, the "first embryo of the species" (104)—which I take to be the preoedipal. This narrative of origins is enacted largely through the Rousseauist fantasy of recovering the "gentle voice" of Mother Nature—a lost maternal voice that once spoke to savage hearts but now remains audible only to those who eschew the vain luxury and empty feminine chatter of the big city.[11]

Hearing the sweet maternal voice through himself, Rousseau confers on it the kind of affective value it has for the infant in what Kaja Silverman calls "the acoustic mirror": the "sonorous envelope" of the mother's voice which precedes the child's entry into the Lacanian "mirror stage" and later into the symbolic order of language.[12] The voice of "our common mother," as Rousseau hears it, preserves within itself the intrinsic value of origin, of the fundamental signified; it resonates with all the beauty, mystery, and vigor of the spoken word. The gentle voice leads back to a space-time of auditory pleasure, self-present speech. It also leads back to the womb of Nature herself.

"The philosophers who have examined the foundations of society have all felt the necessity of going back to the state of nature, but none of them has reached it" (102), declares Rousseau. Yet to seek self-knowledge there, as the *Discourse on the Sciences and Arts* warns, is to risk a "punishment for the arrogant attempts we have made to emerge from the happy ignorance in which eternal wisdom had placed us."

> The heavy veil with which she [Nature] covered all her operations seemed to warn us adequately that she did not destine us for vain studies. . . . Peoples, know once and for all that nature wanted to keep you from being harmed by knowledge just as a mother wrests a dangerous weapon from her child's hands; that all the secrets she hides from you are so many evils from which she protects you, and that the difficulty you find in educating yourselves is not the least of her benefits. *Men are perverse*; they would be even worse if they had the misfortune to be born learned.[13]

And so even good old Mother Nature must be part of the masquerade—the masquerade of femininity. She modestly hides "her operations" to protect man from fatal knowledge, from knowing her as Adam *knew* Eve.[14] Here the veil—that great Rousseauist metaphor, as Jean Starobinski argues, for whatever obstructs sincere human communication and, not least, for the machinations of female deceit—is not the hated obstacle to be overcome but rather the modest maternal screen to be respected.[15] The reasonable man, wrote Rousseau to M. de Franquieres, "stops short and does not touch the veil, content with the [veiled] knowledge that an immense Being lies underneath."[16] For the veil, as Rousseau intimates in a letter to Malesherbes, covers over the abyss where the subject and its signs vanish: "My mind lost in this immensity, I did not think, I did not reason, I did not philosophize." Still, he continues, where there is danger there is pleasure: "I felt with a sort of sensual pleasure overwhelmed with the weight of this universe."[17] Whence the temptation to transgress the original maternal law: "Men are perverse."[18]

Sufficiently screened, Nature becomes a magnificent absence. Contemplation of her is in the realm of the imagination where,[19] as Rousseau so often states in connection with a powerful feminine presence, one puts "imaginary goods in place of the real good,"[20] substitutes the sign/symbol for the thing/referent, Nature for nature—in a phrase, the idea of our common mother (the maternal ideal) for the unnameable mother-origin. Man's proper relation to Nature is at bottom the relation to obstacle: the imaginary good, the veiled woman/mother. The accursed veil is indeed an obstacle but a necessary one; if man removes it, as I have numerous occasions to show, he falls into the abyss.

It is the abyss of signification. Having transgressed the maternal law, savage man was cast out of paradise and compelled to speak, to make a presence of absence. The section on the origin of languages in the *Discourse on Inequality*, which appears at first to be tangential to Rousseau's narrative, is in fact absolutely crucial to his secular tale of the Fall. "May I be allowed to consider for an instant the obstacles to the origin of languages." In question, says Rousseau, is whether "a kind of society [was] already established among the inventors of language" (120). Once again, the philosophers have not gone back far enough and, consequently, they have grafted onto nature what can only be the product of culture. The invention of language was unnecessary at best, useless at worst; it contributed "little . . . to everything men have done to establish social bonds" (126). In the *Essay on the Origin of Languages*, Rousseau goes so far as to imagine that whole societies could have arisen, not very different from those now in existence (but better of course), in which not a word would have been spoken.[21]

At the very least, argues Rousseau, there must have been an "immense distance . . . between the pure state of nature and the need for languages" (121). The *Essay* tells us that even in nascent society or the "age of patriarchs" (composed of isolated families) men spoke in signs (visible objects and gestures) rather than words: "They did not say it, they showed it." Addressed to the eyes, this language was vigorous, unmediated, transparent. "The Sign has said everything before a single word is spoken."[22] In the absence of conventional languages and interfamilial ties, moreover, men "were not bound by any idea of common brotherhood." They had neither the word for nor the idea of it; they could not even distinguish the animal from the human. "Since they had never seen anything other than what was around them, they did not know even that; they did not know themselves. They had the idea of a Father, a son, a brother, but not of a man. Their hut held all those who were like themselves; a stranger, an animal, a monster were all the same to them: outside of themselves and their family, the whole universe was naught to them."[23] If the first men had no idea of a man, they must not have had any idea of a woman either. But did they have an idea of a mother, a daughter, or a sister? And are any of these ideas conceivable in the absence of those of man and woman, of a sociosymbolic sexual difference?

To admit such cultural difference into the putatively biological family would be tantamount to admitting that the social is always already present in the natural; that the very ideas of father, son, and brother exist only in relation to those of mother, daughter, and sister; and that both sets of ideas exist only in relation to the sociolinguistic categories of man and woman. It would be tantamount to admitting that language is the basis of subjectivity and that in language, as Saussure put it, "there are only differences with no positive terms."[24] Rousseau, in contrast, wants to preserve the unity of the subject and the integrity of the signified, both of whose disruption by the signifier amounts to a catastrophe for the fiction of a self-identical identity.[25] He wants to preserve in the sign the myth of origin that guarantees the myth of self-presence, the living presence of the speaker in "natural" language.

To hold off the introduction of the signifier whereby, among other disasters, nature becomes culture—simple sexual needs become dangerous amorous passions—Rousseau posits the isolated family as a presocial modality whose survival was guaranteed by a natural heterosexual instinct: "The distinction between the sexes appeared with age, natural inclinations sufficed to unite them, instinct served in lieu of passion, habit in lieu of predilection." Having said as much, Rousseau is then forced to concede that, in the absence of any interfamilial relations, each family "propagated itself from its own stock alone."[26] He is forced, in other words, to admit that the patriarchal age was one of incest.

That, at least, is what the reader of the *Essay on the Origin of Languages* discovers buried in an amazing footnote—amazing, as Jacques Derrida observes, because Rousseau never names incest but only infers it, and especially so because he never names the mother: "The first men had to marry their sisters." And if we turn to the passage that takes us to the footnote, we find that incest and the mother are not named there either: "[The first] people became man and wife without having ceased to be brother and sister."[27] The sexual relation to the mother remains the unthought, indeed the unthinkable, of the nonprohibition (the incest that would have been incest if it had been forbidden). If access to the mother was forbidden, then the opposition nature/culture cannot hold, for the taboo on incest, as Rousseau himself will show us, marks the birth of civil society. If it was not forbidden, then the Edenic myth of origin cannot hold, for that myth, we have seen, demands that the relation to the maternal origin be suspended, held at a distance by the veil. It is therefore better to leave the mother unnamed. Fortunately, says Rousseau, the age of the nonprohibition was quite orderly. Sexual relations among kin were a reproductive affair bereft of love, pleasure, and desire, a mute affair bereft of any linguistic exchange: "None of this was sufficiently lively to untie tongues."[28] Rousseau calls it a "golden age." But the happiest of times, it turns out, belongs to the somewhat later time of the festival: site of the exchange of words, the exchange of women.

The festival has its origins in Mother Nature but transcends her. It came into existence, Rousseau tells us, "in arid regions, where water could only be had from wells." Thus forced to join together "to dig them, or at least to agree about their use," families were compelled to become sociable. Thus drawn into a world of new objects, "the heart was moved by them and, swayed by an unfamiliar attraction." Around the fountain the sociosymbolic difference between man and woman arose and exogamy was instituted: "Here the first ties between families were established; here the first meetings between the sexes took place." A common language was born as young people found that their diverse domestic vernaculars were insufficient for making "themselves intelligible" to each other; the accented voice was born as they discovered that "an eager gesture no longer proved adequate" for expressing desire.[29]

In the festival, as Claude Lévi-Strauss argues and as the *Essay* confirms, exogamy and language have the same function: communication and integration with others.[30] To the extent that Rousseau views such sociability with immense ambivalence, the objects of exchange (i.e., women and words)—which are the very foundation of a "common brotherhood," of what Carole Pateman calls a fraternal "sexual contract"—symbolize a gain that is always a loss.[31] Still, even as the festival marks a mythic moment when natural man relinquishes his primitive freedom, it marks as well, says Lévi-Strauss, "that fleeting moment when it was permissible to believe that the law of exchange could be evaded, that one could gain without losing, enjoy without sharing." That is why the time, or rather the timelessness, of the festival is a "happy age" for Rousseau. Words are exchanged but they have not yet become the "common property," writes Lévi-Strauss, whereby their "signifying function has supplanted their character as values."[32] Language has not yet perfected itself to its detriment: as Rousseau puts it, that "natural progress [by which] all lettered languages must change character and lose vigor as they gain in clarity" must entropy into "the cold ministry of speech" and become instituted signs.[33]

It is above all in women, however, that the intrinsic value of origin is preserved, the value of the gentle voice of Mother Nature. "For women," as Catherine Clément interprets Lévi-Strauss, "are both sign and value, sign and producer of sign. We know this perfectly well: it happens that women talk, that they step out of their function as sign" (hence Rousseau's concerns about the female spaces of the theater and the salon). Ideally, Clément adds wryly, woman should "remain in childhood, in the original primitive state, to rescue human exchange from an imminent catastrophe owing to the progressive and inescapable entropy of language. . . . At least let women stay as they were in the beginning, talking little but causing men's talk—stay as guardians, because of their mystery, of all language."[34]

One must guard against an autonomous female speech as one must guard against the abuse of words, the misuse of signs, of women as signs. Women as signs are misused, says Lévi-Strauss, when they are not put to the reserved use of signs, which is to be communicated. That is why the prohibition against incest takes root in the festival.[35] For incest is a misuse of women as signs inasmuch as it keeps women out of the masculine economy of exchange.[36] But the festival that institutes the taboo also exceeds it: "Pleasure and desire merged into one and were felt together," writes Rousseau. In the post-patriarchal age (i.e., of brothers rather than fathers) the "first fires of love" sprung "from the pure crystal of the fountains."[37] Nothing will ever again approach that kind of boundless pleasure, of a purely imaginary *volupté*—that is, nothing short of the pleasure and danger that lie behind the veil. Indeed those "symbolic gratifications," says Lévi-Strauss, "in which the incest urge finds its expression . . . do not therefore commemorate an actual event. They are something else, and more, the permanent expression of a desire for disorder, or rather counter-order. Festivals turn social life topsy-turvy, not because it was once like this but because it has never been, and can never be, any different."[38]

The pleasures of the festival are cut short by the rule of law, the prohibition on incest. I return to the amazing footnote:

> The law that abolished it [this incestuous practice] is no less sacred for being by human institution. Those who view it solely in terms of the bond it established between families fail to see its most important aspect. In view of the intimacy between the sexes that inevitably attends upon domestic life, the moment such a *sacred law* ceased to speak to the heart and to awe the senses, men would cease to be upright, and the most frightful morals would soon cause the destruction of mankind.[39]

The absent presence in this passage is, once again, the unnamed mother. "This displacing of the relationship with the mother, with nature, with being as the fundamental signified," writes Derrida, "such indeed is the origin of society and languages." The mother is "the only represented, the only signified whose replacement by its signifier Rousseau prescribes, thus exalting the sanctity of the interdict."[40] But what Derrida calls the "dangerous supplement" (the signifier) is not nearly as menacing as what it (like Nature's "heavy veil") conceals: "The barely covered abyss," as Kristeva writes, "where our identities, images, and words run the risk of being engulfed."[41] The function of the incest taboo, she argues, is to prevent the kind of mingling or confusion of identities which blurs clear lines of demarcation (e.g., feminine/masculine, nature/culture). It is "to ward off the subject's fear of his very own identity sinking irretrievably into the mother."[42]

Indeed, the exchange between families, the economy of kinship laws, as Rousseau himself says above, is not the primary good obtained by the sacred law. The law is sacred not because it creates culture but because it contains a yearning for something beyond the law, for that frightful mingling or confusion just mentioned. But that yearning can only be the effect of the law itself. As the *Discourse on Inequality* puts it, "the very least that ought to be required of the laws is to stop an evil which would not exist without them" (134). This is another way of saying that the law that is supposed to contain disorder actually institutes it, that disorder has its origin in law, in kinship laws—origin of society and languages, of the speaking subject.[43]

The structures of kinship (exogamy and the prohibition on incest) are also the origin of the subjects of sexual difference (a point Lévi-Strauss fails to acknowledge when he assumes that woman as value preexists her circulation as sign).[44] Man and woman, in other words, come into existence through signifying practices. They are born of the sacred law, and each is a signifier of the difference of the other. To be a woman is to be the object of exchange. To be a man is to be the subject but never the object of exchange. That is why, as we see later, the talking woman who exchanges signs confounds the "natural" sociosymbolic order, and why the man who allows himself to be circulated as a sign among talking women loses his constitution.

To be a man, in Rousseau's telling, is to be a subject of representation, but one who always represents himself, who is never signified by an other. The *Discourse on Inequality* confirms and complicates this notion of the masculine subject as self-constituting inasmuch as it shows that the savage only begins to recognize himself, to develop his capacity for self-reflection, by recognizing his sameness and difference from others: "The conformities that time could make him perceive among them [his fellow men], his female, and himself led him to judge of those which he did not perceive." These relationships produced in the savage "some sort of reflection"—a distinctly specular one: "Thus the first glance [look, *le premier regard*] he directed upon himself produced in him the first stirring of pride" (144).

(Primitive) man seeing himself see himself: such is the illusion of the Cartesian consciousness as elaborated by Jacques Lacan. It is an illusion because "what determines me, at the most profound level, in the visible [the scopic field], is the gaze that is outside. It is through the gaze that I enter life and it is from the gaze that I receive its effects."[45] On Lacan's account, the gaze of the other is crucial to the formation of primary narcissism (*l'amour de soi* in Rousseauist parlance); it constitutes the "moi" in the "mirror stage," which aligns the child's image with the first of the countless images around which its identity will coalesce. This "moi," argues Lacan, is an *Idealich* created in an imaginary identification with the wholeness of a body image that is outside the self; it is indeed a source of pride.[46]

Even as the *Discourse on Inequality* posits the subject as self-constituting in that first moment when savage man felt pride at beholding himself, it also shows that the male subject is both dependent on and solicitous of the gaze of others, and not least on and of the female gaze—that he is exhibitionistic, his first impulse is toward self-display. Self-display appears at first to be the root of all vice. Men singing, dancing, and generally showing off belies the desire to be seen and preferred in the gaze of others. What excites this desire to attract the look, we recall, is the first contact between different families, the coming together of the sexes, thus women exhibiting themselves to men, men to women. Sexual desire and gender difference emerge in society; they are not natural facts but performative enactments created in the act of soliciting the look of others in the context of primitive communal life. In the earliest public scenes, writes Rousseau, "each one began to look at the others and to want to be looked at himself, and public esteem had a value." Inequality was born along with "vanity and contempt . . . [as well as] shame and envy" (149). Still, the pleasure of self-adornment was quite innocent: "As long as men were . . . limited to sewing their clothing of skins with thorns or fish bones, adorning themselves with feathers and shells, painting their bodies with various colors [without the help of others] . . . they lived free" (151). It was not "necessary to appear to be other than what one in fact was" (155), even as self-adornment played no small role in constituting what one was.

J. C. Flugel offers an interpretive angle from which to consider the pleasure in self-adornment. The whole psychology of clothes, he argues, consists in the essential opposition between the twin motives of decoration and modesty. Whereas the purpose of decoration is to distinguish oneself from others, to attract their admiring glances (especially those of the sex one wishes to seduce), and to fortify self-esteem, that of modesty is to refrain from the desire for preference and drawing attention to ourselves and our bodies. But—and this is decisive—"modesty," says Flugel, "is secondary; it is a reaction against a more primitive [narcissistic] tendency to self-display." Clothes reconcile these opposing tendencies by allowing us to gratify our desire for exhibitionism under the gesture of concealment.[47]

Flugel observes further that the child's love of decorative ornaments (e.g., feathers, a necklace, or random scraps of clothing) symbolizes its first efforts to distinguish itself from the mother. "Look at me!": such is the nature of the child's first impulse toward self-differentiation. But because garments also symbolize the power of the mother—for it is most often she who imposes clothes on the naked child—to cast off the maternal garb is to cast out the mother and thus once again to affirm that fragile specular imago: "Moi!" For clothes and ornaments, like linguistic signs, are a means of symbolic communication and self-representation. They are "extensions of bodily self" which offer us an increased sense of power and pride, of our difference, first, from the mother and later from others.[48]

This takes us straight back to the frontispiece to the *Discourse* (Rousseau's explanatory note directly precedes his description of men adorning their bodies). Recall that the Hottentot casts off his European attire and goes back to his equals wrapped in a sheepskin and retaining both the cutlass and the necklace. What is the significance of these objects? They have the effect of a sacred law: they secure primal differentiation, masculine self-representation, and the pleasure in self-adornment; they situate the masculine subject in the paternal symbolic ("I shall keep them for love of you") which he both needs and rejects; and thus they mediate the powerful desire to return to Nature, "our common mother."

Furthermore, the frontispiece captures in an image what Flugel calls "The Great Masculine Renunciation" that occurred toward the end of the eighteenth century: man's abandonment of his claim to be beautiful—his renunciation of "all the brighter, gayer, more elaborate, and more varied forms of ornamentation"—in favor of being useful.[49] Foregrounding this association of democracy with the democratization of dress, Rousseau tells us that men must eschew the luxurious attire that is a divisive and dissimulating signifier of rank, status, and wealth. Whereas the sartorial signifiers of excess "announce a wealthy man," says Rousseau, "the healthy, robust man is known by other signs. It is in the rustic clothes of a farmer and not beneath the gilt of a courtier that strength and vigor of the body will be found."[50] To communicate proper political meaning, the body of the citizen must be clothed in simple and functional attire. As Flugel observes, "the whole relatively 'fixed' system of his clothing is, in fact, an outward and visible sign of the strictness of his adherence to the social code."[51] Immorality attaches to the man who retains a taste for finery, but it is woman, as we see next, who comes to stand for the self-display that is the driving force behind dissimulation in human affairs.

The Field of Female Voice and Vision

The *Letter to D'Alembert on the Theatre* is obsessed with the dissimulatress who puts sartorial and linguistic signifiers in the service of other than referential functions. Realm of deception, the theater is the field of female voice and vision. Voice is crucial. It is only through "the successive impression made by discourse, striking with cumulative impact," as the *Essay on the Origin of Languages* argues, that "the scenes of tragedy produce their effect. The passions have their gestures but also their accents; and these accents, which cause us to shudder, these accents to which one cannot close one's ear and which by way of it penetrate to the very depths of the heart, in spite of ourselves convey to it the [e]motions that wring them [from us], and cause us to feel what we hear."[52] Invasive and irresistible, the voice carries to our ears sounds we are unable to shut out (as unable, as *Emile* shows, as the infant is to shut out the voice of the mother). As the vehicle of staged tragedies, the voice heard in the theater is the antithesis of the gentle voice: it communicates not genuine sentiments but rather "feigned miseries."[53] Artificial and secondary, the female voice stands in the *Letter* for the degeneration of "natural" language into the counterfeit meanings Rousseau associates with civilization, commerce, and luxury, with an excess he tries to contain by depriving women of any discursive authority.[54]

The female signifying practices of the theater and the salon "pose a sort of problem" for Rousseau. The ancients "had as their maxim that the land where morals [manners] were purest was the one where they spoke the least of women, and that the best woman was the one about whom the least was said."[55] They preserved the value of women, of the sign, by restraining the circulation of women as signs. In an age when "what was said most vividly was expressed not by words but by signs,"[56] to speak of women was to rob them of their intrinsic value, namely, their purity or virtue.[57] To talk about women is scandalous. Far more scandalous, however, is the woman who talks, who steps out of her function as sign, as the signifier of a "common brotherhood." "It is possible that there are in the world a few women worthy of being listened to by a serious man," concedes Rousseau, but the question is whether it is possible to listen to women without "abasing" one's own sex (47). Masculinity dissipates in the acoustic field of female voice.[58] The "most esteemed woman" among us moderns, says Rousseau, is the one "about whom the most is said" and the one who says the most: "who most imperiously sets the tone, who judges, resolves, decides, pronounces, assigns talents, merit, and virtues their degrees and places, and whose favor is most ignominiously begged for by humble, learned men" (49).

Rousseau's complaint against this "perversion of natural relations" (50) was hardly novel. As Joan Landes argues, Montesquieu and Fenelon (among numerous others) had criticized the salon as the site of bourgeois ennoblement and the salonnières as the instructors of aristocratic values. In an age in which "not birth but commerce, venality of office, and intrigue at court became the new coins of power," she writes, "salon women were particularly important in teaching the appropriate style, dress, manners, language, art, and literature" to non-nobles who sought entry into the culture of polite society. If Rousseau linked the salon to the theater, moreover, it was because the line between them was indistinct. "In this aristocratic world of spectacular relations," Landes observes, "where seeing and being seen was an overriding concern, a favorite sport was to play dress up," to stage "amateur theatrical productions," and generally to revel in the art of the masquerade.[59]

Although Rousseau's critique of the salon merely extends these denouncements of women as the arbiters of aristocratic culture and as the driving force behind luxury, and although his attack on the theater advances well-known arguments about women as the agents of masquerade and imposture, he complicates these debates by infusing them with a sense of urgency that belies his recognition that performance is crucial in the constitution of social and sexual identity, and that it has everything to do with political identity. What Rousseau sees and fears, moreover, is that the "perversion of natural [sexual] relations" is possible because pleasurable. Apart from the woman who assumes a position of mastery in the salon, the men who "weep like women" in the theater and throw themselves at the feet of women outside it are a political problem of the highest order. The major threat to the man and the citizen, in short, is the masculine desire to give oneself over to the imperious woman who seeks to overturn the system of exchange between men.

To explain how it is that a man becomes a woman's "thing," Rousseau shows that identity, especially masculine identity, dissipates in the fields of acoustic and scopic pleasure. The theater is condemned because the spectator loses himself in the spectacle: "Who does not himself become a thief for a minute in being concerned about him" (46)? Such identification is possible because "the stage is, in general, a painting of the human passions, the original of which is in every heart" (18); it is dangerous because we spectators do not have to account for our vicarious pleasure. But such pleasure is itself unthinkable without imagination, the faculty that transports us outside ourselves. Imagination is what makes us human and, Rousseau being Rousseau, what makes us perverse. It is not only that some men "pervert the use of this consoling faculty"[60] but also that perversion attends the imagination when it guards the masculine subject against the female and the abyss.

The imagination protects this subject against what Rousseau's prose constructs as a universal female threat to masculinity and social order. Female desire, as we are told in *Emile* and the *Letter* confirms, is an excess that "drag[s] [men] to death without ever being able to defend themselves."[61] To change the natural "order of attack and defense," to remove the "veil" of female chastity, Rousseau warns, is to unleash the fury of female desire, before which the male goes instantly and utterly limp. What is this chastity, this veil? It is a ruse, a fake, an imaginary good that substitutes for the real good that has never the power to excite but always the power to horrify and destroy. It is the uneasy solution to male performance anxiety and a certain lack of desire. "The apparent obstacle, which seems to keep this object at a distance, is in reality what brings it nearer. The desires, veiled by shame, become only the more seductive; in hindering them, chasteness inflames them. Its fears, its tricks, its reserves, its timid avowals," says Rousseau, "say better what chasteness thinks to hide than passion could have said it without chasteness." So male desire is created in the space of the imagination, which is also the female space of the theater: both require props, masks, veils, obstacles. To be a (certain kind of) woman is to say no so that man can say yes—can say anything—to love. It is to create male desire by hiding that one is a subject of desire; it is to misrepresent oneself. The modest woman is like the actor. "What is the talent of the actor? It is the art of counterfeiting himself, of putting on another character than his own, of appearing different than he is." If the actor "annihilates himself" in a role, the woman who does not act annihilates everything: "Love would no longer be the support of nature but its destroyer and plague" (79–84).

Yet not even the feminine artifice of modesty can ward off the threat of disorder. Perversion inheres in the very faculty of the imagination, "which scandalizes the eye in revealing to it what it sees not only as naked but as something that ought to be clothed. There is no garment so modest that a glance inflamed by imagination does not penetrate with its desires." The irrepressible scopophilic drive will always seek to reach its erotic object: the "absolute nudity [of the female sex]" which, we are told, would create "indifference and perhaps [that is, certainly] distaste"—another way of saying that danger attaches to the immodest woman who hides "part of the object . . . only to set off what is exposed," but also to the modest woman who must play at the game of the veil (134–135). Whatever

Rousseau says about the modest woman, she (like the immodest one) is in the last instance an actress implicated in that greatest of crimes. Supplementing herself ("the real good"), the modest woman puts the sign in place of the thing, the signifier in place of the signified. Then, since on this reading the chaste woman herself is nothing but a simulacrum, she opens up the abyss of signification: the copy that is really a copy of a copy of . . . Enter the professional actress, that "counterfeited sweetness" who lures her unwitting admirer to his destruction at the hands of that other simulacrum of womanly virtue in society. If the *Letter* all but spins out of control, as it so often does, it is because danger (the danger of appearing other than one is, of using all manner of signs to effect a no when one wants to say yes) is written into the Rousseauist ideal of woman. The modest woman as masquerade, the actress as masquerade, the idol of the salon as masquerade. Where does the woman-as-spectacle end?

In the circles, in the space where there is no masquerade because there are no women. (They too have their little societies but—thank heaven—one does not often find men there, and the man who does frequent them is a disgrace to his sex.) Where there is no woman there is no female voice to excite unmanly emotions. The circles preserve a space in which men, because they do not have "to clothe reason in gallantry, can devote themselves to grave and serious discourse" (105). They are the site, in Landes's words, where Rousseau can uphold "the fiction of a 'natural language' against the artificial, stylized discourse [of *le monde*]" and its feminized culture. The salon-nières—and let us not forget that they, like actresses, existed as public women outside the institution of marriage—are guilty, in the Genevan's view, of tampering with language and thus with the natural order.[62] Whereas women of the salons employ artificial signifiers that do violence to truth, the men of the circles, as Thomas Crow puts it, speak "the language of the truth . . . [as found] *dans la Nature toute seule*."[63] Still, even though the "citizen of Geneva" projects all that is culturally debased onto the female voice, he knows that this voice commands and the masculine subject all too happily obeys. That is why, for Rousseau, "the two sexes ought to come together sometimes and to live separated ordinarily." In "a commerce that is too intimate," he warns, men "lose not only their morals [manners], but we lose our morals [manners] and our constitution; . . . the women make us into women" (100).

Such is the danger, such is the scandal. But how exactly does the theater figure in the loss of manly constitution? Once again, by means of a spectatorial identification (as with the thief), only now with the simulacrum of a simulacrum: the modest woman played by the actress in a romance. Her art is to "dispos[e] the soul to feelings which are too tender"—much too tender. Since "however love is depicted for us, it seduces or it is not love," cautions Rousseau, one admires "decent love" in the theater only to find oneself in the grip of "criminal love" in society. "The theater is a treasury of perfect women," and therein lies the danger (51–56). Indeed the power of the actress is at its height when she appropriates the signs of the modest woman and sends out, as it were, false messages from the theatrical place of virtue. In this chaste disguise she effects the most profound subversion of the moral order. For, by the time the male spectator discovers the fake (if he ever does), he is already at the mercy of that other fake in society. But the problem runs even deeper, for the man puts himself at the feet of the imperious woman outside the theater not only because he mistakes her for the passive feminine figure on stage but also, if not precisely, because he identifies with that figure.

Consider Rousseau's reading of Racine's *Berenice*. Here, says the "citizen of Geneva," we have a Roman (Titus) who sways between his duty to country and his love of a mistress. Although the spectator leaves the theater "pitying this sensitive man whom he despised," it is Berenice who claims his heart. At the moment when Berenice can cry no more, the spectators usurp her place and shed volumes of tears at her fate. The result: "The queen departs without the leave of the audience. The Emperor sends her away *invitus invitam* [against his will, against hers]; one might add *invito spectatore* [against the spectator's will]. Titus can very well remain a Roman; he is the only one on his side; all the spectators have married Berenice" (53). One might add, all the spectators have become Berenice, including the male spectators.

Only the sex-segregated circles and societies can protect the masculine subject against his feminine double. "But the moment there is drama, goodby to the *circles*, goodby to the societies!"—more exactly, goodby to the citizen because goodby to the man. "In a republic, *men* are needed" (100–101, my emphasis). That is why the theater must never be allowed inside the gates of Geneva, city of Calvin, of the circles, of sumptuary laws.

The mere institution of a theater in Geneva would destroy the republic. The moment actors and actresses so much as enter the city, "the taste for luxury, adornment, and dissipation" will take hold. Not only are sumptuary laws useless in uprooting luxury where it already exists, the mere sight of "the costumes and jewelry of the players" will immediately introduce luxury as excess where it does not yet exist, an excess that no law could ever contain (57). Then, since luxury is a woman,

> the wives of the Mountaineers, going first to see and then to be seen, will want to be dressed and dressed with distinction. The wife of the chief magistrate will not want to present herself at the theater attired like the schoolmaster's. The schoolmaster's wife will strive to be attired like the chief magistrate's. Out of this will soon emerge a competition in dress which will ruin the husbands, will perhaps win them over, and which will find countless new ways to get around the sumptuary laws. (63)

Danger threatens from inside the walls of the republic: in a flash, wives will want to be seen, men will want to see them, "all the rest is easy to imagine" (63). It appears at first that only constant motion, strenuous work, and strict adherence to the laws can keep this excess at bay, but it turns out that to vanquish the desire for woman-as-spectacle the republic must erect another kind of spectacle.

Rousseau outlines a variety of entertainments (*spectacles*) that would be fitting for citizens. For one thing, socially sanctioned forms of pleasure are necessary so that men "fulfil their duties better, that they torment themselves less over changing their stations" (126n). Rousseau criticizes extreme differences in wealth, but it is less material equality than the sentiment of equality he endorses and wishes to nurture in the republican festivities. Since woman is the master signifier of rank according to the "citizen of Geneva," it is she who must be recoded in the *Letter* as a signifier of fraternity. In the place of the sumptuous idol of the salon stretched out on her couch and the actress passing herself off as the modest woman, Rousseau puts the "Queen of the Ball": the young girl who, at the yearly gathering that brings young persons together to dance under the eyes of the public, is crowned for having "comported herself most decently, most modestly." Since every girl will naturally aspire to be Queen, "the attentions to the adornment of their daughters would be an object of amusement for the women which, in turn, would provide diversion for many others"—pleasure, that is say, for the men. In this way, observes Rousseau, one "can content vanity without offending virtue" (130–131).

Whose vanity? Women's vanity certainly, but also if not especially men's. Rousseau retains and contains not only feminine but also masculine narcissistic and exhibitionist desires in the festivities he recommends: "Why should we not found, on the model of the military prizes, other prizes for gymnastics, wrestling, runnings, discus, and the various bodily exercises? Why should we not animate our boatmen by contests on the lake? Could there be an entertainment in the world more brilliant than seeing, on this vast and superb body of water, hundreds of boats?" So "magnificent" is this spectacle of men, that it will extinguish man's fatal desire to gaze at that other blazing magnificence: the sumptuous body of the salonnière or the actress (127).

The most appealing image of manly pleasure for Rousseau, however, is without doubt the military spectacle he rememorates from his childhood. The scene is in the square of Saint-Gervais where, after a day of military exercises, officers and soldiers have begun to dance together around a fountain: "A dance of men would seem to present nothing very interesting to see," he writes,

> however, the harmony of five or six hundred men in uniform, holding one another by the hand and forming a long ribbon which wound around, serpent-like, in cadence and without confusion, with countless turns and returns, countless sorts of figured evolutions, the excellence of the tunes which animated them, the sound of the drums, the glare of the torches, a certain military pomp in the

> midst of pleasure, all this created a very lively sensation that could
> not be experienced coldly. It was late; the women were in bed; all of
> them got up. Soon the windows were full of female spectators who
> gave a new zeal to the actors; . . . they came down; the wives came
> to their husbands. . . . *The dance was suspended.* . . . My father,
> embracing me, was seized with trembling which I think I still feel
> and share: "Jean-Jacques," he said to me, "love your country. Do
> you see these good Genevans? They are all friends, they are all
> brothers; . . . You are a Genevan." (135n, my emphasis)

In this image of hundreds of men in uniform, holding hands, dancing
in a serpentlike (necklacelike) formation around a fountain—recall
that other fountain, that other scene of unbounded desire in the *Essay
on the Origin of Languages*—in a state of orderly rapture we have the
republican spectacle par excellence. Here the author Rousseau re-
enacts the moment his father spoke his fraternal name and promotes
a spectacle in which "the spectators become an entertainment [*spectacle*] to themselves." Instead of being "suffocat[ed] . . . in sound rooms
well closed" (the salon, 102), instead of being buried alive in the
"gloomy cavern" of the theater (deadly maternal space), men will
take part in festivities "in the open air, under the sky" (125–126).
Uniforms, swords (cutlasses), and whatever else accompanies a "certain military pomp" will guard against the feminine threat yet preserve the masculine pleasure in self-adornment and self-display. At
once spectator and spectacle, man sees himself seeing himself.

   What of the female spectators peering out their windows? It is the
female gaze, as Rousseau tells us, that animates the male pleasure in
self-display. And so it does. But it is a gaze whose power is circum-
scribed by the domestic sphere, a domesticated gaze that knows its
proper place and specular function, which, like the ruse of chastity,
is to reflect man back to himself at twice his original size. And let us
not neglect that the presence of the women who come down to join
the men (each woman joins her husband) guards against another
threat: the manly dance that might very well have transgressed itself
in homoerotic ecstasy. The dance was halted at the moment women
entered the square, as Rousseau himself says, and could not be taken
up anymore.

   The *Letter* would efface the gap between spectacle and spectator, representor and represented, signifier and signified. Yet it is inadequate to assert, as Derrida does, that the text evinces Rousseau's "dream of a mute society, of a society before the origin of languages."[64] His dream, rather, is of a society without female voice, one in which woman remains within her proper function as sign. Rousseau's critique of the signifier, in fact, explicitly links the deadly play of signification (the effacement of the referent or the speaker in the signifier) to woman as signifying subject. That the modest woman masquerades, indeed must masquerade, however, means that there is, finally, no stable referent outside the play of signification that could possibly ground woman as (unified, stable) sign and therefore the natural binarism of masculinity and femininity Rousseau claims to be essential to moral order. This is why the pedagogical construction of gender difference in *Emile* is supplemented by the image of woman in the male imagination: the celestial object that has no earthly referent and, for that very reason, protects man against woman and all her sex.

Making a Man

The educational project of *Emile* is straightforward: to raise a child who "will, in the first place, be a man."[65] Perhaps Emile will be a citizen as well. But he has not the slightest chance of becoming a member of the political community if he does not first become a member of his own sex. Noticeable immediately in the text, as Mary Jacobus observes, is that the man-child "comes into being on the basis of a missing mother."[66] Rousseau himself declares, "Emile is an orphan" (52)—or, more exactly and for all pedagogical purposes, he is orphaned by being placed in infancy in the hands of the tutor. Emile has a mother (as fictive as her son), but apart from her biological function she is redundant. Even her first and most sacred duty to nurse (should she consent to it) is supplemented with a Rousseauist script: "She will be given written instructions, for this advantage has its counter-poise and keeps the governor at something more of a distance from his pupil" (56). The mother-child dyad, in other words, can be overclose, dangerous.

Thus emerges the other face to the nursing mother whom Rousseau raises to the status of a secular idol and contrasts to those big-city mothers who deposit their children with a wet nurse in the country. Rousseau rails for pages in Book I against the "mercenary" practice of wet-nursing, which symbolizes the economy of the supplement and the cash nexus.[67] The child who is farmed out to a hired nurse is swaddled, "hung from a nail like a sack of clothes," and deprived of the maternal breast. And lacking this real good (which Rousseau credits as the source of all felicity, peace, and morals), the child will cry and then fantasize: he will substitute the first of an endless number of imaginary goods that mark the gap between his desires and powers. But if Rousseau holds neglectful mothers to be the cause of all unhappiness, he is just as, if not more, worried by loving mothers who carry their first duty to excess. "Plunging their children into softness," these equally "cruel mothers" prepare them for the sedentary life of a eunuch, lived with women or in their manner (44, 47).[68]

In the place of all mothers Rousseau puts "Thetis [who], to make her son [Achilles] invulnerable, plunged him . . . in the water of the Styx" (47), then puts himself as tutor in the place of the mythical mother. This "lovely" fable is the subject of the frontispiece of *Emile*. It depicts Rousseauist pedagogy as military strategy. To make a man, the sacred mother-child bond must be closely supervised, if not drastically and symbolically severed, in order to prepare the child for battle with "the enemy" who will appear in Book V: the desire for a woman, to be at the feet of woman, if not to be a woman. But just as the mythical Achilles had one weak point (his heel, by which his mother held him when she dipped him in the water, which connected him to his maternal origin), so too is Emile at risk by virtue of being born of woman. The tutor/author, however, knows his mythology well enough to devise safeguards to delay the impending disaster.

The first of these deferral strategies is to replace the mother with a wet nurse, whom the tutor then subjects to relentless visual surveillance in order to ensure that the child be made dependent on things and not on wills. For the very first thing the helpless infant encounters is, of course, absolutely inseparable from human will—that is, a woman's will: the breast is inseparable from her who gives or withholds it and who is, for that reason, the child's first master. Double danger: the infant is not only dependent on the will of a woman but also caught in the sonorous envelope of the (substitute) maternal voice. "I do not disapprove of the nurse's entertaining the child with songs and very gay and varied accents," remarks Rousseau. "But I do disapprove of her making him constantly giddy with a multitude of useless words of which he understands nothing other than the tone she gives them." The child who listens "in swaddling clothes to the prattle of his nurse" confuses the words uttered by the female speaker with reality and soon comes to speak like a woman. The nurse or mother "serve[s] as an interpreter for the city child," whose voice she reduces to mimicry.[69] It is a weak and indistinct voice: "A man who learns to speak only in his bedroom will fail to make himself understood at the head of a battalion," warns the "citizen of Geneva." "First teach children to speak to men; they will know how to speak to women when they have to" (70–73).

The maternal voice is disorienting. "I would want the first articulations which he [the child] is made to hear to be rare, easy, distinct, often repeated," advises the tutor, "and that the words they express relate only to objects of the senses which can in the first place be shown to the child" (70). The child who is taught representative signs before he understands their relation to things loses his originary wholeness in the arbitrary relation between signifier and signified. Thus weakened, he is doomed to become a mouthpiece or actor and to take up his place in the salon or theater amusing women: he can be made to "say whatever one wants" (256)—whatever women want. Double maxim: keep the maternal voice at a distance and keep the child away from books. There is only one book the child needs to learn, "the book of the world" (451). If "we absolutely must have books," says Rousseau, "there exists one which, to my taste, provides the most felicitous treatise on natural education" (184): *Robinson Crusoe*—"that bourgeois parable of masculine self-sufficiency," as Jacobus puts it.[70] Let Emile imagine that "he is Robinson himself, . . . dressed in skins, wearing a large cap, carrying a large saber and all the rest of the character's grotesque equipment," muses Rousseau, "with the exception of the parasol, which he will not need" (185)—of course.

And so (properly attired like that other manly civil-savage of the *Discourse on Inequality*) the child is ready to be taught the value of manual labor. "I absolutely want Emile to learn a trade," declares the tutor. "I do not want him to be an embroiderer, a gilder, or a varnisher, like Locke's gentleman." He should be given a trade that suits his sex and forbidden any that would soften his body. Since we have a choice, says Rousseau, let us choose a trade for its "cleanliness." Let us choose, then, carpentry: "It is clean; it is useful." Whatever trade one prefers, always remember that big manly hands were not made to handle "ribbons, tassels, net, and chenille." So contaminating is such paraphernalia, so fragile is the whole pedagogical code of gender difference by trade, that such crimes against nature should be forbidden by royal decree: "If I were sovereign," declares Rousseau, "I would permit sewing and the needle trades only to women and to cripples reduced to occupations like theirs"; or, if necessary, such crimes should be punished by castration: "And if there absolutely must be true eunuchs, let men who dishonor their sex by taking jobs which do not suit it be reduced to this condition" (197–200).

Immersed in the book of the world, Emile's powers and desires are kept in equilibrium. Another maxim: "The real world has its limits; the imaginary world is infinite. Unable to enlarge the one, let us restrict the other, for it is from the difference between the two alone that are born all the pains which make us truly unhappy" (81). Then, since language operates in the realm of the imagination (the child needs words to signify the real objects it lacks), "in general, never substitute the sign for the thing except when it is impossible for you to show the latter, for the sign absorbs the child's attention and makes him forget the thing represented" (170). Still, it is not quite accurate to say, as Starobinski does, that in *Emile* "discourse . . . follows encounters with real objects."[71] There is one crucial exception to the Rousseauist rule governing the related uses of discourse and the imagination. Not every thing can be shown more safely than the sign, not every "real good" is less dangerous than the imaginary one; one sign is of value precisely because it absorbs the child's attention: "Sophie or the woman."

In Book IV, Emile comes into danger. The moment of crisis has arrived, the decisive moment of his confused sexual awakening. Let us note that this was the moment when the autobiographer's own objectless desires "took a false turn"; the moment when the young Jean-Jacques developed his abject wish to be beaten by a masterful mistress.[72] Warns the tutor, if the child's "pulse rises and his eye is inflamed; if the hand of a woman placed on his makes him shiver; if he gets flustered or is intimidated near her—Ulysses, O wise Ulysses, be careful. The goatskins you closed with so much care are open. The winds are already loose. No longer leave the tiller for an instant, or all is lost." Not about to jump ship, the tutor will play midwife at "the second birth" (212).

Let us reflect on the first appearance of the mythical Ulysses at this point in the text, where *amour-propre* (or "the relative I," 243) comes into play. Everything in Emile's education has thus far been addressed to his *amour de soi* alone. "He has said, 'I love you', to no one" (222); "He does not feel himself to be of any sex, of any species. Man and woman are equally alien to him" (219). In love only with himself but unable to recognize himself (because he recognizes and is recognized by no other), Emile is, so to speak, like the mythical Narcissus, who is entirely within himself and, as Kristeva writes, "does not, in fact, know who he is": "He Loves, he loves Himself—active and passive, subject *and* object."[73] But the ego of narcissism, says Kristeva, is fragile and uncertain because it lacks an object, indeed only barely maintains its borders in relation to a nonobject (the maternal voice, gaze, breast).[74] Emile was dipped in the Styx, but he is not invulnerable. Narcissus, as the fable says, drowned in the pool of his own reflection, fell into the watery maternal element. Ulysses too is on a quest, not of his own image but rather, as Kristeva quotes the *Enneads*, of "the 'fatherland,' for 'it is there that dwells our Father.'" The trajectory "from Narcissus to Ulysses," she writes, "proceeds through *love* and the exclusion of the impure"—the abject.[75] Ulysses does not heed the seductive voice of the Sirens that lured others before him into the abyss, and, as the symbolically appropriate frontispiece to Book V of *Emile* shows us, he triumphs over Circe, who gives herself to the one man she could not debase.[76] Emile too will be sent on a quest for the fatherland, but first he must confront the enemy in himself.

Emile's objectless desires do not arise out of hormonal changes, they "are awakened by the imagination alone. Their need is not properly a physical need. It is not true that it is a true need. If *no lewd object* had ever struck our eyes, if *no indecent idea* had ever entered our minds, perhaps this alleged need would never have made itself felt to us, and we would have remained chaste without temptation, without effort, and without merit" (333, my emphasis). It is true that *Emile*, as Allan Bloom maintains, advances the idea of sublimated sex, but what is sublimated is no instinctual drive; it is rather a perverse desire that is excited by "the memory of objects" from childhood (the nurse, books, women).[77]

"You do not know the fury with which the senses, by the lure of pleasure, drag young men like you into the abyss of the vices," the tutor tells Emile. "Just as Ulysses, moved by the Sirens' song and seduced by the lure of the pleasures, cried out to his crew to unchain him, so you will want to break the bonds which hinder you." To be saved by his guardian, the pupil must first give his duly considered consent. Once "he has, so to speak, signed the contract," the tutor sets about reinforcing the fortress around his young charge. "Removing dangerous objects is nothing, if I do not also remove the memory of them." The tutor comes thus upon the idea of sending Emile on the hunt. "He will lose in it—at least for a time—the dangerous inclinations born of softness. The hunt hardens the heart as well as the body. It accustoms one to blood, to cruelty" (326, 320). It purges the male subject, as Kristeva would say, of the feminine, the abject.

The primary means for erasing the kind of memories that "engend[er] monsters" (325), however, is to plant in Emile's imagination the chaste image of woman. The search for the celestial object begins thus:

> It is unimportant whether the object I depict for him [Emile] is imaginary; it suffices that it make him disgusted with those that could tempt him; it suffices that he everywhere find comparisons which make him prefer his chimera to the real objects that strike his eye. And what is true love itself if it is not chimera, lie, and illusion? We love the image we make for ourselves far more than we love the object to which we apply it. . . . The magic veil drops, and love disappears. (329)

Few knew better than Rousseau that, thanks to the imaginary object, one sex ceases to be anything for the other. In the *Confessions*, the autobiographer tell us that the image of the mother substitute (Madame de Warens) "safeguarded me against her and all her sex." "Fondling her image in my secret heart," writes Rousseau, "and surrounded at night by objects to remind me of her" was not "my undoing" but rather "my salvation."[78] Alfred Binet credited Rousseau with the invention of a form of fetishism that substituted the relic for and preferred it to the woman to whom it originally belonged.[79] Rousseau himself admitted: "It's not at all the vanity produced by estate or rank that attracts me, its sensual delight; a better preserved complexion; a finer, better-made dress, a daintier shoe, ribbons, lace, hair better dressed. I would always prefer the less pretty one as long as she had more of all of that."[80]

Binet's observations help explain why the author Rousseau is immersed in "voluptuous reveries," as Mary Wollstonecraft so astutely put it, "when he describes the pretty foot and enticing airs of his little favourite,"[81] and why Sophie must master "the art of dressing oneself up" (368), of "getting looked at" (373). Sophie "loves adornment" (393). Her natural desire to please begins, as does every girl's, with

> what presents itself to sight and is useful for ornamentation: mirrors, jewels, dresses, particularly dolls. . . . Observe a little girl spending the day around her doll, constantly changing its clothes, dressing and undressing it hundreds and hundreds of times, continuously seeking new combinations of ornaments. . . . you will say, she adorns her doll and not her person. Doubtless. She sees her doll and does not see herself. . . . She is entirely in her doll, and she puts all her coquetry into it. She will not always leave it there. She awaits the moment when she will be her own doll. (367)

If *Emile* can be read as foregrounding "the Great Masculine Renunciation" (and all the psychic inhibitions it entailed for the citizen-subject), then it is more than female vanity that is being gratified in this scene. The narcissistic pleasures the masculine subject denies himself (the tutor forbids his pupil) are projected onto the feminine other who is compelled to love adornment, to make herself a fetish, to become "her own doll." Woman must bear the double burden of *his* desire to see and to be seen, must gratify *his* pleasure in looking and self-display.

Since the pedagogical project of *Emile* is to make a man who renounces aristocratic affectation, not just any kind of female adornment will do. The doll-woman who struts in her elaborate and rich finery stands accused of trafficking in counterfeit goods, of trying "to hide some defects": "I have also noticed that the most sumptuous adornment usually marks ugly women" (372), informs Rousseau.[82] These fakes deceive men and impose the class law of fashion on beautiful women. Attractive or not, the dangerous woman, it turns out, is not so much dissembling as self-sufficient: caught up in her own image, she only appears to please the men who must please her. She is the aristocratic idol who holds court "in the ceremony of the dressing table" surrounded by "the merchants, the salesmen, the fops, the scribblers, the poems, the songs, the pamphlets" (373). Then, since all women are natural coquettes, proper femininity too operates in the realm of deception. But there are two "species of dissimulation," says Rousseau: natural and unnatural, chaste and unchaste, dependent and independent. Women who practice the former kind are commended for "disguising the sentiments that they have"; those who practice the latter are condemned for "feigning those they do not have" (430n).[83] What fascinates and terrifies Rousseau are the narcissistic women who dress up and gaze at their own image but are indifferent to male desire, who "never love [or desire] anything but themselves" (430n). That these women are nothing but the scapegoats of "the Great Masculine Renunciation" is suggested by Flugel's remark that "men with strong exhibitionist desires"—like the autobiographical subject of the *Confessions*—"admire women and at the same time envy their opportunity for bodily and sartorial self-display."[84] That is why the little girl who dresses her doll must be inscribed in the economy of male pleasure, and why Sophie must be made into a dependent coquette who is solicitous of Emile's gaze.

The author/tutor proceeds with his reverie on the imaginary object, telling both reader and pupil that Sophie's "adornment is very modest in appearance and very coquettish in fact." The man whose eyes "roam over her whole person," muses the tutor, cannot help but think that her "very simple attire was put on only to be taken off piece by piece by the imagination" (394). And so female self-representation plays (once again) to the male gaze, to the perverse scopic drive, which means (once again) that it carries the risk of exciting unpleasure. The chaste woman must sustain the endless play of sartorial signifiers, for they alone inhibit the drive from reaching (as we saw in the *Letter*) its erotic object. Female presence is tolerable only as a kind of absence: there must always be one more piece of clothing, one more veil, yet one more obstacle to keep alive the life-saving economy of the fetish, the signifying chain of synecdoches.

Even though the modest woman's great art of the lie is her sacred duty,[85] she may never signify herself as subject, as speaking subject, as a producer of signs—that is, if she is to remain in her function as sign.[86] Thus woman must conceal the production of her femininity, of herself as coquette. Sophie's "art is apparent nowhere" (394), she makes artifice appear natural.[87] So it is that woman effaces herself as subject and thereby upholds herself as referent, as the ground of masculinist self-representation.[88] Men find in Sophie not a radical speaking other, as Joel Schwartz would have it,[89] but rather, as Rousseau tells us time and again, "more or less what they find in their own minds."[90] Indeed Sophie, to borrow Luce Irigaray's account of woman's function in a masculinist symbolic economy, is "the foundation for this specular duplication, giving man back 'his' image and repeating it as the 'same'."[91]

To reflect back to the masculine speaking subject the stable, self-identical image of himself, the symbolic oneness of the I, Sophie must guard him against whatever threatens to encroach on the fragile borders of his identity: the chaste woman must secure the borders of the clean and proper. Proper femininity keeps at bay the abject: that which is opposed to I, that which, in Kristeva's words, "establishes intermixture and disorder," that frightful mingling or confusion.[92] This is why Sophie, as Rousseau tells us, is obsessed with cleanliness. Learned from her mother, she demands it in her "person, her things, her room, her work, her grooming." Sophie's first maxim is to do everything "cleanly," but without any trace of "vain affectation or softness." Of course, Emile too likes things clean, likes his wife-to-be clean. After all, "nothing in the world is more disgusting than an unclean woman, and the husband who is disgusted by her is never wrong."[93] Sophie, fortunately, "is much more than clean. She is pure" (395).

When Emile finally encounters his imaginary object in all her pure and fictive flesh, he barely notices her (although she is sitting at the dinner table with him)—that is, until the mother utters Sophie's name. It is love not at first sight but at first sound. In a matter of moments Emile is ready to camp out in a ditch near her abode, to give "his lessons on his knees before her," to crawl before her. He wants to adorn her, "he needs to adorn her": "As the idolater enriches the object of his worship with treasures that he esteems and adorns on the altar the God he adores, so the lover," writes the tutor, "constantly wants to add new ornaments to her [his mistress Sophie]" (425). Then again, perhaps he wants to add a few of those ornaments to himself. Having renunciated masculine self-adornment as a disgrace to his sex, the Rousseauist lover settles for vicarious pleasure, indeed rechannels his desire to be seen into the desire to see.[94] There is always the possibility, however, that the lover may find himself caught in a kind of psychic cross-dressing, that is to say, in a destabilizing identification with his own woman-as-spectacle.[95]

"Dear Emile," implores the tutor, "it is in vain that I have dipped your soul in the Styx; I was not able to make it everywhere invulnerable. A new enemy is arising which you have not learned to conquer and from which I can no longer save you. This enemy is yourself" (443). Emile "lets himself be governed by women" and is becoming one of them, "softened by an idle life" (431). The tutor has tried all manly means at his disposal to hold off the fatal metamorphosis. But woman's "empire" consists precisely in her power to turn man into his sexual other: "Hercules who believed he raped the fifty daughters of Thespitius was nevertheless constrained to weave [and, in fact, to dress as a woman] while he was with Omphale" (360–361). Rousseau leaves little doubt that the only way to avoid Hercules' fate (not to mention Narcissus's) is to follow the example of Ulysses, and thus to set out on a quest for the fatherland. "Do you know what government, laws, and fatherland are?" the tutor asks his pupil. The answer is clear, the consequence obvious: "Emile, you must leave Sophie" (448).

And so the reluctant pupil is dragged off on a two-year journey and given a crash course in the social contract. He learns the meaning of the body politic, the people, the sovereign, the laws. But he does not, in fact, find the fatherland because it does not exist. Emile declares his choice to remain a man to whom place is irrelevant; a nomad in spirit, he is equally at home among men or without them. The young man has his passions, however, and thus implores the tutor to give him back his "one chain," Sophie (472). The governor restrains his pupil, reminding him that, even though the "social contract has not been observed," "he who does not have a fatherland at least has a country." Should the state call him he must "fulfill the honorable function of citizen" (473–474).

Even though *Emile*, as Judith Shklar rightly argues, is primarily about making not a citizen but rather a man, domestic education would be doomed in the absence of some civic education.[96] Indeed, the chimera of the fatherland comes to the rescue at the moment Emile is most vulnerable (ready to marry and take to the nuptial bed); it is a supplement to that other chimera, the celestial object; and both chimeras are imaginary props whose purpose is to ensure that Emile attain the status of a man—that is, a non-woman. The man and the citizen (like domestic education and civic education) are, in fact, two sides of the same coin to the extent that both entail the renunciation of that which signifies at once the feminine and the aristocratic, and to the extent that neither can succeed in that renunciation alone. Each requires the supplement of the other. Sophie is no Spartan mother, but her modest attire and natural speech are the bedrock of Emile's own forswearing of luxury and strict adherence to the abstract principles of the fatherland, even in its absence: the values of work, duty, and simplicity and the sentiments of fraternity and equality.[97]

What *Emile* teaches, finally, is that cohabitation with women can be lived only with woman: that fiction within a fiction, the chaste image of Sophie that protects Emile against Sophie and all her sex. But the celestial object's earthly referent remains the wild card in Rousseau's pedagogical project. Quite apart from Sophie's unsurprising infidelity in the unfinished sequel to *Emile*—which leads her, as Susan Okin has shown, to the familiar, suicidal "fate of Rousseau's heroines"[98]—her status as a kind of compromise solution to the masterful mistress of the *Confessions* places "the woman" beyond the law. Indeed male pleasure and danger attend the "imperious Sophie," "the severe Sophie," as Rousseau repeatedly describes her. Having learned that the man wants to be on his knees at her feet and how to keep him there, that "imperious girl" (478) makes poor Emile sleep in a separate bed on their wedding night. She is admonished by the tutor for giving her husband cause to complain of her "coldness" (478–479). Her empire, in other words, might very well turn into that of those big-city women, who practice a false species of dissimulation and never love anything but themselves. Whatever its species, however, dissimulation is always just that. There is never any guarantee that men will correctly read the signs of femininity qua coquetry. The latter may be sincere or insincere, put in the service of woman's "natural empire" or "unnatural" female power. The whole foundation of the man or citizen stands on nothing but quicksand. Then again, there is always the social contract: chimera of the fatherland made sacred law.

The Semiotic Republic

Why is woman missing in the *Social Contract*? Leaving aside, for a moment, her unsurprising absence as citizen, let us reflect on her remarkable absence as a topic for political debate in a text that was published almost simultaneously with *Emile*.[99] Indeed, of woman (for once) hardly a word is said; the word itself appears only three times in the entire text.[100] And if we consider that the opening line addressed to men in this treatise on political right ("Man was/is born free, and everywhere he is in chains"; 46) finds its analogue in a line addressed to mothers in that treatise on education ("The first gifts they receive from you are chains"),[101] it seems even more incredible that a blank should mark the place of man's very first master. Taking up the analogy, however, we may speculate that the *Social Contract*, which argues that chains can be made "legitimate" (46), works surreptitiously on the problem of those other chains in *Emile* (and in the *Letter* and the *Discourse*). The Rousseauist citizen-subject will be in "a [desired] condition of bondage," as Hilail Gilden aptly puts it.[102] But the question is, who will be his master? with whom will he contract? with "une maitresse imperieuse" or with other men?

With the preceding remarks in mind, we may speculate that the absence of woman marks her spatial exclusion from the political site of meaning (the enactment and reenactment of the sociosymbolic pact, of legitimate chains), and that woman's permanent exile constitutes an absent presence, and a potentially disruptive one at that. To locate the paradigmatic and unnamed feminine threat, we have only to turn to the second chapter of the text, "On the First Societies": it is Circe, the sorceress. Contesting Aristotle's claim that "some [men] are born for slavery and others for domination," Rousseau observes: "Aristotle was right, but he mistook the effect for the cause. Slaves lose everything in their chains, even the desire to be rid of them. They love their servitude as the companions of Ulysses loved their brutishness. If there are slaves by nature, therefore, it is because there have been slaves contrary to nature. Force made the first slaves; their cowardice perpetuated them" (48). The reference to Ulysses, as Gilden notes, is taken from a work by Plutarch in which the hero "asks Circe to liberate his companions as well as other Greeks whom she had bewitched and transformed into brutes. Circe refuses to do so without their consent. She restores the power of speech to one of her victims and leaves Ulysses alone to speak to him. The beast to whom he speaks argues for the superiority of his transformed condition and refuses to become a man again."[103] Because Ulysses remains a man, says Gilden, he is the model mortal who points to the legislator. Perhaps. But clearly his contented companions—if not the "men as they are" who point to the Rousseauist problem of forming "laws as they can be" (46)—are the men as they might easily become (i.e., as speechless as infants) who point to the very necessity of the laws. And before accepting Gilden's suggestion that the lawgiver is a man like Ulysses, let us not forget that, in Homer's telling at least, even the famed hero is not invulnerable to Circe's charms and in fact barely escapes with his life. He all but forgets his goals of return, Ithaca and the fatherland. If he had not been later tied to the mast, moreover, he would have most surely succumbed to the sweet voices of the Sirens and fallen into the abyss. This feminine call from the beyond can be kept at bay only by the

most extraordinary means, including that most extraordinary of
human beings, the lawgiver.

Simply put, the sacred task of those whom Rousseau calls "Pères
de Nations" is to make men aware of what they themselves desire but
are often unable to discern; it is to articulate the unified inner voice of
reason in every man's heart: the general will that is immutable,
impartial, and never errs. The lawgiver is a quasi-divine figure who,
because he knows all men's passions but feels none of them, can serve
as the "organ" with which the body politic can "enunciate its will"
(67). He is neither Robert Filmer's patriarch nor Thomas Hobbes's
sovereign; he does not have that kind of monopoly on power and
meaning. Let us be clear as well that the wholly conventional voice of
the lawgiver bears no resemblance whatsoever to the original maternal voice. Indeed "Nature's voice" is now deemed, as the first version
of the *Social Contract* (*Geneva Manuscript*) tells us, a "false guide,
working continuously to separate him [the lawgiver] from his people,
and bringing him sooner or later to his downfall or to that of the
State."[104]

Rather than heed Nature, then, the lawgiver must oppose her,
separate his people from her: in short, codify the social pact or
"oath" such that the voice of duty replaces physical impulse, right
replaces appetite.[105] What looks like the Freudian superego is a
fragile achievement at best. Because men are "constantly reminded
of their primitive condition by nature,"[106] all it takes is a small
miscalculation on the part of the legislator as to the type of laws a
people can bear, or the slightest division in the "artificial social body,"
for the whole political edifice to collapse, whereby "invincible nature" regains her "dominion" (76). And if we now note that the
"sacred right that serves as a basis for all the others" (47) assumes but
does not name the sacred law we found buried in the *Essay on the
Origin of Languages*,[107] we can glimpse the magnitude of the lawgiver's
sacred task. To separate men from their "common mother," to wrest
from each individual the *moi humain* and transform it into the *moi
commune*, the lawgiver must, as the *Geneva Manuscript* puts it, "in a
sense mutilate man's constitution in order to strengthen it,"[108] substitute "a partial and moral existence for the physical and independent existence we have all received from nature." He must, so to

speak, build a fortress around the citizen-subject by ensuring that "natural forces are dead and destroyed" (68).

The importance of this act, first of separating and then of keeping separate (that is, of establishing and maintaining a series of symbolic and psychic oppositions: inside/outside, citizen/foreigner, culture/nature, masculine/feminine), can be seen clearly in Rousseau's unbounded admiration for Moses. In *The Government of Poland*—where the author tries his own hand at the role of the great legislator, in accordance with many of the principles of the *Social Contract*—Moses is celebrated for having transformed a "herd of servile emigrants ['wandering about in the wilderness'] into a political society, a free people." Just as the Genevan would secure the Poles against the impending Russian domination and cultural intermixture, so did Moses secure the Israelites against the hostile Philistines, pagan reengulfment:

> Determined that his people should never be *absorbed* by other peoples, Moses devised for them customs and practices that could not be *blended* into those of other nations and weighted them down with rites and peculiar ceremonies. He put countless prohibitions upon them, all calculated *to keep them constantly on their toes*, and to make them, with respect to the rest of mankind, outsiders forever. Each fraternal bond that he established among the individual members of his republic became *a further barrier, separating* them from their neighbors and keeping them from *becoming one* with those neighbors.[109]

The rites, ceremonies, and prohibitions that kept the Israelites vigilant or "on their toes" kept them distinct and separate, prevented the kind of cultural intermingling whereby their identity would have dissipated (as it often came close to doing) into the indistinct pagan environment. These rites included, among numerous others, circumcision (the sign of the covenant for which women cannot be marked and which symbolically separates men from the feminine, the maternal)[110] and the taboo on idols (representation of an invisible God). As Kristeva writes, Moses imposed on his people "a *strategy of identity*, which is, in all strictness, that of monotheism": aimed "to

guarantee the place and law of the One God." And "the place *and* law
of the One," she adds, "do not exist without *a series of separations* . . .
[which relate in the last analysis] to fusion with the mother." Those
rites testify to "the harsh combat Judaism, in order to constitute
itself, must wage against paganism and its maternal cults." What is
more, they carry "into the private lives of everyone the brunt of the
struggle each subject must wage during the entire length of his
personal history in order to become [and remain] separate, that is to
say, to become [and remain] a speaking subject and/or subject to
Law."[111]

Like Moses, Rousseau's secular lawgiver must create a subject
who consents to law, a subject who unites himself with others to
create the one: the unity of the artificial social body, its common ego
and voice. That is why it is not enough for the great legislator to draft
the laws; he must also communicate them such that they penetrate to
the very hearts of the citizens, who will then preserve them in their
cultural practices. This he does, in part, not by employing force or
reason, both of which Rousseau strictly forbids him, but rather by
speaking in the mute eloquence of Signs, those "crude but august
monuments of the sanctity of contracts."[112] The Jews' prophets, says
Rousseau, were masters of this archaic language,[113] but the political
uses of Signs are not in any way exclusive to biblical or ecclesiastical
communities. Indeed, as Rousseau indicates in *Emile*, the Sign is the
very lifeblood of monarchies and, not least, of republics. To cite one
example, the genius of Antony was to eschew the letter for the Sign
when he had the bloody corpse of Caesar "brought in" for all to see:
"What rhetoric!"[114]

Of particular interest, however, is a less gruesome version of the
Sign, in which the law is engraved on the hearts of citizens, the image
of the fatherland kept constantly before their eyes, through "spectacular display,"[115] better known as the secular ceremonies and rites
of manly passage in which the social is secured through the sartorial
contract: "How great was the attention that the Romans paid to the
language of signs! Different clothing according to ages and according
to stations—togas, sagums, praetexts, bullas, laticlaves; thrones,
lictors, fasces, axes; crowns of gold or of herbs or of leaves; ovations,

triumphs. Everything with them was display, show, ceremony, and everything made an impression on the hearts of citizens."[116] The hierarchic features of dress mark and sustain differences among men in the midst of unity; the individual identifies with but is not lost within the manly crowd; the masculine pleasure in self-adornment is indulged without betraying any effeminacy. Finally, let us note and reserve comment on a more sexually ambiguous version of the Sign: "The Doge of Venice [is] without power, without authority, but rendered sacred by his pomp and dressed up in a woman's hairdo under his ducal bonnet."[117]

One place where the semiotics of the Roman republic and those of the Jewish state meet those of the social contract, where the Sign prevents the kind of mingling that is the death of the body politic and the citizen-subject, is in Rousseau's detailed proposal for preserving Poland against the foreign threat. Above all, the citizenry must develop "an instinctive distaste for mingling with the peoples of other countries." Therefore, Rousseau advises, all national customs must "be purely Polish." For example, "the Poles [should] have a distinctive mode of dress. . . . See to it that your king, your senators, everyone in public life, never wear anything but distinctively Polish clothing."[118] And, to guard against class mingling, "I should like each rank, each employment, each honorific reward, to be dignified with its own external badge or emblem. I should like you to permit no officeholder to move about *incognito*, so that the marks of a man's rank or position shall accompany him wherever he goes."[119] And so forth.

Even as this amazingly precise semiotics evinces the "dream of a transparent society, visible and legible in each of its parts," in Michel Foucault's words, it also contests inherited class position, the signifying economy of landed property.[120] All "active members of the republic," advises Rousseau, are to be divided into three classes, each of which is to have "a distinctive emblem that its members will wear on their persons." These emblems, however, are to "be struck out of distinct metals, whose intrinsic value would be in inverse proportion to the wearer's rank." Then, since signifiers of aristocratic privilege are also those of counterfeit masculinity, "the ribbons and jewels" that have served as the insignia of "knighthoods"—and were conferred on the basis of "royal favor"—are to be strictly forbidden: they "have overtones of finery and womanish adornment that we must avoid in the institution we are creating."[121]

In the place of such unmanly marks, Rousseau puts "the stamp of the knightly tournaments," which are to reconfigure the male body as the spectacular site of republican virtue and individual merit. Because "delight in physical exercise discourages the dangerous kind of idleness, unmanly pleasures, and luxury of spirit," Poland should promote a variety of "open-air spectacles" in which men of all classes compete for prizes (yet other emblems) and display their "bodily-strength and skill." These public games—in which "different ranks would be carefully distinguished," "the people never actually mingle with the rulers"—would challenge those of noble birth to prove their worth in a communal scopic field. All claims to superior rank would be evidenced by "external signs," which must be legible enough to be read by the people, public enough to prevent those who govern from becoming "unmanly and corrupt."[122]

"Spectacular display," then, makes at once the man *and* the citizen; the citizen *and* the man are produced at once through the republican spectacle.[123] This is why the masculine pleasure in self-display is not in any way forbidden by Rousseau but rather strictly regulated: "Let us look with a tolerant eye on military display, which is a matter of weapons and horses [not to mention the rest of the martial paraphernalia that characterized the festive scene in the square of Saint-Gervais]. But let all kinds of womanish adornment be held in contempt. And if you cannot bring women themselves to renounce it [or rather men to renounce their vicarious pleasure in it], let them at least be taught to disapprove of it, and view it with disdain, in men."[124] At stake is "The Great Masculine Renunciation," which is to say the man, the citizen, the republic. Sumptuary laws alone are powerless against the masculine desire for sumptuous self-display. No law could possibly contain that kind of excess, that kind of disorder in men; not even the prohibition on "gambling, the theater, comedies, operas—everything that makes men unmanly."[125]

To be in any way effective—effective at keeping the feminine other at bay—sumptuary laws and the taboo on disgraceful spectacles must be combined, at each and every moment, with hard work,

strict adherence to the laws, constant vigilance, in a word, obstacles
to dangerous idleness and unmanly pleasures. That is why freedom
for Rousseau, as Benjamin Barber writes, "entails permanent and
necessary tension, ineluctable conflict. It requires not the absence
but the presence of obstacles; for without them there can be no
tension, no overcoming, and consequently, no freedom."[126] In the
absence of all obstacles there is only the permeability of the ego or, as
the *Social Contract* tells us, of the "moral and collective body," its
"unity" and "common self" (53).

Thus, in addition to the natural obstacles to self-preservation that
bring men together in the first place, there is the obstacle of private
wills: "If there were no different interests, the common interest,
which would never encounter any obstacle, would scarcely be felt"
(61). Invincible Nature would take its place; the abject feminine
other would take its place. Then there is the obstacle of the weather
that guards men against the ravages of luxury: "In climates where
seasonal changes are abrupt and violent, clothes are better and sim-
pler" (94). A certain deprivation is necessary in the republic, not so
much to foment revolution, but enough to keep men on their toes.[127]

Above all, the republic must regulate the use of money, that
secular idol—the other being woman—that "merely supplements
men." For one thing, "that which supplements is never so valuable as
that which is supplemented."[128] For another, what is supplemented
soon ceases to exist. "Is it necessary to march to battle? They [the
citizens] pay troops and stay home. Is it necessary to attend the
council? They name deputies and stay home." Money promotes
"softness and the love of comforts." It is the beginning of the end:
"Give money and you will soon have chains." With his purse in the
place of himself, the masculine subject vanishes as a citizen, vanishes
as a man. He forgoes active participation in the public duties and
ceremonies that alone safeguard against the feminine threat: military
service (masculinist self-display) and the "periodic assemblies" (reenactment of the contract, 106–107). Money breeds the fatal economy of the representative, the parasite that is the "death of the body
politic." Fact: The moment a people allows itself to be represented,
"it is no longer free, it no longer exists." Reason: "Sovereignty cannot
be represented. . . . It consists essentially in the general will [the one,

the I], and the will cannot be represented. Either it is itself [the one, the I] or it is something else; there is no middle ground." None at all—that is, nothing short of the something else, the chaos or abyss of the unmanly passions. Indeed, the slightest spacing between the citizen-subject and his political voice introduces a momentary non-coincidence that is nothing less than calamitous: "The general will becomes mute" (98–109).

The republic, then, must be small, tight, fortresslike. Since any slackening of the social bond spells disaster, each citizen must remain, as Derrida observes, "within earshot" of all the others, within the acoustic field of the one, the celestial voice.[129] A man is either with the community or against it, a citizen or a foreigner. There is nothing in between short of the dissolution of the social pact. And let us not forget, "Whoever refuses to obey the general will shall be constrained to do so by the entire body; which means only that he will be forced to be free. For this is the condition that, by giving each citizen to the homeland, guarantees him against all personal dependence" (55). This contentious Rousseauist maxim makes profound sense inasmuch as one state of bondage substitutes for another; compared to enslavement to a feminine authority, not to mention to one's own femininity, it is an act of secular grace when the republic compels a man to be free—to be a citizen qua man.

Woman is not simply missing in the *Social Contract*; she is, rather, the absent presence that constitutes but mostly unsettles the boundaries of the semiotic republic. She is, in fact, as dangerous as money (if not more so): a supplement, simulacrum, or idol. Inscribed in the very crime of representation, compelled to make of herself a fetish, woman always exceeds the Rousseauist terms of her containment. Like money, woman is that which, in Kristeva's words, "impinges on symbolic oneness,"[130] the I of the masculine speaking subject, the I of the *moi commune*. The celestial object undercuts the celestial voice. Inhabiting the citizen-subject as otherness, woman haunts a social (sartorial/linguistic) contract which is as unstable as the masculinist signs that constitute it are arbitrary. Rousseau may insist that "we are not our clothes,"[131] but his version of "The Great Masculine Renunciation" teaches just that. And, "if it is clothes alone, i.e., a cultural sign, an institution, which determine our reading of . . . masculinity and femininity and insure sexual opposition," as Shoshana Felman asks; "if indeed clothes make the *man*—or the woman—, are not sex roles as such, inherently, but travesties?"[132] "Jean-Jacques Rousseau, citizen of Geneva," has already given us his insightful if fearful answer to that very rhetorical question.

CHAPTER THREE

The "Furies of Hell": Woman
in Burke's "French Revolution"

In my opinion all that you say of the Queen is pure foppery.
—Philip Francis to Edmund Burke

Am I obliged to prove juridically the Virtues of all those I shall see suffering every kind of wrong, and contumely, and risk of Life, . . . before I endeavour to excite an horror against midnight assassins at back stairs, and their more wicked abettors in Pulpits? What, are not high Rank, great Splendour of descent, great personal Elegance and outward accomplishments ingredients of moment in forming the interest we take in the Misfortunes of Men? The minds of those who do not feel thus are not even Dramatically right.
—Edmund Burke to Philip Francis

Reflections on a Revolution in France is a dramatic text. And the distinctive features of Edmund Burke's rhetorical style are nowhere better displayed than in the literary recreation of that "atrocious spectacle" of "the morning of the 6th of October 1789," when the king and queen of France were "forced to abandon the sanctuary of the most splendid palace in the world" under threat of assassination.[1] As Isaac Kramnick has written, these few pages, which set the stage for the emotional effusion that characterizes Burke's poetic evocation of Marie Antoinette, cast the "humiliation of the queen as the dramatic embodiment of Jacobin evil."[2] That Burke was quick to play the part of knight-errant, on whose literary potency the honor of women depended, was not unusual. The figure of a lady in distress is an all too common trope in Burke's writings and speeches.[3]

The political meaning of Burke's gendered coding of social crisis, however, turns, in part, on the question of how much importance we can attribute to what appears to some readers as nothing more than a bombastic deployment of feminine tropes, which admittedly lent high drama but presumably added little substance to Burke's political theory. Although Burke's masterful use of figural language remains undisputed, there is a curious tendency in political theory scholarship to regard such prose as an almost inexplicable poetic digression. Treating Burke's flights into rhetoric as instances of an imagination out of control,[4] or as regrettable expressions of the author's "natural ardour,"[5] many informed critical readings of Burke see in his theatrical language and chivalric posturing little more than what Thomas Paine aptly coined a "dramatic performance."[6]

Yet Paine's critical view of the "stage-effect" produced by "Mr. Burke's Horrid Paintings" suggests that literary artifice is not incidental but rather crucial to what W. J. T. Mitchell has called the "politics of sensibility."[7] Burke himself notes this in his letter to Philip Francis when he explains the importance of dramatic form in the development of a conservative counter-rhetoric. As Frans De Bruyn puts it, for Burke "the articulation of a political ideology is equally the art of telling a story."[8] And the task of the master storyteller, as Burke observed in his 1757 essay on aesthetics, *Enquiry into the Origins of our Ideas of the Sublime and the Beautiful*, "is to affect rather by sympathy than imitation; to display rather the effect of things on the mind of the speaker . . . than to present a clear idea of the things themselves." Because "we yield to sympathy, what we refuse to description," said Burke, the great writer is he who manipulates the magical power of words to draw the reader into his emotional universe—a universe populated by seductive and terrifying, crowded and confused verbal images.[9]

Taking up the *Enquiry's* theory of writing and aesthetic response, De Bruyn shows that Burke drew extensively on eighteenth-century gothic and sublime literary conventions to tell highly charged tales of social and sexual transgression. And at the heart of Burke's nightmarish tale of Jacobinism, he argues like Kramnick, is a portrayal of woman as the innocent victim of male sexual aggression and commercial avarice.[10] Yet, if the *Reflections* depicts woman as the passive object of lewd male sensibilities and the Jacobin attack on landed property, what amounts to a literary *construction* of endangered femininity in his texts emerges in relation to, and needs to be squared with, another representation of woman: the aggressive political woman whose threat to the sexual economy of chivalry and the aristocratic order is both evoked and managed in the author's prose.

Examining the recurring tropes of female monstrosity that organize Burke's account of the French Revolution as a sublime tale of horror, I consider the *Reflections* as an attempt to make sense not only of what Ronald Paulson calls the "seemingly unthinkable political phenomenon"[11] of Jacobinism but also of the seemingly unthinkable phenomenon of political women. If Burke's "French Revolution" transforms the great historical event it appears to describe,[12] it tells as well a tale of the writer's efforts to contain a confused social world and an inverted symbolic order in which femininity no longer signifies what Burke would have it signify—beauty, order, and submission. What comes apart in the French Revolution, I argue, is a gendered semiotic code, outlined in the *Enquiry*, which organizes the traditional moral order around the binary opposition of the feminine beautiful and the masculine sublime. Burke's political prose defends a traditional world in which feminine and masculine figures, like Marie Antoinette and her monarch husband, cannot be dissolved into the play of signifiers in which, as Burke puts it, "a king is but a man; a queen is but a woman; a woman is but an animal; and an animal not of the highest order."[13]

The act of writing a political theory of the Revolution, of organizing a plethora of "astonishing" events into a linear narrative of tragic proportions, however, implicates the author of the *Reflections* in questions of gender and political rhetoric that involve but cannot be reduced to his stated authorial intent—his conscious effort to contest, with words, the actions of "midnight assassins at back stairs, and their more wicked abettors in Pulpits." As De Bruyn rightly notes, Burke's use of gothic and sublime aesthetic modes far outstrips the author's "need for narrative clarity and focus."[14] We can discern moments when Burke's hysterical defense of moderation exceeds the terms of his own rhetorical strategy of figurative excess, and when Burkean political discourse is swept up by the revolutionary play of signification that the *Reflections* would contain with the pleasing illusion of woman as proper femininity.

Burke's recreation of the assault on the royal family at Versailles, which draws on a dark and repressed image of brute passions unconstrained by the civilizing conventions of chivalry and feminine beauty, figures woman as the site of chaos that is at once social and symbolic. In Burke's telling, the incursion of women into public space undermines the symbolic foundation of the Old Regime: the feminine beautiful and the masculine sublime. To account for that which disrupts the moral order (public women), Burke will call on the literary trope of the sublime to figure something that by its essential nature cannot be sublime (woman) but that must be accounted for both politically and symbolically. Once woman is sublime, however, Burke's French Revolution spins out of control, having lost its mooring in the binary relation just mentioned. To contain the uncanny feminine sublime, Burke will transform the unfamiliar figure of public woman into a familiar, beautiful figure of femininity: the 1789 October march of "Amazonian" sans culottes into the 1774 ethereal vision of Marie Antoinette, the horrible spectacle of the "furies of hell" into the chivalric spectacle of the lady in distress. The political activity of women, we find, is the uncanny for Burke: an unknown that is first encoded as "sublime" and then rendered safe—if only rhetorically and far from reassuringly—as "beautiful."

Terror and Delight

On the face of it, Burke's 1757 *Enquiry* stands as an attempt to develop "an exact theory of our passions, or a knowledge of their genuine sources."[15] The massive confusion that characterizes treatises on this subject, says Burke, stems largely from a failure to distinguish properly between the two great poles of aesthetic experience: the beautiful and the sublime. A precise, even scientific, theory of the passions is possible, he argues, because the "origin of these ideas" of the sublime and the beautiful is in the intrinsic qualities of objects (5). Inasmuch as Burke accepts the tenets of Lockean epistemology, however, he agrees that, when "we go but one step beyond the immediately sensible qualities of things, we go out of our depth" (129–130). He thus concedes that whatever we take to be the essential properties of objects is only what we surmise to be their properties based on the universal effects those objects produce in subjects.

Fending off the possibility that a subject-oriented theory of aesthetic response must lead to relativism and, consequently, to further conceptual confusion, Burke writes: "It must necessarily be allowed, that the pleasures and the pains which every object excites in one man it must raise in all mankind, whilst it operates naturally, simply, and by its proper powers only; for if we deny this, we must imagine that the same cause operating in the same manner, and on subjects of the same kind, will produce different effects, which would be highly absurd" (13–14). Even though this tautology proves nothing, it intimates the urgency of Burke's project to produce, under the shadow of Lockean sensationism, a foundation—or better, a transcendent foundation—on which to build a theory that is at once aesthetic and moral.[16] In the *Enquiry*, that foundation goes under the name of the "agreement of mankind" (15), which is a tacit emotive contract of sorts: a consensus of our senses that is both evidenced and reproduced in habits and manners—in a word, custom—and that is crucial to social order. "For if there were not some principles of judgment as well as of sentiment common to all mankind," writes Burke, "no hold could possibly be taken either on their reason or their passions, sufficient to maintain the ordinary correspondence of life" (11).

To demonstrate the agreement of mankind, Burke organizes his text around the "remarkable contrast" of the beautiful and the sublime. For instance:

> Sublime objects are vast in their dimensions, beautiful ones comparatively small; beauty should be smooth, and polished; the great, rugged and negligent; . . . beauty should not be obscure; the great ought to be dark and gloomy; beauty should be light and delicate; the great ought to be solid and even massive. They are indeed ideas of a very different nature, one being founded on pain [the sublime], the other on pleasure [the beautiful]; and however they may vary afterwards from the direct nature of their causes, yet these causes keep up an *eternal distinction* between them, a distinction never to be forgotten by any whose business it is to affect the passions. (124, my emphasis)

Even as Burke suggests that the intrinsic properties of objects maintain the eternal distinction between the sublime and the beautiful, he is also concerned that this distinction not be neglected by the author who would excite the human passions: "Beauty *should be* light and delicate," the sublime *"ought to be* solid and even massive," and so forth—which is another way of saying that the dichotomy itself is not so eternal that one need not even think about it. On the contrary, constant cultural work is required to keep the difference between the beautiful and the sublime. The supposedly objective features that distinguish the two are produced discursively and maintained through cultural representations, not the least of which is the Burkean representation of an incommensurable sexual difference.

The gender analogues of the remarkable contrast emerge clearly in Burke's claim that, just as there are two classes of aesthetic object, so are there two classes of virtue: the "great" and the "subordinate." The former "turn principally on dangers, punishments, and troubles," the latter "on reliefs, gratifications, and indulgences." The former produce terror and fear, the latter affection and love. Then, to bring the point home, so to speak, Burke offers the following example of the difference between what is "highly venerable" and what is "inferior in dignity":

> The authority of a father, so useful to our well-being, and so justly venerable upon all accounts, hinders us from having that entire love for him that we have for our mothers, where the parental authority is almost melted down into the mother's fondness and indulgence. But we generally have a great love for our grandfathers, in whom this authority is removed a degree from us, and where the weakness of age mellows it into something of a feminine partiality. (111)

This passage follows and is followed by extensive discussions of womanly beauty, which Burke contrasts repeatedly with the manly sublime. So obvious are the gendered examples of the "remarkable contrast" that Burke interjects: "In short, the ideas of the sublime and the beautiful stand on foundations so different, that it is hard, I had almost said impossible, to think of reconciling them in the same subject, without considerably lessening the effect of the one or the other upon the passions" (113–114). Mixing the sublime and the beautiful, for example, produces the quasi-feminized figure of the grandfather, whose attenuated authority makes him lovable but not lovely and certainly not venerable.

To bring the (masculine) sublime and the (feminine) beautiful into mere textual proximity, then, is to undercut the singular affective powers of each. Burke also insists that, if their "qualities . . . are sometimes found united," this in no way proves "that they are any way allied." On the contrary, they remain eternally "opposite and contradictory" (124–125). The urgency that characterizes Burke's insistence on the difference belies the possibility that the (feminine) beautiful and the (masculine) sublime exist, not in a clear relation of pure antithesis, an "eternal distinction," but rather in an uneasy relation of interdependence. The fact that one term (the sublime) is dominant in the "remarkable contrast" suggests further that each term derives its meaning from, and signifies the difference of, the other; the meanings of the (masculine) sublime and the (feminine) beautiful are produced through the vigorous articulation of the masculine sublime/feminine beautiful opposition in the space of representation of the *Enquiry*.[17]

At this point, several questions arise. Why is Burke at pains to establish, and then to keep at each and every moment, the difference between two aesthetic categories (the sublime and the beautiful) which are also categories of identity (the masculine and the feminine)? What is at stake in these binary oppositions for the "agreement of mankind"? And, finally, how stable are the aesthetic qua gendered terms of the "remarkable contrast"?

These questions can be usefully explored by turning to the insights of another theorist of the sublime and the beautiful, Freud. Indeed, in the spirit of Burke's *Enquiry*, Freud's essay "The Uncanny" takes "the subject of aesthetics" as an occasion to advance a "theory of the qualities of feeling." What makes the Freudian category of the uncanny especially relevant for our purposes is that, like the Burkean sublime, it concerns the class of objects that are frightening, that excite in the subject dread and horror.[18] Freud's claim that the uncanny (*unheimlich*) is not distinct from but rather interconnected with its etymological opposite, canny (*heimlich*), moreover, sheds some light on (I say "some" because Freud's essay raises its own set of problems) the "eternal distinction" between the (feminine) beautiful and the (masculine) sublime.

Freud claims that "as good as nothing is to be found upon this subject [of terror] in comprehensive treatises on aesthetics," which generally treat the sublime as a species of the beautiful and thus are concerned with objects that call forth "feelings of a positive nature" rather than with ones that elicit "the opposite feelings of repulsion and distress."[19] Obviously Freud had not read the *Enquiry*. For it was Burke who changed the terms of aesthetic theory by insisting that "terror is . . . the ruling principle of the sublime" (58). To cite the famous definition, "Whatever is fitted in any sort to excite the ideas of pain, and danger, that is to say, whatever is in any sort terrible, or is conversant about terrible objects, or operates in any manner analogous to terror, is a source of the *sublime*; that is, it is productive of the strongest emotion which the mind is capable of feeling" (39).

Burke is uncompromising in his claim that terror attends the sublime. "Admiration, reverence, and respect" are but "inferior effects." In its highest degree, the sublime produces "astonishment": "that state of the soul, in which all its motions are suspended, with some degree of horror." The subject is frozen, paralyzed with fear: "The mind is so entirely filled with its object, that it cannot entertain any other, nor by consequence reason on that object which employs it" (57). The sublime, in Burke's telling, is violent, fierce; the encounter with it is at bottom the subject's fantasized relation with death.

But it is not only Burke's insistence on terror that makes the *Enquiry* so remarkable and original. It is also his claim that, when pain and danger do not press too close, the sublime produces "a sort of delightful horror, a sort of tranquillity tinged with terror" (136). Vastness, infinity, succession, and repetition are all powerful sources of this "delight," which is a distinct mode of affect associated with an excess on the plane of signifiers—a kind of implosion of meaning, a "great profusion of things," "a sort of fireworks."[20] When one gazes at "the starry heaven," for instance, the eye is overwhelmed by innumerable stars, which "lye in such apparent confusion, as makes it impossible . . . to reckon them." A similar effect is produced in works of poetry, oratory, and rhetoric, "which owe their sublimity to a richness and profusion of images, in which the mind is so dazzled as to make it impossible to attend to that exact coherence and agreement of the allusions" (78).

Similarly, "to make any thing very terrible," writes Burke, "obscurity seems in general to be necessary" (58). The moment the eyes become accustomed to the sight of a dangerous object, the sense of dread practically vanishes. Clarity and light belong to the beautiful; they destroy the sublime. What is sacred, for example, is almost always shrouded in obscurity, kept "from the public eye." On this principle, "heathen temples were dark," and "even in the barbarous temples of the Americans at this day, they keep their idol in a dark part of the hut, which is consecrated to his worship" (59). To clinch his point about obscurity, Burke offers the following "description of Death" from *Paradise Lost*:

> The other shape,
> If shape it might be called that shape had none
> Distinguishable, in member, joint, or limb;
> Or substance might be called that shadow seemed,
> For each seemed either; black he stood as night;
> Fierce as ten furies; terrible as hell;
> And shook a deadly dart. What seemed his head
> The likeliness of a kingly crown had on. (59)

"In this description all is dark, uncertain, confused, terrible, and sublime to the last degree," Burke adds. "The king of terrors [Death]" takes an undefined shape, a sexually ambiguous shape. He is "fierce as ten furies," those raging female spirits who are represented in ancient art and poetry, as H. J. Rose writes, as "formidable beings, stern of aspect, carrying torches and scourges, and generally wreathed with serpents, or having serpents in their hair or carried in their hands."[21] In Greek mythology they are called the Erinyes, and they often appear in connection with other menacing underworld female powers—such as the harpies, which gives in *Paradise Lost* the combined figure of the "harpy-footed Furies" (2.596)—and are linked to the forces of fertility. Above all, they are avengers of blood crimes who relentlessly pursue and punish the individual who has desecrated the ties of kinship (e.g., Orestes for the murder of Clytemnestra).[22] In the *Eumenides* they are ferocious cannibals and, as Apollo's words emphasize, are clearly on the nether side of the clean and proper: "You should make your dwelling in the cave of some blood-gorged lion instead of coming to defile others by inflicting your foulness in this temple of prophecy."[23] They are also figured in Greek myth as embodied curses, a destructive frenzy that seizes and drives the individual toward catastrophe. In this sense the Erinyes are associated again with "the daemonic power of defilement," which, as Jean-Pierre Vernant and Pierre Vidal-Naquet write, "is contiguous and attaches itself, over and beyond the individual to his whole lineage."[24]

I have more to say about these Erinyes or Furies—the Burkean trope for Jacobin frenzy and defilement par excellence. But for now we might read them as intimating the presence of the menacing feminine in the masculine sublime. For they introduce ambiguity into the "remarkable contrast," a sexual undecidability into the logic of terror which can be explored further by turning back to Freud. The word *heimlich*, he writes, is ambiguous: "On the one hand it means what is familiar and agreeable [homelike, domestic], and on the other, what is concealed and kept out of sight." Its opposite, *unheimlich*, is commonly taken to signify only the second meaning (in Burke's terms, what is obscure and sacred, kept out of the public eye). Interrogating the common distinction between the familiar and the unfamiliar, the pleasing and the terrible, the feminine and the masculine, Freud suggests that "*heimlich* is a word the meaning of which develops in the direction of ambivalence, until it finally coincides with its opposite, *unheimlich*." Interested in the meaning of the prefix *un*, Freud argues that the experience of terror is the recurrence of something that has been repressed, something that may have been not originally frightening but rather familiar. What we call uncanny is not in fact an object but an effect produced through an unconscious *process*.[25]

In his reading of E. T. A. Hoffmann's "The Sand Man," Freud suggests that terror is an effect that belongs to the anxiety of "the castration complex of childhood."[26] But this theory of *das Unheimliche* is complicated by another example, which "furnishes a beautiful confirmation of our theory of the uncanny": "It often happens that neurotic men declare that they feel there is something uncanny about the female genital organs. This *unheimlich* place, however, is the entrance to the former *Heim* [home] of all human beings, to the place where each one of us lived once upon a time. . . . In this case too, then, the *unheimlich* is what was once *heimisch*, familiar; the prefix '*un*' is the token of repression."[27]

Having invoked this amazing example to prove that "everything is *unheimlich* that ought to have remained secret and hidden but has come to light," to show that "what is *heimlich* thus comes to be *unheimlich*,"[28] Freud then proceeds to bury it beneath the classic oedipal narrative. The example itself speaks to Freud's well-known tendency to reduce the preoedipal terror of undifferentiation to the masculine subject's oedipal horror of female castration.[29] The fearful submission to paternal authority, in Freud's telling, rescues the masculine subject from another kind of terror: the maternal *heim* that can only be figured as a lack, as *unheimlich*—in a word, as abject.

Had Freud read the *Enquiry*, he would have found a model for the rather desperate rhetorical move that brings the terror of undifferentiation, of the preobjectal, back home to the father. What threatens the masculine subject, in Burke's account, is the passion of "imitation," which "forms our manners, our opinions, our lives." "Yet if men gave themselves up to imitation entirely," he continues,

and each followed the other, and so on in an *eternal circle*, it is easy to see that there never could be any improvement amongst them. Men must remain as brutes do, the same at the end as they are at this day, and that they were in the beginning of the world. To prevent this, God has planted in man a sense of ambition. . . . It is this passion that drives men to all the ways we see in use of signalizing themselves, and that tends to make whatever excites in a man the idea of this distinction so very pleasant. . . . It is on this principle that flattery is so prevalent. . . . Now whatever . . . tends to raise a man in his own opinion, produces a sort of *swelling* and triumph that is extremely grateful to the human mind; and this *swelling* is never more perceived, nor operates with more force, than when without danger we are conversant with terrible objects, the mind always claiming to itself some part of the dignity and importance of the things which it contemplates. (49–51)

The sublime, then, rescues the masculine subject from the eternal circle in which he would remain like a brute: speechless, undifferentiated, nameless. Contrary to what Thomas Weiskel argues, the delightful "swelling" afforded by the sublime entails something more than the release from "an unconscious fantasy of parricide" through identification with an all-powerful paternal figure.[30] For the moment of "sublimation," in Julia Kristeva's words, "is nothing else than the possibility of naming the pre-nominal, the pre-objectal." Caught in the timeless void of imitation, the masculine subject, she writes, is trapped in "a *land of oblivion* [maternal space] that is constantly remembered," crushed under "a weight of meaninglessness."[31] This is akin to what Burke calls "absolute indifference" (104), a common human condition that can easily slide into a "languid inactive state" that is at once psychic and physiological: "Melancholy, dejection, despair, and often self-murder, is the consequence of the gloomy view we take of things in this relaxed state of the body" (135). And the cathartic solution, argues Burke, is the terror of the sublime.

One can put the same process in Kristevan terms:

In the symptom [of melancholy, dejection], the abject permeates me. Through sublimation I keep it under control. The abject is edged with the sublime. . . . For the sublime has no object either. When the starry sky, a vista of open seas . . . fascinate me, there is a cluster of meaning, of colors, of words . . . that arise, shroud me, carry me away. . . . The "sublime" object dissolves in the raptures of a bottomless memory. It is such a memory, which, from stopping point to stopping point, remembrance to remembrance, . . . transfers that object to the refulgent point of the dazzlement in which I stray in order to be. As soon as I perceive it, as soon as I name it, the sublime triggers—it has always already triggered—a spree of perceptions and words that expands memory boundlessly. I then . . . find myself removed to a secondary universe, set off from where "I" am—delight and loss. Not at all short of but always with and through perception and words, the sublime is *something added* that expands us, overstrains us, and causes us to be both *here*, as dejects, and *there*, as others and sparkling.[32]

Lifted by the sublime from the abyss of the uncanny, clammy abject, the subject encounters a proliferation of signifiers that overwhelm it but are nonetheless a paternal godsend for all that. Over-strained by the sheer excess of perceptions and words, the subject moves from imitation to ambition, dejection to delight, speechless-ness to speech, namelessness to identity. For what Burke calls "diffi-culty" (77) is, as he argues, a source of greatness that inheres in the sublime object and is claimed by the terrified subject who struggles to make sense of the "great profusion" of words or things. Swelled with pride, this subject is confirmed as a masculine speaking subject in the paternal symbolic order.

What then of beauty? Where does the beautiful figure in the logic of terror and identity? Or, rather, how does one sustain the differ-ence between the feminine beautiful and the maternal abject, be-tween that which confirms the masculine subject and that which menaces him? To keep what is *heimlich* from becoming *unheimlich*, to keep what ought to remain secret and hidden from coming to light, in short, to keep woman as the ground for "a sort of swelling and triumph," a fair degree of feminine artifice is required. This is why, as Burke argues, we wrongly think of beauty as identical with perfec-tion: "This quality, where it is highest in the female sex, almost always carries with it an idea of weakness and imperfection. Women are very sensible of this; for which reason, they learn to lisp, to totter in their walk, to counterfeit weakness, and even sickness. . . . Beauty in distress is much the most affecting beauty" (110).[33] And so the feminine beautiful, supposedly eternally distinct from the masculine sublime, comes down to nothing more than a cultural performance of endangered femininity. Let us not underestimate the womanly de-vice of "strategic mistakeness"[34] in the phallic theater: "We submit to what we admire, but we love what submits to us; in the one case we are forced, in the other we are flattered into compliance" (113), swelled with a sense of "our" importance. The "agreement of man-kind," the very foundation of a universal aesthetic that is also a universal moral order, then, stands on nothing but a fraud: it is as unstable as the gendered semiotic code that governs "our" response to objects is arbitrary.

But the code is unstable in yet another way. Not even the machina-tions of feminine deceit can guarantee the Burkean moral aesthetic, not even the masquerade of femininity can protect the masculine subject against the abyss that subtends the "remarkable contrast." For one thing, the fragile beauty of woman that flatters the male ego also "acts by relaxing the solids of the whole system": the subject is thus not swelled but "softened, relaxed, enervated, dissolved, melted away by pleasure" (149–150). Melancholy, dejection, and despair are not far behind, and with them abjection. For another, what appears beautiful ceases to be so once the pleasing illusion is desecrated by the desire for knowledge: disentangled from "the allurements of the object," the enlightened subject peers into "the artifice of its contrivance." At that point the beautiful becomes "odious and distasteful" (108)—uncanny, abject.

We might say, then, that the Burkean aesthetic is menaced by the abject, against which the *Enquiry* obsessively maps the "remarkable contrast" of the beautiful and sublime; an "eternal distinction" that is nothing other than, in Kristeva's words, the "demarcating imperative" of abjection. And we next see that the defilement rites—which build up lines between nature and culture, the feminine and the masculine, the profane and the sacred, the pure and the impure—are akin to the rite of writing that produces Burke's French Revolution. For "writing," as Kristeva argues, "implies an ability to imagine the abject, that is, to see oneself in its place and to thrust it aside only by means of the displacements of verbal play."[35] Above all, language is the vehicle of sublimity with which the author of the *Reflections* tries to tame female signifying practices that do not conform to the Burkean foundational principle of "beauty in distress," and that thus destroy the "agreement of mankind."

Burke's *Reflections* as Self-Reflections

Burke's political task of the *Reflections* was in important respects a literary one. The English, who were not witness to the "astonishing" spectacle on the Continent, were subjected instead to a simulacrum: to a representation of the Revolution in the words of such men as the Reverend Dr. Price. Indeed, the preacher's sermon of 4 November 1789, as the subtitle of the *Reflections* makes clear, was the representation that served as the referent, so to speak, of Burke's French

Revolution.[36] Re-presenting that sermon, the conservative writer would produce, among other discursive objects of defilement, "the Theban and Thracian Orgies acted in France and applauded," with "enthusiastick ejaculation," in the "Old Jewry" (85).

In contrast to the "perverted" Price and his "lay flock," who "exult"—delight—in the terrible spectacle of human tragedy, "natural" men, said Burke, are first filled with "melancholy sentiments" and then "alarmed into reflexion; our minds . . . are purified by terror and pity" (93–94). And yet, if "there is no spectacle we so eagerly pursue, as that of some uncommon and grievous calamity," to cite the *Enquiry*, and if the spectacle of another's misfortune "always touches [us] with delight," what was to ensure that the sublime Burkean spectacle would excite in its readers sympathy rather than the voyeur's delightful horror? In 1757, the writer's answer was this: "The pain we feel, prompts us to relieve ourselves in relieving those who suffer."[37] But in 1790, Burke observed, the "strange scene" on the Continent, which ought to produce "contempt and indignation," inspired in some "no other sentiments than those of exultation and rapture" (22).

And so the theorist of terror and delight would try to contain this inexplicable perversity not by eschewing the powers of verbal sublimity but by deploying them in the service of a conservative sensibility. Just as language mediates terrible objects to produce the reader's delight, the writer's feeling mediates language to produce the reader's sympathy. Burke had argued as much in 1757. In 1790, however, the overflow of writerly emotion would exceed what some commentators read as a classic Burkean rhetorical strategy of instilling terror and pity in the reader by means of crowded and confused images. The sublime narrative of social and political transgression would give way to an almost unsignifiable "universe of Death"[38]— populated by harpies and furies and other such feminine tropes of frenzy and pollution—that needs to be taken into account both politically and symbolically.

To situate the *Reflections* strictly within a thematic of authorial intention, moreover, neglects the possibility that in staging horror the writing subject himself is "purified by terror"—purged, as Kristeva argues, of what is opposed to I. Still, the didactic distance Burke struggles to maintain between himself and his objects often collapses under the very textual mechanisms that generate the narrative pleasure (i.e., authorial and readerly delight) to be had in those extraordinary scenes of cannibalism, murder, and sexual violation that are the literary hallmark of his 1790 masterpiece. I examine several of these passages below. Here I suggest that, if the conservative political persona of "Edmund Burke" is created discursively in the writings and speeches on the French Revolution, so too is that persona unsettled by the writerly act of naming Jacobin abomination.[39]

This reading of the *Reflections* focuses on the "voice" of the author—a voice whose dialogic ambiguity emerges through a multiplicity of literary modes, a virtual battle of social languages that undercut any single enunciative authority. For Burke not only draws on eighteenth-century sublime and gothic literary conventions, he also interweaves a discourse of the sacred and the profane, a carnivalesque language of the masquerade, literary satire and parody, detailed historical narrative and political analysis, and, of course, intensely personal commentary.[40] This melange has led to multiple interpretations of Burke's text: ones that find evidence for Burke as master dramatist, as the defender of natural law, or as the rightful heir to John Locke.[41] But when political theory scholars pose the question of interpretation as "Who is the real Burke?" they risk overlooking the remarkable, troubling, and ambiguous achievement of the *Reflections*—the manner in which its discursive elaboration of the confused mode of the aesthetic generates the politics of sensibility, whereby persuasion is primarily a matter of inducing the reader to share in the author's feelings.

To investigate the dialogic workings of the *Reflections*, that is, as Mikhail Bakhtin argues, of language as both an intersubjective and intrasubjective form of communication, we might begin with the origins of the text itself.[42] Although it is often noted that the *Reflections* began as a letter to Charles-Jean-François Depont, it is seldom considered why Burke chose to publish his manuscript as a letter, despite his claim that a different plan might have been "more favourable to a commodious division and distribution of his matter." "Having thrown down his first thoughts in the form of a letter," Burke wrote in his preface to the reader, the "author" "found it difficult to change the form of address" (13). Perhaps the letter was retained for other reasons: "Indulging myself in the freedom of epistolary intercourse, I beg leave to throw out my thoughts, . . . just as they arise in my mind, with very little attention to formal method" (21).

Even if the epistolary form of the *Reflections* justifies (if inadequately for both hostile readers like Paine and more sympathetic ones like Francis) the author's personal style, we might nevertheless ask: If Burke's text was a letter, then who was its addressee? It was Depont, it was England—but it was also the author himself. Burkean political discourse, to invoke Kristeva's formulation of Bakhtinean dialogism, evinces a *Spaltung*, a split subject: the *Reflections* "belongs doubly to an 'I' and to the other."[43] As a letter, then, the text can be read as sustaining a conversation with the reader as well as with the writer himself—a conversation in which the writing subject works through, in dialogic form, the effects of that sublime historical object (the French Revolution) and its English representations.

"I have had my Eyes turned with great Curiosity to the astonishing scene now displayed in France," wrote Burke to Depont in 1789. "It has certainly given rise in my Mind to many Reflexions, and to some Emotions."[44] What would amount a year later to an amazing understatement in the context of Burke's passionate political crusade against Jacobinism is telling. If "reflexions" was the eighteenth-century word for ideas, so too was it a word used to express, as Locke wrote, "that notice which the Mind takes of its own Operations."[45] "Reflexions," then, can be taken to mean not only the relationship between sensations and ideas but also the self-reflections of a mind whose autonomy had been undermined by Lockean sensationism. For "the mind," as Weiskel has written of the Lockean model, "is not its own place, but the space in which semiotic sublimations occur. It cannot control the making of meaning." What is more, he adds, "if sensations are withdrawn, consciousness knows only a vacancy,"[46] an absence or emptiness that produces boredom or what Burke called indifference and, ultimately, melancholy. And the astonishment produced by the sublime, as Burke argued in the *Enquiry*, is a cathartic antidote to passivity, to languor and despair.

"It looks to me as if I were in a great crisis," wrote Burke as he asked the reader to forgive his emotional rhetoric, "not of the affairs of France alone, but of all Europe, perhaps of more than Europe" (21–22). To consider the writer's coding of a crisis that was at once psychic and political, I now turn to his reflections on the collapse of the "remarkable contrast" and thus the universal "agreement of mankind." The familiar Burkean image of a beautiful femininity, which made the masculinist "reflexion" on woman a self-constituting act, was shattered by a confusion of aesthetic signals: the feminine in the guise of the masculine, beauty as sublimity—simply, by political women.

Breaking the Code

Let us begin our excursion into the gendered imagery of the *Reflections* by noting that Burke's articulation of proper (passive and beautiful) femininity as the foundation of moral order was conservative but far from idiosyncratic. In a social world as marked by the great dividing line of aristocracy and peasantry as it was by the subtle signs of graduated statuses within the middle orders, women occupied a central place in the complex grammar of class relations.[47] The common law tradition of coverture—in which the family was seen as being governed by the single will of the paterfamilias—had secured in both England and France a patrilineal form of inheritance. Subsuming the identity of the wife into that of the husband, coverture denied a married woman any legal right either to property or to her own children. Lord Hardewick's 1753 Marriage Act sought to buttress this model of the family against the challenges that came from a variety of social quarters and especially from the plebeian population.[48]

Burke's vigorous opposition to the repeal of the Marriage Act is interesting for our purposes because, by linking sexual to economic to political transgression in a chain of metonymic and metaphoric associations, his rhetoric foreshadowed his narrative account of the collapse of the Old Regime. In a 1781 speech, for instance, Burke rebuked his parliamentary colleagues for worrying too much about the accumulation of wealth in great families and too little about the semiotics of property—that is, of "the monied" versus "the landed interest." Even though the act allowed the aristocracy to arrange their children's marriages and thus enabled them to enlarge their estates, said Burke, "still we must have laws to secure property, and still we must have ranks and distinctions and magistracy in the state." In guarding against the "avarice of the father," the House of Commons was letting loose "another species of avarice,—that of the fortune-hunter." "Who has heard of a man running away with a woman not worth sixpence?" Burke answered his own rhetorical question with a metaphoric substitution that countered the principles of affective individualism: "Do not call this by the name of the sweet and best passion,—love. It is robbery,—not a jot better than any other."[49]

Burke's opposition to change in family law was rooted in the English moral and political discourse that came under attack by parliamentary activists who contested the twin analogies of kings/fathers and subjects/children.[50] One might say, then, that Burke's defense of the traditional family was simply a defense of the state as a "mortmain," a "family settlement," through which, he wrote in the *Reflections*, "we transmit our government and our privileges, in the same manner in which we enjoy and transmit our property and our lives" (45). As J. G. A. Pocock writes, Burke makes "the State not only a family, but a trust; not so much a biological unity, or the image of one, as an undying *persona ficta*": a set of artificial institutions—grounded in the ancient constitution and preserved in the social institutions of landed property and the patriarchal family—that transcend generational time. This "positive, recorded, *hereditary* title" which secures our liberty, property, and so on, writes Burke, "carries an imposing and majestic aspect. It has a pedigree and illustrating ancestors. It has its bearings and ensigns armorial. It has its gallery of portraits; its monumental inscriptions; its records, evidence, and titles" (44–46). Burke creates this *persona ficta*, says Pocock, "by the simple device—the most superb of all legal fictions—of identifying the principles of political liberty with the principles of our law of landed property." He would make sense of the Burkean family/state analogy by seeking its "historical genesis" in English common law and "in the chain of association formed by the words 'entail', 'family settlement', 'mortmain', 'incorporation'."[51] But this reading neglects another chain of meaning: the material origins of the modern state, property, and family that bind the master trope of *persona ficta* to that other master trope of paterfamilias; that tie the "superb legal fiction" of property and liberty to the patriarchal legal fiction of paternity; and that thus connect state, family, and landed property to men's property in women.[52]

Consider, for example, the domestic scenes of transgression that form no small part of Burke's *Letter to a Member of the National Assembly* (1791). The Jacobins stand accused of calling on "the rising generation in France" to execute the revolution in property by seeking their fortunes in the homes of the landed nobility. Sending out an aggressive army of "pert, petulant literators, . . . who betray the most awful family trusts *and* vitiate their female pupils," the Jacobins teach that "debauchers of virgins . . . [are] fit guardians of the honor of those husbands who succeed legally to the office which the young literators had preoccupied without asking leave of law or conscience."[53] So it is that the semantic connection between the crime against property and that against women, established by a conjunction ("and"), takes the form of metaphoric language: women are that property, their chastity is that "awful family trust." Indeed, the enterprising pedagogue, agent of the monied interest, usurps the legal place of the aristocratic husband in the "office" of the female body. From that place the Jacobins wage their profane assault on sacred family trusts, on landed property, and ultimately on the state.

The point becomes even more obvious, the rhetoric more sublime, when we consider Burke's figuration, in the *Letter*, of the unguarded female body as the site of the collapse of class distinctions and the defilement of aristocratic blood.

When the fence from the gallantry of preceptors is broken down . . . there is but one step to a frightful corruption. The rulers in the National Assembly are in good hopes that the females of the first families in France may become an easy prey to dancing-masters, fiddlers, pattern-drawers, friseurs, [etc.] . . . who, having the entry into your houses, and being half domesticated by their situation, may be blended with you by regular and irregular relations. By a law they have made these people their equals.[54]

Note the feminized figures who aggressively enter, first, the sacred domain of the landed estate and, then, the aristocratic female body. The breakdown of the "venerable castle" of the paterfamilias and of the *persona ficta* leads first to sexual debauchery, then to blood inter-mixture, then to the collapse of the pure/impure dichotomy, then to the effacement of the landed/monied interest distinction, and inevitably to the confounding of all signs of social status: "In this manner these great legislators complete their plan of levelling."[55]

Burke takes up the same theme in the *Reflections*, only now he links the intermixture of monied and landed blood, once again by the medium of the female body, to the transformation of land into money, to the seizure of church properties, and finally to the frenzied production of assignats. In accordance with "ancient usages," writes Burke, "the general circulation of property, and in particular the mutual convertibility of land into money, and of money into land, had always been a matter of difficulty." Then, in a passage that evokes the "eternal distinction" of the beautiful and the sublime, Burke adds: strict "family settlements, . . . the great mass of landed property held by the crown . . . [and] the vast estates of the ecclesias-tic corporations,—all these had kept the landed and monied interests more separated in France, less miscible, and the owners of the two distinct species of property not so well disposed to each other as they are in this country" (122–123). That what is landed is sacred, and what is monied, profane, emerges in Burke's claim that "the monied property was long looked on with rather an evil eye by the people"— not just by plebians but by those members of the aristocracy whose "unendowed pedigrees and naked titles" were "eclipsed, by the splendour of an ostentatious luxury." This pretentious signifier of monied wealth, this blasphemous simulacrum of nobility, polluted the great families that were forced either to interbreed or to perish: "Even when the nobility, which represented the more permanent landed interest, united themselves by marriage . . . with the other description, the wealth which saved the family from ruin, was sup-posed to contaminate and degrade it" (123).

Although Burke's rhetorical association of blood defilement with aristocratic shame was far from unusual, his insistence that the monied and the propertied interests be kept at all times separate took on an obsessive character that needs to be accounted for in terms of his symbolic economy of Jacobin abomination. The monied interest struck at the nobility through not only the family but also the church. Claiming that "ecclesiastics are fictitious persons" (120), the Jacobins confiscated the vast tracts of church property, an insane project that led to more "madness": the creation of "a new paper currency [assignats]," which was spewed out by "the *Bank of discount* [the Caisse d'Escompte], the great machine, or paper-mill, of their fictitious wealth" (135). In contrast to the "real" coin of the landed interest, whose production and circulation was controlled through such sacred laws as the Marriage Act, the "fake" currency of the monied interest was unmoored from tradition and, especially, from the sanctity of matrimony. Even as "the sworn guardians of property must look upon with horror" this "depreciated paper which is stamped with the indelible character of sacrilege," they too were forced to participate in the "pillage" by being compelled to use that paper in all payments (136–137). Assignats became the carriers of the contagion of Jacobin blasphemy.

In contrast to those "who have wished to pledge the societies of Paris in the cup of their abominations," writes Burke, the mass of the English people are horrified and alarmed by these "confiscators [who] truly have made some allowance to their victims from the scraps and fragments of their own tables from which they have been so harshly driven, and which have been so bountifully spread for a feast to the harpies of usury" (118–119). Rightly anticipating that assignats would benefit a class of speculators, the master dramatist certainly made good use of his ancient mythology. But surely the trope of the harpies of usury suggests more than a greedy bunch of men. For the harpies were birdlike creatures with the faces of women, and highly menacing ones at that. In the *Odyssey* they carried away the orphaned daughters of Pandareos, who had been under the protection of Aphrodite, and gave the girls as servants to—who else?—the Erinyes (furies). In the *Aeneid* they appeared in a far more abominable form: "modelled on carrion-feeding birds," as Rose writes, and "represented as not only hideous and ravenous, but as so disgustingly filthy that such food as they did carry off was left totally uneatable."[56] We again encounter this fully abject image of the harpies in Burke's all-out war on Jacobinism: *Letters on a Regicide Peace.*

As we saw with the presence of the Furies in the sexually indistinct figure of Death in the *Enquiry*, the Burkean trope of the harpies cannot be explained adequately either as a mere rhetorical flourish, expendible to political meaning, or as a conscious image of horror staged by Burke the master dramatist. It points rather to the likewise indistinct figure of Jacobin abomination Burke everywhere associates with the collapse of the Old Regime; it intimates that woman may be not beautiful and passive but rather sublime and aggressive if not abject.

Burke's representations of an endangered feminine virtue and the revolution in property need to be squared with another kind of political qua sexual transgression. The familiar Burkean trope of woman as victim, in short, might be read (initially at least) through the "topos of the woman-on-top," to borrow Natalie Davis's famous phrase.[57] For if 1789 was sublime, it was so, in Burke's view, because it was carnivalesque: plebeian "country clowns" acting the part of distinguished magistrates and especially women acting that of public men.

In France the Burkean semiotic code—whereby the beauty of woman (or the domestic figure of mother) signifies (excites ideas of) tenderness, love, and affection in masculine subjects—is disrupted both in the larger Jacobin practice of exploding the conventional usage of words (like "mother") and in the "unheard of" practice of divorce. "Those monsters" of the "Constituent Assembly of 1789," writes Burke in *Letters on a Regicide Peace*, have "employed the same or greater industry to *desecrate and degrade* that state, which other legislators have used to render it holy and honorable. By a strange, uncalled-for declaration, they pronounced that marriage was no better than a common civil contract." Quasi-religious filial pieties are then tempered by a more reasoned passage in which we are presented with the facts, with the ratio of divorces to marriages in the year 1793—a ratio, Burke comments, "not much less than one to three: a thing unexampled, I believe, among mankind."[58] And so indeed it was, in England at least. As Keith Thomas has shown, from the end of the seventeenth century through 1857 "there were only a little over 200 divorces granted." And "only about a half dozen were granted at the suit of a woman."[59]

That in France, however, primarily women, but also some men, pressed the National Assembly to relax divorce laws[60] may not be inconsequential to the passage that immediately follows such reasoned calculation—a passage in which arithmetical observation gives way to horror and disgust of a distinctly abject kind:

> Mothers are taught that tenderness is no part of their character, and, to demonstrate their attachment to their party, that they ought to make no scruple to rake with their bloody hands in the bowels of those who came from their own.
>
> To all this let us join the practice of cannibalism. . . . By cannibalism I mean their devouring, as a nutriment of their ferocity, some part of the bodies of those they have murdered, their drinking the blood of their victims, and forcing the victims themselves to drink the blood of their kindred slaughtered before their faces. By cannibalism I mean also to signify all their nameless, unmanly, and abominable insults on the bodies of those they slaughter.[61]

Classic Burke—master dramatist? Certainly, but also something else. There are few passages in the entire corpus of his writings that can begin to approach this scene of Jacobin abomination. We are already far from gender inversion (if we were ever there), from the recognizable topus of the woman on top. In Kristevan terms, the Jacobin assault on the symbolic order unleashes the semiotic body, an orgasmic and devouring body. Their abominable and unmanly insults amount "to tampering with the mother. Defilement is incest considered as a transgression of what is clean and proper."[62] Once the sanctity of matrimony is defiled by the practice of divorce, nothing can contain the raging frenzy of the (profane) maternal and its assault on (sacred) paternal law. Nothing can control the abject that sweeps away the entire social symbolic order: in Burkean parlance, the feminine beautiful/masculine sublime, the eternal distinction, the remarkable contrast, the agreement of mankind. Nothing, that is, short of writing. The unsignifiable can be named, the abject tamed: it is "nameless, unmanly, and abominable."

The symbolic figure of the frenzied mother or woman that haunts Burke's rhetorical universe represents a confounded social world, populated by public women, in which reproduction outside marriage destroys property and all other forms of masculinist self-representation, including the *persona ficta* of the state, by destroying the legal fiction of paternity. In accordance with Burke's critique of the Jacobin explosion of the traditional significations of words, "the prostitute," he writes, is "called by the affected name of 'a mother without being a wife.'" This mother who is no wife produces children with no father and then steps into the public space of the National Assembly to call "for a repeal of the incapacities which in civilized states are put upon bastards." Supposedly freed from the "tyranny of parents and of husbands," all such women are granted the same "profligate equity," "the same licentious power."[63]

When Burke's French Revolution is understood as a semiotic chaos, it can also be seen to be a reproductive chaos. The frenzied prostitute/mother is figured as the embodied equivalent of the political economic nightmare Pocock has identified as the motivating force of Burke's impassioned rhetoric: the multiplication of paper credit. Assignats "might end by destroying the value and the meaning of property," as Pocock writes, but for Burke disorganized reproduction was the more fundamental source of the chaos in value.[64] For property, in whatever form, is meaningless if it cannot be transmitted in an orderly fashion, if it cannot be attached to a paternal name.

"It is not necessary to observe upon the horrible consequences of taking one half of the species wholly out of the guardianship and protection of the other," wrote Burke of Jacobin France.[65] A woman's chastity was the most precious form of property; it was at the center of a political theory of the state understood as a "mortmain," as "perpetual ownership," as a "family settlement"; it was the male sex-right that ensured the orderly transmission and inheritance of economic and political power. Without it, the entire historical panoply of "records," "acts of parliament, and journals of parliament," which Burke rather desperately invoked to secure "canonized forefathers" against Jacobin abomination, were nothing. Without it, the "positive, recorded *hereditary* title" of the ancient constitution was little better than the "paltry, blurred shreds of paper about the rights of man" (99–100). Without it, the state as *persona ficta*—its "pedigree and illustrating ancestors," "bearings and ensigns armorial," "gallery of portraits," "monumental inscriptions"—in short, the whole museum of masculinist symbolic representations—was a collection of meaningless artifacts.

That was one reason why the conservative writer would trans-figure aggressive femininity into beauty in distress—and why the beautiful would be accorded a far more momentous role in the *Reflections* than it had held in the *Enquiry*. The canny spectacle of endangered femininity would be invoked rhetorically to tame the uncanny spectacle of political women, and to manage the writerly horror of the feminine sublime.

The Furies at Versailles

"Burke's originality," writes Peter Hughes, "which is so caught up with obsessive notions of ancestry, generation, and origins, re-quires—by an understandable paradox—an allusive literary, even histrionic style, a style that serves as its and *his* own genealogy."[66] The anxiety-ridden rite that is Burke's writing does indeed produce such a genealogy in producing, time and again, the "records, evi-dences, and titles"—in a word, the signs—of sacred paternal author-ity. And it does so, I have suggested, to shore up the venerable castle of *persona ficta* and paterfamilias, not to mention the boundaries of the masculine speaking subject, against a profane genealogy that can only be called maternal, against Jacobin abomination figured as the disorderly woman: frenzied, cannibalistic mothers, harpies, and furies of hell.

Moreover, Burke's hysterical defense of tradition, which is to say of a certain kind of genealogy, involves another, related rhetorical strategy: the appropriation of "feminine sensibility" in which mas-culine displays of emotion are framed by a larger rhetoric of chiv-alry—a rhetoric in which it appears to be the woman, rather than the narrator himself, who is endangered, the lady, rather than her knight, who is in distress.

Burke found his woman and his cause in what was to become the condensed moment of that "revolution in sentiments, manners, and moral opinions"—a moment Burke dated from the "atrocious specta-cle of the 6th of October" (93). Most would like to forget that day;

"history," however, "who keeps a durable record of all our acts," says the writer, "will not forget." When summoned by the theorist, history could bear witness to the authenticity of an account that loathsome others would leave "to feed the living ulcer of a corroding memory": "History will record, that on the morning of the 6th of October 1789, the king and queen of France . . . lay down . . . to indulge nature in a few hours of respite, and troubled melancholy repose" (83–84). So begins the spectacle of all Burkean spectacles: the sublime assault on the beautiful, the profane on the sacred—the Jacobin assault on Marie Antoinette.

"History," however, like the "letter," became the pretext for the display of emotion that characterizes Burke's literary recreation of a historical event:

> From this sleep the queen was first startled by the voice of the centinel at her door. . . . A band of cruel ruffians and assassins . . . rushed into the chamber of the queen, and pierced with an hundred strokes of bayonets and poniards the bed, from whence this persecuted woman had but just time to fly almost naked, and through ways unknown to the murderers had escaped to seek refuge at the feet of a king and husband, not secure of his own life for a moment.
>
> This king, to say no more of him, and this queen . . . were then forced to abandon the sanctuary of the most splendid palace in the world, which they left swimming in blood, polluted by massacre, and strewed with scattered limbs and mutilated carcasses. Thence they were conducted into the capital of the kingdom. . . . The royal captives . . . were slowly moved along, amidst the horrid yells, and shrilling screams, and frantic dances, and infamous contumelies, and all the unutterable abominations of the furies of hell, in the abused shape of the vilest of women. (84–85)

At this point, let us note that, to the extent that there is *any* gendered figure in this atavistic scene of Jacobin defilement, it is the figure of woman—or rather the unutterable that is made nameable by being symbolized as the furies of hell. The masterful rhetorical delivery that utters the unutterable tames the abject by naming it. Perhaps the sheer horror of it produces a kind of writerly delight? Not quite the "holy ejaculations" (86) of a Price, but perhaps a rather swelling feeling nevertheless?

A similar possibility could be put somewhat differently. Consider that this famous passage is itself almost immediately *preceded* by another, in which the king, "to say no more of him," is once more nothing but a powerless monarch, helpless to prevent the fatal course of events. In the space of a few lines, Burke iterates three times the impotent image of the "captive king" (82–83). The king is not only the prisoner of Jacobin France; he is the captive of Burke's political prose. For the passage about this captive king refers to the agreement reached on October 6, *after* the early morning assault on the palace, which established that the monarch would live under popular surveillance.[67] But once the king, "to say no more of him," is exiled to the outlands of Burke's narrative reordering of the French Revolution, there is left none other than the author himself to defend the queen's honor: "I thought ten thousand swords must have leaped from their scabbards to avenge even a look that threatened her with insult" (89). In the historical absence of chivalry and the textual absence of the king, it would be the words qua swords of the writer that avenged the lady.

Defend her honor against whom? Against what Kramnick, in his provocative reading of these passages, suggests are Jacobin phallic ravishers? Perhaps, but also something else. If we look at the social actors and the political events that led to the sixth of October, we find that the narrative atavism occasioned by the assault on the "almost naked" queen is not simply the creature of Jacobin "unleashed masculinity." I am referring to the famous October 5 Women's March on Versailles: a march of approximately six thousand women—market women, wage earners, wives of artisans, craftswomen, small business women, and some women from the middle classes—exercising their time-honored right as mothers to demand bread for their families; a march that provoked the municiple government to send the National Guard to hold off counterrevolution by bringing the king to Paris; a march that, in the early hours of the sixth, would lead "a crowd of women and a *few* men," as Ruth Graham writes, to enter "the palace door leading to the queen's chambers."[68]

The momentous historical scene Burke's prose reconstructs and figures as the spectacle of Jacobin frenzy, then, entails something other than the clash of the masculine sublime (phallic ravishers) and the feminine beautiful (the queen of France); it entails rather that of the feminine sublime (political women) and endangered femininity (the "almost naked" queen). It is a battle of one kind of woman against another kind, Burke's "furies of hell" against "Marie Antoinette." This means, to press further the same point about this Burkean symbolic economy, that if the "hundred strokes of bayonets and poniards"—which supposedly "pierced" the "bed, from whence this persecuted woman had but just time to fly almost naked"—can be read as phallic imagery, it can just as well be read as phallic femininity. And when passive (beautiful) femininity becomes phallic (sublime) femininity, what is left but for woman to be figured as the abyss: the "horrid yells, and shrilling screams, and frantic dances, and infamous contumelies, and all the unutterable abominations."

Speaking of this "almost naked" queen and the frenzied scene that immediately follows, or rather is unleashed by, her exposure, the famous *Moniteur* account of 6 October did not record anything like the queen's nakedness. But no eye-witness account is going to stop the fecundity of the writer's imagination. The figure of the "almost naked" queen was crucial to Burke's French Revolution. The terror that attends this figure, however, entails more than the kind of social leveling whereby "Marie is no different from any other woman."[69] What excites terror and horror in the writer, rather, are the political women who explode the "pleasing illusions" of feminine artifice, not simply of the queen but of woman as a signifier of masculinity and as the ground of the Burkean symbolic order. And let us not forget to mention another kind of terror, the distinctly masculine kind of terror observed by Freud: the *unheimlichkeit* of the maternal *heim*. Once woman is not clothed in "the wardrobe of a moral imagination," once "the decent drapery of life is . . . rudely torn off," *once the queen is not "almost naked" but naked*, there is nothing left but the "defects of our [or rather her] naked shivering nature" (90). And there is nothing to halt the play of signifiers that destroys the remarkable contrast and, with it, the boundary between culture and nature: "A king is but a man; a queen is but a woman; a woman is but an animal;

and an animal not of the highest order."[70] That is why, as Burke tells us in the very next passage, "in the groves of *their* [the Jacobin's] academy, at the end of every visto, you see nothing but the gallows"—the abyss (91). That is also why, in the writer's moral imagination, the queen cannot be naked but rather "almost naked," clothed with language, that master fetish.

What will stop "the unutterable abominations of the furies of hell"? Writing, of course: a rite that halts this excess on the plane of signifiers, resolves the breakdown of discourse and the social symbolic order, by means of a substitution, a metaphor. Having displaced the uncanny spectacle of the "famous 5th of October" march of "Amazonian" Parisians[71] onto the more familiar spectacle of the endangered femininity of the sixth, that rite then further contains the symbolic chaos by transcoding the anthropophagous 1789 visto of the "furies of hell" into the reassuring 1774 visto of the dauphiness at Versailles.

> It is now sixteen or seventeen years since I saw the queen of France, then the dauphiness, at Versailles; and surely never lighted on this orb, which she hardly seemed to touch, a more delightful vision. I saw her just above the horizon, decorating and cheering the elevated sphere she just began to move in,—glittering like the morning-star, full of life, and splendor, and joy. Oh! what a revolution! and what an heart must I have, to contemplate without emotion that elevation and that fall! (89)

And so the transfiguration would seem to be complete: uncanny has been refigured as canny femininity, as nothing more than "beauty in distress," that "most affecting beauty."

The beauty that contains symbolic chaos also produces the man of "natural feeling." Burke told Francis: "I tell you again that the recollection of the manner in which I saw the Queen of France in the year 1774 . . . did draw Tears from me and wetted my Paper. These Tears came again into my Eyes almost as often as I lookd at the description. They may again. . . . I tell you it is truth—and that it is true, and will be true, when you and I are no more."[72] The writer's sensibility is beyond truth claims, beyond the opinions of Francis, beyond the words of Price, beyond Jacobin assassins and Amazonian Parisians, and beyond politics.

On a closer reading, however, the metaphor that produces the man of natural feeling, that contains symbolic chaos, and that slows the excess of signifiers produces another kind of excess: that of the signified. Overwhelmed by the image and the melancholy sentiments it occasions, the writer all but lapses out of discourse ("Oh! What a revolution!"; 89). He is in danger of stasis, obsessive fixation.[73] Following Paul de Man's insights on romanticism, we could say that Burke's recollection of the queen seems "to come so close to giving in completely to the nostalgia for the object that it becomes difficult to distinguish between object and image, between imagination and perception." In its "desire to draw closer and closer to the ontological status of the object," Burke's language seems to appropriate it completely.[74] The writer so identifies with the very figure whom his words violate and rescue as to all but usurp her place. More than *almost naked* in his emotive epistolary address, is not the knight himself the lady in distress?

"Excuse me," Burke begs the reader, "if I have dwelt too long on the atrocious spectacle of the sixth of October 1789, or have given too much scope to the reflections which have arisen in my mind. . . . As things now stand, with every thing respectable destroyed without us," he added, "one is almost forced to apologize for harbouring the common feelings of men" (93). 1789 was abominable enough, but by 1792, after France had declared war on Prussia and Austria, the country that had once been "*gentis incunabula nostrae*" (93) became the "mother of monsters, more prolific than the country of old called *ferax monstrorum*." No image of feminine beauty or endangered femininity could possibly contain that kind of profligacy. It was rather a manly matter of whether "the fallow of peace comes to recruit her fertility."[75] And so Edmund Burke, the man of feeling, would take up the stance of the warrior.

Postscript: The Maternal Republic

"I hope that those who yet wear royal, imperial, and ducal crowns will learn to feel as men and as kings," wrote Burke in his *Letters on a*

Regicide Peace; "if not, I predict to them, they will not long exist as kings or as men."[76] The *Letters* were a virile cry to arms against France, whose imperialist intentions, in Burke's view, gave the lie to the olive branch with which she would lure and then destroy the English crown. Seduced by her "deceitful representations," Parliament was proceeding as if that "dire goddess . . . with a murderous spear in her hand, and a gorgon at her breast, was a coquette to be flirted with." A sort of "impious hierarchy" is to be erected, said Burke, "of which France is to be the head and the guardian." Breeding revolutions that appear to respect the sovereignty of states, the real object of Jacobinism is to make them all "dependent ostensibly, as well as substantially, on the will of the mother republic to which they owe their origin."[77]

It was, in other words, a question of genealogy. Republican France was not "a new power of an old kind" but rather "a new power of a new species"[78]: a fecund maternal power compared to which all the signs—the records and journals of Parliament and acts of Parliament—of canonized forefathers were like so many moldy shreds of paper; a vigorous power compared to which "sluggish, inert, and timid" landed property was like a decayed fortress;[79] an aggressive power against which the "frivolous effeminacy" and the "cold sluggishness" of the English national character was like the timorous beautiful in the presence of the awesome sublime.[80] Quite simply: "If we meet this energy with commonplace proceedings, . . . with doubts, fears and suspicions, with a languid, uncertain hesitation, with a formal official spirit," Burke warned, "down we go into the abyss."[81]

As Don Herzog and Michael Mosher have both argued, by 1796 Burke had departed from the political principle of moderation and was willing to throw England into debt to wage holy war on Jacobin France.[82] In "Letter to a Noble Lord" (1796), Burke attacked the duke of Bedford for his languid spirit and unearned wealth. The feeble, feminized duke, and by extension the landed interest, would be ravaged by the "always vigilant, active, enterprizing" Jacobin—that is, as Mosher rightly notes, "were it not for [manly] men of talent like Burke."[83] But Burke's amazing assault on sacred family settlements and on the paternal authority of the landed nobility—in a word, his warrior stance—can hardly be understood apart from his figuration, in the "Letter," of what Herzog calls "the contagion of revolutionary principles."[84] It demands the closest reading:

> The Revolution harpies of France, sprung from Night and Hell, or from that chaotic Anarchy which generates equivocally "all monstrous, all prodigious things," cuckoo-like, adulterously lay their eggs and brood over, and hatch them in the nest of every neighboring state. These obscene harpies, who deck themselves in I know not what divine attributes, but who in reality are foul and ravenous birds of prey, (*both mothers and daughters*), flutter over our heads, and souse down upon our tables, and leave nothing unrent, unrifled, unravaged, or unpolluted with the slime of their filthy offal.
> [Burke next cites the following verse from the *Aeneid*, for which I give an English translation.]
>
> > No monster
> > More shocking, no pest or embodied wrath of gods,
> > More fierce than they arose from Stygian waters.
> > They have the face of virgins; from their bellies
> > Flows out the vilest discharge, and their hands
> > Are talon-like, their features always pallid
> > With hunger.
>
> [Burke again]
> Here the poet breaks the line, because he . . . had not verse or language to describe that monster even as he had conceived her. Had he lived to our time, he would have been more overpowered with the reality than he was with the imagination. . . . Had he lived to see the revolutionists and constitutionalists of France, he would have had more horrid and disgusting features of his harpies to describe, and more frequent failures in the attempt to describe them.[85]

There is something fully abject in Burke's symbolic economy that far exceeds even his most powerful images of disgust and horror in the *Reflections*. The "eternal distinction" between the (feminine) beautiful and the (masculine) sublime—not to mention that between the pure and the impure, the sacred and the profane—has so completely broken down that it is utterly absent. In the first segment, Burke's prose moves from France to the fecund maternal to chaotic anarchy to uncanny breeding to surrogate gestation to an inescapable abjection. There is nothing like a border, a margin, or a boundary here. The harpies are upon us, they are polluting our food, contaminating our country, effacing our speech. The abject, in other words, is not outside, not over there on the Continent; it is rather inside, right here breeding within our nation, breeding within ourselves. It is deadly and ravenous ("their features always pallid with hunger"); nothing can stop it—not even writing. For it exceeds the writer's powers of signification. Like the poet, Burke "has not verse or language to describe that monster as he had conceived her." She, *if* she it can be called, remains outside meaning; the disgusting figure of the harpie can hardly signify this threat, which is connected with a complete collapse of outside and inside, of the clean and proper, of the nameable and the unnameable, and thus, as Kristeva writes, of the ever "ambiguous opposition I/Other."[86]

The writer is abject: "Viewing things in this light, I have frequently sunk into a degree of despondency and dejection hardly to be described." The writer confronts the abject: "Yet out of the profoundest depths of this despair, an impulse which I have in vain endeavoured to resist had urged me to raise one feeble cry against the unfortunate coalition which is formed at home, in order to make a coalition with France."[87] Not every man can face up to that kind of profligate, maternal power; most men are driven away from her by "fatigue," "disgust," "unsurmountable nausea." But not "Edmund Burke." He assumes the part of true heroes, "who watch day and night by the bedside of their delirious country,—who, for their love to that dear and venerable name, bear all the disgusts and all the buffets they receive from their frantic mother."[88] For in that abject scene on the Continent were all the Burkean elements of a "swelling scene."

And so, like "Ulysses in the unravelling point of the epic story," so stood forth Burke in the mid-1790s.[89] Then again, perhaps this writer who overcame his melancholy to cry out against the deadly coalition with murderous Mother France was more akin to that other figure in the *Odyssey*, Menelaus, the surrogate father for Telemachus, who initiates the son of Odysseus into the paternal rites of the clean and proper. It is Menelaus who, in raising "the calamituous fate of his friends, and his own manner of feeling it," as the *Enquiry* tells us, "owns indeed, that he often gives himself some intermission from such melancholy reflections, but he observes too, that melancholy as they are, they give him pleasure."[90]

CHAPTER FOUR

The "Innocent Magdalen":
Woman in Mill's Symbolic Economy

I was seated at a table . . . with a woman at my left hand & a young man
opposite—the young man said, quoting somebody for the saying, "there are
two excellent & rare things to find in a woman, a sincere friend & a sincere
Magdalen." I answered "the best would be to find both in one"—on which
the woman said "no, that would be *too* vain"—whereupon I broke out "do
you suppose when one speaks of what is good in itself, one must be thinking
of one's own paltry self-interest? no, I spoke of what is abstractly good &
admirable." How queer to dream stupid mock mots, & of a kind totally unlike
one's own ways or character. According to the usual oddity of dreams—when
the man made the quotation I recognised it & thought he had quoted it wrong
& the *right* words were "an *innocent magdalen*" not perceiving the
contradiction.

—John Stuart Mill to Harriet Taylor Mill

As dreams go, Mill's of "some speculation on animal nature" lends
itself to numerous interpretations.[1] When situated in their historical
context, however, those "mock mots" take on a specific significance:
they point to a culturally contingent, and fundamentally ambiguous,
symbolic resolution of the contradiction that inhered in representations of the Victorian domestic ideal. It was an ideal of asexual
femininity in which persisted the figure of woman as willful bodily
appetite. It was a middle-class ideal in which a "sexless, moralized
angel and an aggressive, carnal magdalen" existed in a precarious but
necessary balance:[2] precarious, because the sexualized woman that
presumably lurked beneath her virtuous double undercut the domestic ideal as a cultural symbol of middle-class moral superiority;
necessary, because the supposedly disruptive effects of female sexuality provided a justification for the gendered separation of spheres.

For John Stuart Mill the sheer incoherence of cultural claims about woman was an occasion to expose the "angel in the house" as a patriarchal euphemism for the "domestic slave," coverture as the "legal slavery" of woman. No one knows the essence of woman, argued Mill, and those men who claimed to know it were continually stumbling over the logical inconsistencies of their own statements on proper femininity. Victorian representations of woman were unstable and dangerous masculinist constructions designed to service the "government of the male sex."[3]

In light of his critique of the domestic ideal as a vehicle of male power, commentators have puzzled over the shortcomings of Mill's most sustained indictment of patriarchy, *The Subjection of Women*. Susan Okin, Jean Elshtain, and Zillah Eisenstein have called our attention to how Mill's feminist prose runs aground on his own homilies to woman's "highest destiny,"[4] on his all-too-Victorian praise of female sexual restraint, and on his curious failure even to question the gendered division of labor in the family.[5] Whereas these critics locate Mill's blindness to the extralegal sources of women's oppression in his liberalism, Mary Shanley has argued that it is unfair to fault Mill for failing to "address issues not put forward by conditions and concerns of his own society." She submits further that, had Mill seen that the division of labor was an obstacle to sexual equality, he would have "altered his view of practicable domestic arrangements."[6]

In this chapter, I advance another reading of Mill and show that the extent to which he remained hostage to the very ideal of femininity he condemned reflects neither his inadequate understanding of how the model of a domesticated, feminized morality sustained sexual inequality nor the inevitable shortcomings of liberal theory itself.[7] Rather, I argue, the problems in Mill's feminism emerge despite and because of the rhetorical features of his own powerful arguments against woman's domestic slavery, and they bespeak the deep implication of asexual femininity as a moralizing force in the articulation of Mill's political vision.

It was a vision of an enlightened citizenry and a rational public sphere wrought in the context of the intense class struggles that characterized the tumultuous period between the First and Second

Reform Bills; a vision that identified bodily appetite as the primary cause of class conflict, poverty, and unemployment, hence as a major obstacle to social progress; a vision articulated through competing, class-laden, and gendered images of the "higher" and the "lower natures." It was a vision that documented Mill's contempt for the money-grubbing middle class, demonstrated his awareness of the effects of proletarianization on the working class, yet translated, finally, class inequality into moral difference—the difference between those who exercise "prudence" and "restraint" and those who "follow their brute instincts without due consideration."[8]

Whereas Mill's disdain for those enslaved to their base passions has been the subject of numerous debates,[9] little attention has been paid to the discursive uses of woman in framing the nature and scope of the problem of industrial and political reform as one of self-discipline and self-help in *Principles of Political Economy* and *Considerations on Representative Government*. What emerges in these writings are a series of contradictory arguments about the wage labor system and the extension of the franchise which locate, indeed figure, the female body as the site not only of gender but of class conflict, and not only of social progress but of cultural apocalypse. Alternately passive and active, transgressed and transgressive, that body takes on a highly ambivalent meaning in Mill's political narratives. It is deployed rhetorically to articulate Mill's radical case against woman's domestic slavery, but also to authorize his moral Malthusianism, his defense of Poor Law reform, and his delimited conception of representative democracy.

Attending to the symbolic figuration of the female body in Mill's discourses on class helps us explain the persistence of the domestic ideal in his vision of social progress. Because Mill held that individuals can be liberated from their dangerous desires, therefore from class, by reason,[10] he rejected the fatalistic Malthusianism of his conservative contemporaries and argued that political, economic, and social reform would weaken what he saw as the degrading appetites. But the almost demonic force with which Mill's political narratives invest those appetites casts doubt on the possibility that the working class could speedily be made rational beings, and it symbolically aligns their unruly passions with the impeding deterioration of humanity that was the other face of Mill's optimistic account of social progress.

This rhetorical slippage—whereby the laboring masses are first cast as the victims of larger social and cultural forces and then come to figure as the agents of the very social evils for which they were initially seen to be the effect—evinces an anxiety that individuals are not in fact the authors of their own actions, that they are determined rather by forces beyond human control. There is, moreover, a profound sense in Mill's writings that the fallenness of the masses is menacing to culture and contaminating to their social betters. Even though Mill would call for social reform, it was often for the kind of reform that can only be called a middle-class strategy of containment. Mill's dread of the masses would lead him to propose fairly elaborate devices to compensate for the extension of the franchise. It would also lead him to advocate a series of disciplinary mechanisms that increase the power of the state, place the working-class family under middle-class surveillance, underwrite the factory system as an instrument of moral reform, and uphold, at times, a less than enlightened public opinion.

These mechanisms pose serious problems for, indeed *produce*, Mill's passionate concern with individual liberty, and it is in relation to them that the shortcomings of his feminism emerge. One way of mitigating the dangers associated with the "power which can be legitimately exercised by society over the individual" is to advocate the Victorian solution, in the present state of things, of a self-regulating femininity as a check on animal instinct, therefore on class conflict.[11] So it is that woman (or rather the middle-class woman) comes to occupy an active, but none the less troubling, role as the vigilant superintendent not only of the private but of the public sphere, not only of the bourgeois but of the working-class family. The primary task of the Millean "angel in and out of the house" is to anchor an aggressive male sexuality and to reclaim the "dangerous classes."

However, to obtain the figure of woman as agent of culture rather than chaos, to obtain his "innocent magdalen," Mill must write out the sexualized figure of woman that was written into the domestic ideal. We can discern this woman who defies the rational public sphere, and her symbolic transfiguration into the woman who upholds it, most clearly in Mill's response to the legislation that aimed to regulate the disruptive sexuality of the "magdalen,"[12] and that posed a threat both to the domestic ideal and to personal liberty: the Contagious Diseases Acts.

Political Economy of the Body

On the face of it, Mill's *Principles of Political Economy, with Some of Their Applications to Social Philosophy*, appears to be an abstract scholarly treatise on the laws of the production and distribution of wealth. And yet, written as it was in the social context of the widespread unemployment and class conflict that characterized the "hungry forties," the text lends itself to another angle of interpretation, suggested by the subtitle itself. Indeed "the design of the book," Mill tells the reader in his 1848 preface, "is different from that of any treatise on political economy which has been produced in England since the work of Adam Smith."[13] Like Smith, Mill wishes to enlarge Political Economy "as a branch of abstract speculation" to embrace "other branches of social philosophy" (xci); his task is not only a theoretical but a practical one. It is, among other things, to put forth a "true theory of the causes of poverty" (352n) which might recast the increasingly divisive political terms of the Condition of England debate.

The extent to which Mill envisions such a role for his science becomes evident in the chapter titled "Of Property." It is here that Mill takes up the critique put forth by communists and socialists. If there be merit to the argument that both would destroy the "incentive to work," says Mill, so too must it be admitted that "under the present system of industry this incitement . . . does not exist," for the wage laborer "has no personal interest in the matter at all." Apart from the fact that "the labourer who loses his employment by idleness and negligence, has nothing worse to suffer . . . than the discipline of a workhouse" (a reference to the 1834 Poor Laws), the vagaries of the market keep all workers in a state of perpetual insecurity, laboring incessantly for low wages with no chance of acquiring property.[14] For these reasons, "the restraints of Communism would be freedom in comparison with the present condition of the majority of the human race. The generality of labourers in this and most other countries, have as little choice of occupation or freedom of locomotion, are practically as dependent on fixed rules and on the will of others, as they could be on any system short of actual slavery; to say nothing of the entire domestic subjection of one half of the species" (204–209).

It is well known that one of Mill's reasons for sympathizing with Owenism and other forms of socialism was that they "assign equal rights, in all respects, with those of the hitherto dominant sex" (209).[15] In this context, however, it is valuable to focus on the twin radical analogies of the woman/slave and the worker/slave. As in the radical tracts of the Owenites, in Mill's text these images are deployed to expose as illusory the respective patriarchal and bourgeois notions that domestic labor is naturally self-fulfilling and that wage labor is voluntarily self-alienating. The paternal despotism of the home is no more benevolent than the economic inequality of the market is consensual; woman's labor in the family is no more self-lessly given than a worker's labor in the factory is properly remunerated. Both domestic and wage laborers are the victims of unjust laws and the slaves of economic necessity.

Yet Mill, it turns out, is unwilling to accept the idea that individuals are the helpless victims, the mere effects, of larger economic and cultural forces. The social determinism of the Owenites forecloses the question of individual responsibility and moral choice; it throws into question the possibility of human agency and autonomy.[16] In contrast to Owen, Mill argues that the institution of private property must no more render workers virtual slaves than the institution of marriage must render women so. Just as Mill fends off the necessity of abolishing the former because "the principle of private property has never yet had a fair trial in any country" (207),[17] so does he fend off the necessity of abolishing the latter because "marriage has not had a fair trial."[18] It is not quite optimism about the unrealized possibilities of both institutions which shapes such claims, as can be seen in his defense of the doctrine of free labor.

On the one hand, writes Mill, a "stationary state of capital" is preferable to "the trampling, crushing, elbowing, and treading on each other's heels, which form the existing type of social life." On the other hand, this deplorable spectacle of a humanity divided against itself is "a necessary stage in the progress of civilization." For coarse minds, he laments, "require coarse stimuli." "That the energies of mankind should be kept in employment by the struggle for riches . . . until the better minds succeed in educating the others into better things, is undoubtedly more desirable than that they should rust and stagnate" (753–754). The moment human beings are assured of their material existence, argues Mill, they not only stagnate but deteriorate, and fairly quickly at that. Thus, he concludes, "competition may not be the best conceivable stimulus, but it is at present a necessary one, and no one can foresee the time when it will not be indispensable to progress" (795).

When read as a necessary stage in the cultivation of the uncultivated, Mill's remarks help explain why he inverted Owen (and Marx) by claiming that communism is only practical "among the *elite* of mankind."[19] For Mill, the threat of stagnation was not only more troubling than the market economy and its system of hired labor, it was the problem to be solved by both. If one is not yet one of "the better minds," it is more advantageous to compete than to stagnate, or rather to deteriorate and to take those who remain industrious along into the undifferentiated mass. Indeed, such an immanent danger to civilization is the "natural indolence of mankind," says Mill, that "every restriction of it [competition] is an evil, and every extension of it, even if for the time injuriously affecting some class of labourers, is always an ultimate good" (795).

Putting aside for a moment the implicit problems that such unlimited competition raises for social community, what we detect in the preceding remarks is not a blatant apology for capitalism but rather elements of a conception of "civilized life as a perpetual and tension-filled striving against the forces of decay" which Christine Di Stefano has shown to be the defining feature of Mill's worldview.[20] Di Stefano develops her analysis through a reading of, among other Millean texts, an 1850 essay titled "Nature," whose central claim is this: "Nearly every respectable attribute of humanity is the result not of instinct, but of a victory over instinct."[21] Mill's passionate antipastoral rhetoric, she argues persuasively, evinces anxieties about nature as an archaic maternal power that holds men in an infantile state of passivity. The call for "self-dependence," obtained by "the power of artificial discipline,"[22] as Mill put it, emerges in relation to his fear, says Di Stefano, of a "feminized" nature which "stands in sharp and threatening contrast to the morality and rationality of the civilized world."[23]

As in the *Principles*, there is a profound sense in Mill's essay that, the moment humankind so much as rests on the laurels of civility, all is lost. Stagnation gives way to deterioration and to a fate too horrible to contemplate: a virtual apocalypse of culture, a leveling of the distinction between the human and the animal. In Mill's view, as Di Stefano argues, only constant activity and eternal vigilance can keep the hostile (maternal) forces of nature at bay.[24] A closer look at the essay, however, suggests further that Mill's symbolic figuration of nature is articulated through a discourse not only of gender but also of class. For nature exerts her destructive power first and foremost through the working-class body that remains on the nether side of the clean and proper, at once savage and menacing.

That the walled fortress of the Victorian civilized self is threatened by the laboring masses' putatively brutish character can be glimpsed in what Mill gives as clear evidence for his argument that culture is the "triumph over instinct," "the quality of cleanliness." Mill invokes the "artificial" love of cleanliness and its psychic corollary, the powerful feeling of "disgust" (that is, abjection), as instances of "one of the most radical of the moral distinctions between human beings and most of the lower animals." He then goes on to argue that "the lower classes of most countries, seem to be actually fond of dirt."[25] Cast as being naturally drawn to it, the poor are associated with filth not only metonymically, by virtue of their social location in the slums; they are associated metaphorically: they *are* pigs.[26] Physical depravity signifies moral depravity in yet another sense: like cleanliness, adds Mill, the "power of sacrificing a present desire to a distant object . . . is most unnatural to the undisciplined human being," as may be seen in "savages . . . and in a somewhat less degree in nearly the whole of the poorer classes in this and many other countries."[27] Symbolically aligned with the primitive if not with the lower ani-

mals, the bestiality of the poor situates them at the unstable boundary of nature and culture, where their animal instincts constitute the
problem to be solved by, among other things, the system of hired
labor.

What we witness in Mill's essay on nature, and locate in the
Principles, is a rhetorical slippage which, as Amanda Anderson argues, was characteristic of Victorian social reform discourse: "Metonymic associations between subjects and their social environments
are displaced by metaphoric ones."[28] Part of the symbolic work of
this displacement was to account for mid-century social inequality
and widespread poverty by drawing clear moral lines of demarcation
between the middle classes and the destitute masses. The casual poor
(those without any steady employment) came to be seen by their
social betters as "the dangerous class," indeed, as recalcitrant savages
living at the margins of civilized culture. In London and other urban
areas, the casual poor were perceived as inhabiting, in Gareth Stedman Jones's phrase, an "immense *terra incognita*" akin to the state of
nature, the breeding ground of disease, criminality, and vice.[29]

Representations of the poor which cast them first as victims and
then as the agents of their own immiseration worked to diffuse the
political claims of a radicalized working class and to account for the
social effects of proletarianization in the bourgeois terms of self-help
and self-discipline. Naturalized moral distinctions (e.g., the lower
classes are fond of dirt, the middle of cleanliness) worked to produce
a unified middle class in the course of the nineteenth century and to
secure the civilized identity of the bourgeoisie, its own clean and
proper self, against an abject social other.[30] Following Julia Kristeva,
one can argue further that cleanliness came to figure as a dominant
trope of middle-class moral superiority partly because the abject
menaces the bourgeois subject from within the borders of its own
identity. Abjection, she writes, can concern

"moral matters—an *abjection* in the face of a crime [e.g., the degradation of an individual that so concerns Mill], for example. But it is
an extremely strong feeling which is at once somatic and symbolic,
and which is above all a revolt of the person against an external
menace from which one wants to keep oneself at a distance, but of

which one has the impression that it is not only an external menace but that it may menace us from the inside. So it is a desire for separation, for becoming autonomous and also the feeling of an impossibility of doing so—whence the element of crisis which the notion of abjection carries within it.[31]

Kristeva's remarks help account for the intensity of moral outrage and physical disgust that many proper Victorians, including Mill, felt toward the casual poor. The spatial and moral distance that ought to mark and keep the difference between classes stands in perpetual danger of collapse; what is opposed to the I, to one's own clean and proper self, threatens the borders of bourgeois identity. This always already fragile distance between the bourgeois subject and its abject other bespeaks the irreducible alterity that inhabits the subject and mocks its claim to moral autonomy and authority. It is a distance that must be and yet cannot be maintained. Attending to that struggle and that paradox, we may understand part of the immense ambivalence that characterizes Mill's stance toward the casual poor.

Turning back to the *Principles*, we witness how a rhetorical slippage from the metonymic to the metaphoric is played out, once again, through a metanarrative of civilization's "struggle against the animal instincts" (367). This tale articulates the alternately ominous and auspicious messages of Millean political economy and, especially, Mill's attack on the well-meaning but misguided advocates of the "New Philanthropy." These advocates would have the state keep wages artificially high; but the solution to poverty, Mill reminds his readers, cannot be "fix[ing] a minimum of wages" (356) because low wages are not the true cause of poverty. Rather, "poverty, like most social evils, exists because men [or rather a certain class of men] follow their brute instincts without due consideration" (367).

The moral Malthusianism that is the *dernier mot* of Millean political economy could be read from a variety of interpretive angles.[32] One could attribute it to Mill's reliance in the 1840s on Ricardian wages fund theory;[33] to the concern he shared with Owen to stem the rapid multiplication of the laboring population which helped to keep wages at below subsistence levels;[34] or to his feminist concern to liberate women from their enslavement to "one physical function"

(373).[35] Although correct in many respects, none of these interpretations explains why Mill's own account of the proletarianization that was the real historical force behind the rise in population should have given way to an anxiety-ridden narrative of a society driven to the brink of extinction by the "animal power of multiplication" (354).[36] What is at stake between those two narratives? The first explains laborers' procreative habits as a rational response to the low wages that made large families an expedient means of obtaining more income;[37] the second explains them as an irrational mode of behavior caused by moral—not social—poverty.

Consider Mill's response to those who advocated a minimum of wages and a guarantee of employment through "a forced increase of the wages-fund; by a compulsory saving." "Such a proposition," says Mill, "would have no more strenuous supporter than myself." That is,

> if this claim on society could be limited to the existing generation; if nothing more were necessary than a compulsory accumulation, sufficient to provide permanent employment at ample wages for the existing numbers of the people. . . .
>
> But it is another thing altogether, when those who have produced and accumulated are called upon to abstain from consuming until they have given food and clothing, not only to all who now exist, but to all whom these or their descendants may think fit to call into existence. Such an obligation acknowledged and acted upon, would suspend all checks, both positive and preventative; there would be nothing to hinder population from starting forward at its rapidest rate; and as the natural increase of capital would, at the best, not be more rapid than before, taxation, to make up the growing deficiency, must advance with the same gigantic strides. The attempt would of course be made to exact labour in exchange for support. But experience has shown the sort of work to be expected from recipients of public charity. . . . ; to extract real work from day-labourers without the power of dismissal, is only practicable by the power of the lash. (356–357)

The final comment is telling. Wage slavery is deplorable, but to give pay for no work is to create the conditions for actual slavery.[38]

Subjecting workers to impersonal market forces, the wage labor system is all that holds off the otherwise certain death of the rational forces of production at the bodies of the irrational forces of reproduction. Yet so impotent is capital vis-à-vis the fecundity of labor, "if the market for our manufacturers should, I do not say fall off, but even cease to expand at the rapid rate of the last fifty years, there is no certainty that this fate may not be reserved for us" (351).

This grim Malthusian scenario, then, frames Mill's quarrel with the New Philanthropy: "An absolute right to be supported at the cost of other people . . . relax[es] the springs of industry and the restraints of prudence."[39] If honored, that right would undermine the entire system of reward for abstinence and thrift, thereby collapsing the prudent into the improvident: "The payers and the receivers would be melted down into one mass." And with class meltdown, as the very next sentence of text makes quite clear, so that of civilization itself: "The check to population either by death or prudence, could not then be staved off any longer, but must come into operation suddenly and at once; everything which places mankind above a nest of ants or a colony of beavers, having perished in the interval" (358–360).

What we have in these passages is the articulation of a population anxiety whose chain of signification begins with, but then quickly exceeds, the logic of wages fund theory, raising the specter of a willful, ungovernable body whose sexual appetites not only immiserate workers but obliterate culture by collapsing, first, class distinctions and, ultimately, the boundaries between the human and the animal. There is a profound sense here that the unregulated body can lead humanity into the abyss precisely because its archaic sexual drives and immense procreative power are under no one's control: the human body destroys the social body because it "recognizes" no master (thus poses the problem of slavery). Or, to formulate the issue in Kristevan terms, at the threshold of culture and nature there is no stable, masterful and rational subject, only a desiring, semiotic body that apparently evades, mocks, and defies sublimation and therefore destroys civilization—the symbolic order of law and language. The semiotic body is a generative body, the restraint of whose disruptive animal instinct of multiplication must involve more than the laissez-faire prophylactic of (unsubsidized) wages.

Although this casting of the body as beyond the law, hence as "an absolute social problem," in Catherine Gallagher's phrase,[40] was the legacy of the *Essay on the Principles of Population* (1798), Mill departs significantly and in characteristically Victorian fashion from Malthus by coding the body, specifically its sexual appetites, as base, as the origin of all social evils, and as the enemy of human progress. Indeed, whereas Malthus could not imagine a more just society that did not take proper account of the legitimate claims and sensual pleasures of the body,[41] Mill cannot imagine one that did not regulate and even extirpate presumably natural bodily appetites, including "those which are necessary to our preservation"—"or rather," he adds, "(what can be done even to an instinct) to starve them by disuse."[42]

That Mill thinks such a remarkable strategy to be necessary speaks, not only to the fact that the *Principles* is indebted somewhat less to Malthus than to such Enlightenment advocates of a disembodied human perfectibility as Godwin and Condorcet, but also to the ways in which Mill's text contributed to, indeed was deeply implicated in, what Michel Foucault calls "bio-power."[43] This new technology of the body put it in the service of economic growth and middle-class ideas of social progress by regulating the sexual drive Mill assumed to be archaic and Foucault shows to be a historical, discursive construction: bio-power, and by extension the *Principles*, then, involved "the production of [a certain kind of] sexuality rather than the repression of sex."[44]

Foucault's claim is buttressed by Mill's own account, which shows that the problem of the body and its appetites was at once class- and gender-specific: it was not *the* body that was put into the discourse of political economy but rather the differences between working-class and middle-class bodies, male and female bodies; it was not some abstract notion of sexual instinct that was invoked in the *Principles* but rather the difference between an unregulated working-class and a regulated middle-class sexuality, an aggressive male and a passive female sexuality.

The poor have a right to social justice, affirms Mill. But he also argues that they seek higher wages and less work to indulge in sensuality.[45] Mill's explanation of imprudent procreative practices in terms of moral depravity also entails a specific attack on the patriarchal despotism he finds implicit in the arguments of those who overlook

> the law of wages, or . . . dismiss it in a parenthesis, with such terms as 'hard-hearted Malthusianism'; as if it were not a thousand times more hard-hearted to tell human beings that they may, than that they may not, call into existence swarms of creatures who are sure to be miserable, and most likely to be depraved; and forgetting that the conduct, which it is reckoned so cruel to disapprove, is a degrading slavery to a brute instinct in one of the persons concerned, and most commonly, in the other, helpless submission to a revolting abuse of power. (352)[46]

This is a radical critique of male power—and something else. Apart from the language of abjection that characterizes here, as elsewhere, Mill's remarks on procreation and male sex-right, and apart from the claim that being born into the working class dooms one not only to social misery but also to moral depravity, Mill's invocation of the Victorian opposition between a passive female and an aggressive male sexuality elides the political issue of overpopulation. It substitutes an ahistorical male lust for the historical relations of proletarianization; it effaces the relationship between class exploitation and sex-class oppression, capitalism and patriarchy.

Furthermore, Mill's rhetorical deployment of the familiar Victorian figure of woman as helpless (asexual) victim denies whatever social power women held in the working-class family—a power that was, on some accounts, not only considerable but considerably more than that held by middle-class women, whose husbands were, in Mary Ryan's phrase, "prudent procreators."[47] If this is correct, then the possibility arises that, just as there was buried beneath Mill's representation of woman as "the victim of the man's animal instinct"[48] the more unsettling one of woman as active subject of desire,[49] so too was there buried beneath the political-economic image of a disruptive working-class body (which presumably brings into existence poverty, misery, and depravity) a body whose generative power was irreducibly female. To suggest as much is to consider the female body's active rather than passive place in Mill's tale of the conflict between production and reproduction, that is, in the impending cultural catastrophe. That place becomes visible in Mill's staunch and unpopular defense of Poor Law reform.

Political Economy of the Female Body

Mill's unqualified praise for the 1834 Poor Law Amendment Act, writes Fred Berger, demonstrates his conviction that "the poor have a *right* to subsistence income to be provided through government channels."[50] Actually, a closer look at Poor Law reform reveals Mill's stance on it to be far more complicated. Mill defended the act against conservatives, who had argued that charity destroys the incentive to work; but he also defended the original Poor Law commissioners against advocates of the destitute who had accused them of being hostile to the very principle of legal relief.[51] The policymakers of 1834, wrote Mill, should be praised for having shown that "the guarantee of support could be freed from its injurious effects upon the minds and habits of the people, if the relief . . . was accompanied with conditions which they disliked, consisting of some restraints upon their freedom, and the privation of some indulgences" (360).

Those restraints and privations were written into the 1834 Poor Law Amendment Act, whose main objective was to deny relief to "able-bodied" men (those deemed physically and mentally capable of employment) outside the union workhouses. Assuming that unemployment was by and large voluntary, the commissioners held the strict discipline of the workhouses to be essential to instilling in the able-bodied the habits of industry and to giving them an incentive to seek work in the market economy.[52]

That Mill accepted the Poor Law commissioners' notion of self-willed pauperism can be seen from two 1835 newspaper articles. What is valuable in the act, wrote Mill, is that it prevents the able-bodied pauper from starving while keeping him "in a condition inferior to that of the labourer subsisting honestly on his own industry."[53] To those who had argued that to place the pauper family in the workhouse was to "make their poverty a disgrace," Mill countered: "It is simply to make their poverty *known*, or rather to make the fact known that they are living upon the labour of others." Moreover, as "the independent labourer earns so little," he added, "you cannot give the pauper less; you can only give him that little on harder terms." Apart from insisting that class distinctions between the laboring and unemployed poor had to be upheld if society was to maintain the incentive to work, Mill contended that the privations and "discipline of a well-regulated workhouse, are quite sufficient . . . to make every able-bodied pauper desire to extricate himself from pauperism; and wherever this has been tried, all, or nearly all, the able-bodied paupers have speedily found employment."[54]

This argument was already difficult to defend in the context of the emerging economic crisis of the 1830s, and it became increasingly absurd in the "hungry forties," when low wages and recurrent unemployment assumed critical dimensions while the *Principles* stood firm on the justice of Poor Law reform. What is more, much as the commissioners redefined the economic reality of the 1830s in terms of the moral reality of lower-class indolence, so too, argues Pat Thane, did they identify the able-bodied male pauper as the problem to be solved by the 1834 act by taking "for granted the universality of the stable two-parent family, primarily dependent upon the father's wage, and the primacy of the family as a source of welfare." Silent on female paupers, the commissioners' report assumed women to be financial dependents.[55]

There was, however, one exception to female invisibility: the woman who was a mother but no wife. The Bastardy Clauses of the 1834 report stated that a bastard is "what Providence appears to have ordained that it should be, a burthen on its mother, and, where she cannot maintain it, on her parents."[56] Assuming that the rise in illegitimacy could be stemmed by imposing the double standard, the commissioners singled out "lewd women" for public opprobrium. To combat female unchastity, they absolved fathers from all moral and financial obligations to unwed mothers and their children.[57] The report's references to depraved women, as breeders of those swarms of creatures that were to be maintained at public expense, made explicit the threat posed by female sexuality unconstrained by proper femininity to property, social order, and public morality.[58] Taken together with the separation of the sexes in the workhouses, and with the more draconian measures aimed to curtail illegitimacy and improvident marriages (all of which Mill supported), the problem to be solved by Poor Law reform was the generative power of the female body.[59] The hidden Malthusian agenda was to prevent, in Mill's concise phrase, "paupers from breeding hereditary paupers" (358).[60]

The female pauper, then, was not a marginal but a central (if mostly invisible) figure in the texts of Poor Law reform and in Millean political economy. Her body was figured, at times explicitly but more often implicitly, as the threat to the social body, as the site of reckless breeding, as the origin (in both senses of the word) of working-class poverty. Whether she was seen as the victim of the man's "animal instinct" or as the agent of the irrational forces of reproduction (more often as both), the subjectivity of the female pauper was continually effaced by her symbolic status in Victorian social reform discourse.

In light of Mill's extensive knowledge of and praise for the 1834 act, it is intriguing that he failed to comment on the special status of the female pauper in the texts and practices of Poor Law reform. Part of the reason is that Mill, like other social reformers, appears to have been uncertain as to how to categorize the female pauper, and thus he simply subsumed her under the category of the pauper (as he would often subsume working-class women under that of the working class and at other times under that of women). To some extent, cultural figurations of the female pauper (as victim or threat) were akin to those of the casual poor at large. Yet in an age that herald the asexual domestic ideal, the pauper woman posed a specific problem of symbolic representation. On the one hand, her active sexuality had to be accounted for; on the other, her public presence. Inasmuch as the unregulated female body came to stand not only for immorality but also for the uncontrolled breeding that spelled the death of the social body, the pauper woman was located at the explosive intersection of mid-century debates about gender and class.

Angel in the House

Apart from the question of how to figure her sexuality (aggressive or passive), the pauper woman posed a specific problem for social reformers like Mill because they remained uncertain as to whether

her proper place was in the wage labor force or in the home. Female pauperism itself was largely an effect of the ideology of female domesticity, which was tied, of course, to the needs of the wage labor economy and which placed limits on women's freedom of contract and justified paying those who could find work bare subsistence wages at best.[61] In the 1840s, many advocates of protective legislation were Tories, who mixed the languages of social paternalism and domestic ideology, combining Arthur Helps's *The Claims of Labour* (1844) and Sarah Ellis's *Mothers of England* (1843). Lord Anthony Ashley, a prominent Tory spokesman of reform, made it quite clear that beneath both the paternalist polemic against female exploitation in the workplace and the domestic pieties about moral motherhood was a fear of "unnatural women," a concern about their economic power.[62] Female pauperism was threatening; more threatening, however, was the female wage labor that undermined the emerging symbolic order of the Victorian economy: it hindered the consolidation of separate spheres; it revealed the arbitrary nature of the gendered distinction between different kinds of work (paid and unpaid, alienating and self-fulfilling); and it destroyed the illusion of the home as the nurturing alternative to the brutish world of the market.[63]

Exposing what underlay protectionist rhetoric, Mill argued that the Factory Acts subsumed women, like children, under the category of dependents. Not only were women quite capable of making their own decisions, their so-called protectors were those persons against whom women needed protection (761). Moreover, if women had control over their persons and property, writes Mill, "there would be no plea for limiting their hours of labouring for themselves, in order that they might have time to labour for the husband, in what is called . . . *his* home. Women employed in factories are the only women in the labouring rank of life whose position is not that of slaves and drudges; precisely because they cannot easily be compelled to work and earn wages in factories against their will" (953). The defense of women's right to make contracts contests social paternalism and domestic ideology.[64] But, while criticizing male despotism in the home, Mill creates, once again, an unrealistic image of the market as the sphere of freedom and consent.

The distinction between free female laborers and enslaved domestic drudges effaces Mill's more radical analogy between wage slaves and domestic slaves. It also speaks to his deep fear of the working-class home as the site of barbarism, male despotism, and vice. That fear led Mill to advocate women's industrial and political rights, but also to support the kind of middle-class intervention into the working-class family called for in Edwin Chadwick's *Report . . . on an Inquiry into the Sanitary Conditions of the Working Classes* (1842): a key reform text, as Peter Stallybrass and Allon White summarize, which insisted that the regulation of the poor "depended upon breaking down those architectural barriers which kept the immoral 'secluded from superior inspection and from common observation.'"[65] Chadwick argued—and Mill agreed—that because the "fever nests and seats of physical depravity are also the seats of moral depravity, disorder, and crime," they create a laboring population that is "short lived, improvident, reckless, and intemperate, and with an habitual avidity for sensual gratifications."[66]

Many of the concerns that led Mill to advocate state intervention into "the domestic life of domestic tyrants" (952), then, also led him to advocate the wage labor system and controversial forms of state intervention into the working-class family.[67] But if Mill wove his feminist attack on patriarchy into the fabric of classical political economy, Millean political economy also posed significant problems for his feminism. Women should be given access to independent industrial employment, says Mill, primarily as a matter of principle but also because it will lead to "a great diminution of the evil of over-population." For the "animal instinct in question is nursed into . . . [a] disproportionate preponderance" when women are confined to the performance of "that exclusive function" (765–766). Mill's argument for women's right to compete, however, comes face to face with the problem written into the Malthusian logic of wages fund theory: excessive numbers as the true cause of low wages.

Even as Mill argues that unrestricted industrial employment for women will lead eventually to a decrease in population, hence to an increase in wages for all workers, he maintains that, in the short run, female (and child) labor depresses wages—a fact "authenticated by the inquiries of the Handloom Weavers Commission."[68] Mill quickly qualifies however:

No argument can be hence derived for the exclusion of women from the liberty of competing in the labour market: since, even when no more is earned by the labour of a man and a woman than would have been earned by the man alone, the advantage to the woman of not depending on a master for subsistence may be more than an equivalent. It cannot, however, be considered desirable as a *permanent* element in the condition of a labouring class, that the mother of the family (the case of a single woman is totally different) should be under the necessity of working for subsistence, at least elsewhere than in their place of abode. (394)[69]

Here Mill shares what many other defenders of female employment shared, curiously enough, with their conservative foes: the view that women would work in the market only out of economic necessity; that unpaid domestic labor was unlike and preferable to wage labor; and that it was natural for a wife to be dependent on her husband's wage. The case of the single woman was indeed totally different at mid-century because—as the 1851 census "redundant women" statistics would verify—there were not enough men to guarantee domestic bliss to all women.[70] Moreover, Mill sees that many married women had to work because wages were low, as was the moral state of their husbands. For these reasons, then, we are told that *even though* it has been "authenticated" that female labor depresses wages, women should be allowed to compete. But the entire argument for the dependence of wages on numbers—that is, the entire argument about reckless breeding as the true cause of poverty—works against Mill's feminism. A tension has built up in the text, and it is revealed in his ambivalence about the working-class mother's proper place, which is not in an overstocked labor market but in the home.[71]

Mill had yet other reasons for upholding the domestic ideal. In the 1840s all that distinguished the indolent pauper from the honest laborer was that the former was confined to the workhouse. According to Poor Law logic, the unemployed were impoverished because they were unwilling to work; according to the political-economic law of wages, all workers were impoverished because there were too many of them looking for work. Poverty, Mill argued, could not be eradicated "without requiring the exercise, either enforced or voluntary, of any self-restraint, or any greater control than at present, over the animal power of multiplication" (354). But "if a prudent regulation of population be not reconcilable with the system of hired labor," he added, if overpopulation is attributable to proletarianization, other "arrangements of property" must be found. This was a rhetorical problem, the expected response to which was "But there exists no such incompatibility" (373).

The problem is rhetorical, the response expected, because both are already given in a text that translates the more radical association of poverty with proletarianization into the ahistorical language of animal instinct and the moral language of abstinence. Thus, apart from offering the social remedies of a national system of education, state-financed emigration for the working classes, and small landholdings for those who had already proven that they were prudent and responsible (374–378), Mill puts forth another solution: "spontaneous restraints" on population through the mechanism of an enlightened public opinion. He asks his readers to imagine what social change might occur if each labourer came to look "upon every other who had more than the number of children which the circumstances of society allowed to each, as doing him a wrong—as filling up the place which he was entitled to share." What is more, Mill added, "the opinion here in question . . . would have powerful auxiliaries in the great majority of women. It is seldom by the choice of the wife that families are too numerous. . . . Among the barbarisms which law and morals have not yet ceased to sanction, the most disgusting surely is, that any human being should be permitted to consider himself as having a *right* to the person of another" (371–372).

This passage illustrates Kristeva's claims that (1) social anxieties about overpopulation are often tied to a fear of the generative power of women; (2) social taboos for restraining reproduction are connected to other rites for mapping the clean and proper body; and (3) a language of abjection ("disgusting") in the face of the moral crime of brute procreation bespeaks a dread of the archaic maternal body.[72] Note, too, with the pauper woman in mind, that Mill's radical attack on male sex-right may entail a rhetorical displacement of cultural anxieties about an aggressive female sexuality onto the brutishness of the working-class male.

What is truly striking about this passage is the idea that women, because they are free of sexual desire and oppressed by male lust, might serve as the "auxiliaries," if not the guardians, of an ideology of self-help that associates poverty with the sexual relations of reproduction instead of with the sexual/class relations of production, with reckless breeding instead of market forces. So "the *status* of hired labourers," writes Mill, "will gradually tend to confine itself to the description of workpeople whose low moral qualities render them unfit for anything more independent" (769).

Mill's social vision in the *Principles* of a far more desirable "stationary state of capital" and more just distribution of wealth requires "a stationary state of . . . population" (752–753). Yet, if civilization "has not brought the instinct of population under as much restraint as is needful," he tells the reader, "we must remember that it has never seriously tried." The ceaseless reproduction of capital necessary to compensate for the ceaseless reproduction of bodies can be halted because "man is not necessarily a brute" (367–368). And the control (some) women have over their own sexual desires—if any desires they have—might serve as a model of artificial self-discipline for men, who have heretofore compelled only women to be chaste.[73] Put somewhat differently, the sheer artificiality of asexual femininity is a sign of the triumph of the rational forces of culture over the irrational ones of nature, of reason over the "reckless abandonment to brute instincts" (768). If the asexual character of woman could transform the aggressive sexual character of man, then divisive competition—necessary to prevent cultural stagnation and deterioration yet destructive of social community—would give way to a better society modeled on the domestic life woman enables men of all classes to share.[74]

The Millean domestic ideal, then, emerges as a solution to class conflict defined in terms of a recalcitrant working-class body, a semiotic and abjected body. For Mill, in Kristeva's words, "the body must bear no trace of its debt to nature: it must be clean and proper in order to be fully symbolic"—that is, fully rational and moral, without any trace of the semiotic or the disruption of desire. And "maternal authority," she adds, "is the trustee of that mapping of the self's

clean and proper body."[75] Indeed, at the threshold of nature and culture, at the place of the willful and generative body that defies sublimation and thus destroys civilization, Mill puts the self-regulating
female body and woman as rational, moral subject. Guardian of the
clean and proper, woman is guardian of the moral order and of social
progress.

In contrast to defenders of the domestic ideal, however, Mill
argues that, as long as woman is confined to the home, she will be
deprived of her right to social justice and unable to perform her
"highest destiny," which is not only moral motherhood but the moral
reform of society at large. Thus women must be admitted "to the
same rights of citizenship with men" (372–373). Yet, inasmuch as
Mill's view of woman was tied to his fear of the working classes,
of nature out of control, of sexuality, of a loss of identity in the
undifferentiated mass, his case for female suffrage could not be
unattenuated.

Angel out of the House

The problem of too many bodies competing for a fixed economic
space resurfaces in *Considerations on Representative Government*[76] as one
of too many voices competing for a contested political space—one
that could be enlarged gradually to the extent that those voices could
be made rational, the working class made rational, moral beings. As
Mill summarized the magnitude of the task in "Thoughts On Parliamentary Reform,"

> none are so illiberal, none so bigoted in their hostility to improve-
> ment, . . . as the uneducated. None are so unscrupulous, none so
> eager to clutch at whatever they have not and others have, as the
> uneducated in possession of power. An uneducated mind is almost
> incapable of clearly conceiving the rights of others. . . . No lover
> of improvement can desire that the *predominant* power should be
> turned over to persons in the mental and moral condition of the
> English working classes.[77]

Mill's dread of the mass of brute ignorance was a fear not of social revolution but of a legislative class tyranny—above all, it was a dread of cultural stagnation. The question, he asks at the outset the *Considerations*, is "which of two common types of character, for the general good of humanity, it is most desirable should predominate—the active, or the passive type." There is an acute sense in the text that the latter is contaminating to the former. Apart from the fact that the indolent character, rather than try to raise itself, "delights in bringing others down to its own level," "it is much easier for an active mind to acquire the virtues of patience, than for a passive one to assume those of energy." Indolence—which "retains in a savage or semi-savage state the great majority of the human race"—is contagious: a permanent threat even to those who have attained the very upper rungs of the evolutionary ladder. To avoid becoming its passive other, then, the active type must "keep moving," on its toes (190–195).

Mill's distinctly political solution to the spread of indolence throughout the civilized social body was to include the masses in the active management of their affairs. He defended a graduated suffrage and sought to elevate the working classes so that the franchise could be extended safely to them. But he also sought means, in Gallagher's words, for "reorganizing the franchise to compensate for its extension."[78] For, far from being passive, the working classes were actively and at times aggressively demanding political reform, and, as the aftermath of the First Reform Bill had made clear, they were less than receptive to middle-class leadership.[79] Deeply worried that a prematurely enfranchised working class would advance its "sinister interests,"[80] Mill departed from the descriptive model of representation outlined in his father's *Essay on Government* (1820).[81] Refuting the idea that the accumulation of private interests would translate into the public interest—what James Mill had called "enlightened self-interest"—J. S. Mill insisted on the importance of citizen disinterestedness and on a political system that would promote it and give cultural authority to those who stood for it.[82]

"The multitude," observes Mill, "have often a true instinct for distinguishing an able man, when he has the means of displaying his ability in a fair field before them." The problem, however, is that existing "institutions . . . keep him out of sight" (261). Assuming that by merely gazing upward at this superior human being the inferior person would be insensibly raised to a higher moral level, Mill wanted to get the able man in the view of the masses. This was one reason Mill was eager to support, initially, Thomas Hare's complex scheme for the proportional representation of minorities, and, somewhat later, a "plurality scheme" that would give extra votes to those who demonstrated "mental [qua moral] superiority" (284).[83]

Even more intriguing than Mill's argument for either of these well-known plans is his case against the secret ballot. Arguing that, by the 1860s, society was no longer characterized by social deference, Mill says that the ballot does not protect the voter against intimidation; rather, it provides the "shield of secrecy" that promotes his selfishness. Furthermore, the ballot deprives the disenfranchised of their legitimate right to indirect political influence. Taking up the example of women, Mill begins by insisting that a man's female relatives are entitled to know how he votes on matters that concern their interests (e.g., legislation on domestic violence). He then goes on (with what amounts to a rhetorical slippage) to contest the objection brought by "democratic reformers": "Whoever is fit to influence electors, is fit to be an elector." Mill casts doubt on this radical political claim by pointing to the "present state of morals and intelligence," not in the sex class of women but in, once again, the "poorest and rudest class of labourers"—which includes, of course, some members of that sex class. "All who are fit to influence electors are not, for that reason, fit to be themselves electors," he concludes (304–309).

Leaving aside for a moment the possibility that such statements might play into the hands of those who opposed not only manhood but also women's suffrage, let us reflect on what Mill calls "a still deeper consideration":

> The notion is itself unfounded, that publicity, and the sense of being answerable to the public, are of no use unless the public are qualified to form a sound judgement. It is a very superficial view of the utility of public opinion, to suppose that it does good, only when it succeeds in enforcing a servile conformity to itself. To be under the eyes of others—to have to defend oneself to others—is

never more important than to those who act in opposition to the opinion of others. . . . If any one thinks that the mere obligation of preserving decency is not a very considerable check on the abuse of power, he has never had his attention called to the conduct of those who do not feel under the necessity of observing that restraint. (309)

Striking here, especially in light of Mill's contempt for the "mediocrity of respectability," is the power he assigns to the public gaze and to an opinion he himself admits is far from enlightened.[84] He comes close to immersing the voter—as Chadwick would immerse the working-class family, Bentham the inmate of his model prison, the Panopticon—in a "field of total visibility," to borrow Foucault's phrase. Mill seems to assume, not only that to be under the eyes of others forces one to give an account of one's actions, but also (and in true Benthamite fashion) that the gaze can prevent even the possibility of wrongdoing.[85] There is a profound sense here, once again, that the darker side of human character breeds in spaces of secrecy. Those who cannot sublimate their private interest to that of the public have not interiorized the power of moral sanction, of artificial self-discipline. Thus arises the need for keeping each voter under the surveillance of the whole community, even if that means merely preserving decency.

Mill associated the kind of self-regarding behavior promoted by the concealment afforded by the ballot with that promoted by the privacy of the patriarchal family. The sinister sex-class interests of men which endangered women were the foundation of the sinister interests which endangered politics. If one wanted to root out the selfishness of the electorate, Mill argued, one had to do more than advocate plural voting and oppose the ballot; one had to attack the "citadel" of male selfishness in the home.[86] In short, one had to admit women to the franchise.

Even though part of Mill's argument for women's suffrage extends to the accident of sex his broader attack on the arbitrariness of the traditional signs of political right, that argument cannot sustain his feminism, partly because Mill himself argues against basing political rights (for the working classes) on natural equality. The centerpiece of Mill's plea for women's political rights, it turns out, is not equality but "self-protection."[87] Women, like men, "do not need political rights in order that they may govern, but in order that they may not be misgoverned." Although Mill asserts that "no one now holds that women should be in personal servitude," he also shows that this is precisely their condition, one symbolized by that ever recurring Millean trope, the domestic slave. The tenacity of patriarchal despotism and women's physical weakness, he argues, make women "more dependent on law and society for protection," hence most in need of the suffrage (290–291).

Maintaining that "where there is life there is egotism," Mill explicitly rejected his father's self-satisfied claim that the interests of women are contained wholly in those of their male relatives.[88] For Mill, the most damning example of male egotism was the appalling and pervasive reality of domestic violence.[89] Although clearly aware of and troubled by the crimes perpetrated against women of all classes, Mill was also of the mind that "the brutal part of the population [which] can still maltreat, not to say kill, their wives, with the next thing to impunity" was composed of those whom "democratic reformers" would immediately enfranchise, not to mention those whom no one but socialists would enfranchise, the large pauper population.[90]

Mill would grant political rights to working-class women on the same graduated terms he would grant them to working-class men, but those in "receipt of parish relief" would be "disqualified" by virtue of being "dependent on the remaining members of the community for actual subsistence" (280). Mill's complete exclusion of paupers, as well as of the numbers of illiterates, becomes troubling, even illogical, given his claim that the suffrage was a means for ending women's legal servitude and a form of "bodily-protection." For if the female pauper was a virtual appendage to her husband in the practices of poor relief, and if women of the lowest order of society were most brutalized, as Mill maintained, then these women were most in need of political rights.

Attending to the invisibility of female paupers (illiterates, and other such cases), we begin to see that Mill's category of sex class, as Eisenstein argues, is constructed through a whole series of exclusions that reveal the middle-class bias of his feminism.[91] But the problem runs even deeper, for those exclusions destabilize Mill's larger *protective* case for female suffrage insofar as that case is built on maintaining that women *as* women constitute an endangered and distinct class, a sex class. Sex class, it turns out, is a gloss on economic class—a category that can be maintained only by substituting, once again, a gender similarity for the more divisive class differences between women; a category that must be maintained if women electors are to mitigate class conflict and represent the other-regarding values Mill would have them represent.

There is yet another problem written into Mill's (unstable because illusory) monolith of sex class: it risks underscoring the concern that women's suffrage would lead to sex-class war. Parliamentary debates around the time of the Second Reform Bill articulated worries about the intrinsic divisiveness of "women's interests."[92] Liberal antisuffragists feared that women would return Tories to Parliament, and conservatives worried that women's partisan bias would lead them to return representatives intent on pursuing a philanthropic political agenda. Besides, as one member of parliament put it in 1867, he was quite certain that "nine men out of ten—nay, . . . nine women out of ten—was opposed" to female suffrage.[93] This retort to Mill's 1867 amendment proposal for admitting single women who met the property qualification made quite clear that the real fear was a male fear of "strong-minded women," and that the real danger was the danger to legal patriarchal right, to coverture.[94]

So Mill tried to unravel these antisuffrage arguments. To dispel fears of those "strong-minded women," as Mill observed in a letter to Mrs. Peter Alfred Taylor, it is "extremely desirable that the ladies who lead the movement should make themselves visible to the public, their very appearance being a refutation of the vulgar nonsense talked about 'women's rights women,' and their manner of looking, moving, and speaking being sure to make a favourable impression from the purely feminine as well as from the human point of view."[95] By creating the right impression in public, these women would do more than prove antisuffragist allegations false; their refined and feminine presence would also have a moralizing influence on the laboring population. To behold these women was akin to beholding the able man: it was to be raised up by the spectacle of civility, by the public display of higher culture.

Even though middle-class women figure prominently in Mill's plans for educating the masses so that the franchise could be extended to them, he was not exactly convinced that those women would exercise the suffrage in accordance with the principle of disinterestedness. Feminist commentators have called our attention to the Millean image of woman as a retarding influence on an enlightened democracy, if not on civilization itself.[96] The wife, he lamented in *The Subjection of Women*, is often a "drag," "a perpetual dead weight," on her husband's social conscience.[97] This ambivalence translates, in the *Considerations*, into a host of reasons why women are and are not likely to exert a moral influence on politics. So, in one breath, Mill tells us that, if the woman were given the vote, "the man would often be obliged to find honest reasons for his vote, such as might induce [in him] a more upright and impartial character"; in the next breath, he admits, "often, indeed, it would be used, not on the side of public principle, but of the personal interest or worldly vanity of the family."[98] Mill then counters his own concession to the antisuffrage point, saying that woman's direct agency would be far less mischievous than her indirect influence: "Give the woman a vote, and she comes under the operation of the political point of honour" (292–293). But why should women—why should "domestic slaves," "sexual slaves"—exercise the vote more honorably than any other oppressed and disenfranchised class?[99]

However suspicious he was of women's parochial interests, and however vivid was his depiction of male brutality, Mill had to write out the more aggressive image of the female citizen because to do otherwise would be to concede the antisuffragist point. But that was not the only reason. As Mill noted in an 1868 letter to Charles Eliot Norton, "the political enfranchisement of women, whenever it takes place, will further strengthen the influences opposed to violence and bloodshed."[100] That enigmatic remark seemed to assume, once again, that sex-class interests were not divisive as were class interests, and that women's suffrage would not lead to increased domestic antagonism. So Mill could reassure the antisuffragist Florence Nightingale that, "if men come to look upon women as a large number of unamiable but powerful opponents and a small number of dearly loved and charming persons, I think men will think more highly of women, and will feel less disposed to use badly any superior power."[101] Yet the question remained: If gender relations in the household were as bitter as Mill held, then why should women not be disposed to use *their* newly won power—the power of the franchise—badly?

One solution to the dilemma was to rework the fierce image of women as a mass of unamiable opponents into the more conciliatory one of a small group of charming persons; to articulate the case for female suffrage through the Victorian discourse of the domestic ideal; in short, to cast the angel in the house as the angel out of the house. So, in an 1869 speech to the Women's Suffrage Society, Mill remarked: "If home is a woman's natural sphere (and I am not at all called upon to contradict this assertion) those departments of politics which need the faculties that can only be acquired at home, are a woman's natural sphere too. But there are great spheres and little spheres; and some people want women to be always content with the little spheres. I don't."[102] Here Mill is cleverly exploiting the domestic ideal for feminist ends. If woman's place *was* in the family, her role domestic, then, as Denise Riley puts the familiar middle-class feminist strategy, "let the social world become a great arena for domesticated intervention, where the empathies supposedly peculiar to the sex might flourish on a broad and visible scale."[103]

Mill's argument for women's intervention in the social, then, appears to be an argument for female suffrage. On closer examination, however, his argument for the suffrage turns out to be justification for increased intervention into the social. Women would be the executors of reform, the volunteers who would reduce the crushing expense of reform, and the superintendents of Poor Law reform.

"From the moment when society takes upon itself the duties required of it by the present state of civilization," Mill told his audience, "it cannot do without the intelligent co-operation of women." Take education: "When we set about really teaching the children of all ranks of the people . . . we shall need a vastly greater number of schoolmasters than we can afford to pay"—that is, "if we reject the [voluntary] assistance of half . . . the available force." Take nursing the destitute: here "our poor-law, instead of doing too much, does not do nearly enough." "There are numbers of women who, from their domestic occupations, cannot give all their time, but would willingly give part of it, either as volunteers or at a small renumeration, for work which would be too costly if paid for at the value of the time of medical men in good private practice." Finally, take the "management of the poor," "those in receipt of public relief—the pauper population," a case that merits fuller quotation:

> That formidable difficulty is weighing upon the spirits of all our thinkers. . . . A wide experience has taught to thoughtful men that the right principle of a poor-law, is to give relief . . . nowhere but in public establishments—workhouses, and, for those who need them, hospitals. And this method has been tried: but the workhouses and the workhouse hospitals have been so execrably managed . . . that the system has broken down, and public feeling shrinks from enforcing it. If this is ever remedied, it will be when pauper establishments are looked after by capable women. . . . *The fittest person to manage a workhouse is the person who best knows how to manage a house. The woman who has learnt to govern her own servants, will know how to do the same with workhouse servants.* . . . Every experienced traveller knows that there are few comfortable inns where there is no hostess.[104]

Quite apart from the last remark, which needs no comment, and apart from Mill's acceptance of the Victorian notion that middle-class women could volunteer because the majority had neither the need nor the desire to earn their own wage,[105] it was in fact the case that by 1869 the Poor Laws had fallen into even further social disrepute. The 1834 act had seriously underestimated the number of "deserving" poor, and it had not delivered on its promise to reduce poverty by giving the "undeserving" an incentive to work. Consequently, the numbers receiving out-door relief had not dwindled but increased, the costs had not declined but risen continuously, and the overcrowded workhouses had not been able to maintain order or to instill the middle-class habits of abstinence and industry.

It was middle-class women who were at the forefront of the attack on the workhouses, which they criticized as being cruel, ineffective, and destructive of the working-class family. These women occupied a central place in the philanthropic organizations that developed between 1850 and 1860 in response to the wretched conditions of state institutions, and in the 1870s to the growing numbers who could no longer qualify for out-door relief, many of whom were women with children.[106] Female reformers, in short, contrasted their approach to the destitute with that of the inhumane Poor Law commissioner, and their personal rescue work with the impersonal regime of the repressive workhouses.[107]

That Mill was concerned about this approach to combating social evils can be seen in his remarks to the Women's Suffrage Society. Women's real talent, Mill told his audience, lies in managing "all those parts of the business of life which depend on the vigilant super-intendence and accurate estimation of details," thus they would make fine administrators of state institutions.[108] Having argued for installing middle-class women in what appears to be the quasi-panoptical position of the workhouse overseer,[109] Mill then queries as to "whether women will discriminate well between good and bad modes of combatting evils, and will not be apt to mistake the most direct mode for the most efficacious."[110] This cryptic remark inti-mated that women's "addiction to philanthropy,"[111] which had trans-lated into female reformers' opposition to the Poor Laws, might lead women to prefer charity over the kind of legal relief Mill preferred: relief in the well-regulated workhouse. Then again, "this would only be a real objection," Mill added, "if we were going to disenfranchise the men, and turn over the whole power to women." Just as there was little danger of *that*, so was there "little danger that the over-zeal of women will not be quite sufficiently tempered by the over-caution of men."[112]

Mill's supervisory stance toward the poor entailed a deep worry that the charity work of female reformers would promote working-class indolence and reckless breeding, which in turn would consume wealth and, ultimately, destroy civilization.[113] It also concerned his fear that the middle-class philanthropist who ventures into the neth-erworld of the destitute might very well find herself contaminated by it, and that her antipathy toward the state and her work on behalf of the masses would undermine the movement for women's suffrage.

These fears surfaced in Mill's response to women's organized opposition to the legislation which, unlike the Poor Laws, he also vigorously condemned: the Contagious Diseases Acts.

The Innocent Magdalen

In 1871 Mill was called on to testify before the Royal Commission on the Contagious Diseases Acts (C.D.A.). Mill formulated his opposition to the acts in terms that related to the central problem he had posed in *On Liberty* (1859): "the nature and limits of the power which can be legitimately exercised by society over the individual."[114] The C.D.A. seemed to provide Mill with an urgent and practical case for linking his feminist concerns to his famous defense of personal liberty. The acts were a chilling example of the second-class status of women, the power of the state, and the tyranny of public opinion.

And yet Mill's essay also contained a qualification that could be read as having brought him, curiously and paradoxically enough, into an unwitting alliance with proponents of the very legislation he opposed. The qualification was this: the "only purpose for which power can be rightfully exercised over any member of a civilized community, against his will, is to prevent harm to others."[115] The Royal Commission repeatedly invoked, and reminded Mill of, the principle of collective self-protection. Because the diseased prostitute's body constituted a threat to the health of the larger social body, it was a legitimate site of state intervention. Citing their charge to prevent harm to "innocent persons," the commissioners asked Mill whether the state was not in fact justified in apprehending for medical examination and police registration any woman suspected of being a prostitute and, should she prove to be infected, in forcibly confining her to a lock hospital.

That very paradox speaks not only to the significant problems left unresolved in Mill's defense of personal liberty[116] but also to woman's vulnerable position vis-à-vis the patriarchal state and Victorian public opinion. Although Mill was critical of both, we have seen that he too contributed to cultural notions of proper femininity and supported the right of the state to intervene in the family, especially the lower-class family, and in the social sphere. Contrary to what Gertrude Himmelfarb argues, *On Liberty* was not at all ahead of its time in raising the specter of the sovereign individual under siege.[117] That specter was already foregrounded in the disciplinary and surveillance mechanisms that were designed to reform and contain "the dangerous classes." Mill's classic essay, then, can be read as an impassioned response to the threat to personal liberty that was in many respects *produced* by his own advocacy of such mechanisms. And Mill's testimony on the C.D.A. can be read as evincing his deep concern in *On Liberty* that, because those who need surveillance create the need for it, they constitute a threat to the liberty of those who do not.

If the C.D.A. realized in legislative practice the warning Mill had issued in *On Liberty*, they also showed quite clearly that in Victorian social practice liberty had always been a strictly gendered and classed affair. Inasmuch as they targeted not men but women, problematized not male but female sexuality, the acts highlighted, more than any other piece of legislation, the limits that could be placed on women's access to the public sphere in the name of social reform. Likewise, inasmuch as they targeted not middle-class but working-class women, not the sheltered domestic angel but the street-walking magdalen, the acts underscored the central place occupied by the unregulated lower-class female body in nineteenth-century arguments for the enlargement of the state's powers and for extending its control and surveillance capacities over the casual poor.[118]

The 1867 proposals for the extension of the original 1864 act to the civilian population appealed to the propertied classes' standing concern to maintain order. But the very fact that women *as* women could be arrested on suspicion, should they dare to venture out in public unaccompanied by male relatives, transformed the class issue of prostitution into a sex-class issue of women's basic civil rights. At the forefront of the repeal movement was the Ladies' National Association (L.N.A.), headed by Josephine Butler, which pointed to the increasingly policed and centralized state which troubled liberal male repealers, but also, as Nancy Woods writes, "to the patriarchal character of governmental structures and practices which the Acts represented."[119]

The L.N.A. was quick to seize on the forced medical examination of prostitutes as telling evidence both of the state's designs on women's bodies and, more generally, of the double standard that assumed as natural an aggressive male lust and cast the female body as the agent of contagion. Citing Judy Walkowitz's landmark study on prostitution, Woods notes the "brilliant rhetorical manouvre [with which] the L.N.A. turned the argument about female transmission of venereal disease on its head and depicted prostitutes 'as the *victims* of male pollution, as women who had been invaded by men's bodies, men's laws, and by that "steel penis", the speculum.' "[120]

Although sympathetic to the basic objectives of the L.N.A., Mill was also deeply worried that C.D.A. agitation would prove fatal to the movement for women's suffrage.[121] On the one hand, Mill's fears were far from unfounded. Maligned in the press as "shrieking sisters," "frenzied, unsexed, and utterly without shame," repealers like Butler stood accused of being prostitutes—or even, as Sir James Elphinstone told the House of Commons in 1872, of being "worse than prostitutes"—by virtue of having taken up the cause of the magdalen as that of all women.[122] As Mill put it in correspondence to George Croom Robertson, "To the mass of the English people the union of the C.D.A. agitation with that for the suffrage, condemns the latter utterly, because they look upon it as indelicate and unfeminine."[123] On the other hand, Mill was not exactly immune to seeing L.N.A. members as being guilty of such improper behavior: "The C.D.A. agitation itself would never have become the objectionable thing many people feel it, had it been carried on by people who had more knowledge of the world, and more consideration for the feelings of others." What is more, Mill told Robertson, "these same people would soon contrive to make the agitation for the suffrage vulgar and ridiculous." Now, "if the only object were to lead into noisy activity those and those only who go all lengths in favour of women's rights," said Mill, "their policy would be excellent"; but since the majority of the English were adverse to "giving women any rights at all," he concluded, it was "simply suicidal."[124]

Mill's concern to distance the polite and respectable London National Association for Women's Suffrage—whose members' "feminine" way of moving and speaking in public was to raise the tone of public morality—from the noisy and vulgar L.N.A. was an intelligent political strategy for combating sexual inequality. But it was also more than that. It was an attempt to distance the modest middle-class woman from the immodest working-class prostitute. Indeed, whereas members of the L.N.A. sought to expose the sex-class issue of the acts by taking up the prostitute's cause as their own, by identifying with the "fallen" woman, Mill sought to uphold the moral distinctions among women which, he maintained, the practical enforcement of the acts had all but effaced.

Mill's testimony rested on an uncritical acceptance of the nineteenth-century binary opposition between the depraved and the modest woman. The contagious disease legislation, Mill remarked in his opening statement to the commission, takes personal liberty away "almost entirely from a particular class of women intentionally, but incidentally and unintentionally . . . from all women whatever, inasmuch as it enables a woman to be apprehended by the police on suspicion." Asked whether his objection was confined to such instances of mistaken identity, Mill responded: "That is a very great part of my objection. . . . What number of cases there have been in which modest women, or women at any rate not prostitutes, have been apprehended by the police on suspicion, I do not know."[125] Butler understood the assault on women's liberty rather differently: "Ladies who ride in their carriages through the streets at night are in little danger of being molested [by the police]. But what of working women?"[126]

Mill's concern that the modest woman could be mistaken for the immodest one reflected cultural anxieties about the clandestine prostitute—the prostitute who also passed as a "respectable" woman. Whereas proponents of the acts assumed that a prostitute could be identified on sight, the very possibility that the lady could be taken for a streetwalker highlighted the unreadability and instability of, in Anderson's phrase, the "marks of virtue or impurity."[127] A series of mid-century reports excited and confirmed the middle-class consternation about the mobility and secrecy with which some women went from the depravity of the streets to the respectability of marriage.[128] The prostitute came to be figured as a threat to polite society not only because she was seen as the carrier of syphilitic infection but also because she was seen as being cunning and mobile rather than tragic and fallen. Far from remaining at an unbridgeable distance from her social betters, the clandestine prostitute aggressively if covertly entered their ranks. Posing as the lady, she disrupted the symbolic economy of Victorian society: she unsettled signifiers of class difference, she blurred the distinction between the moral and the depraved.

What made the prostitute, in Walkowitz's words, the literal and figurative "conduit of infection to respectable society," then, was her transgression of class boundaries, which implicated her as well in the destruction of the bourgeois family. A central argument for interfering solely with the prostitute's personal liberty was that she was the origin of the chain of contagion that destroyed the lives of innocent persons—and, besides, men would never accept being subjected to that kind of espionage. Attacking the double standard, Mill advanced the position of the L.N.A.: "a woman cannot communicate the disease but to a person who seeks it," so "it must be the man who communicates it to innocent women and children afterwards."[129] Concerned as his testimony was almost exclusively with the modest woman, however, Mill neglected the L.N.A.'s more radical point: it was often the man who communicated disease, not only to his wife and children, but to the prostitute herself.

One reason Mill, like many other Victorians, figured the prostitute as the origin of the chain of contagion was that the chain itself seemed to have neither origin nor end and recognized neither class boundaries nor moral differences. The figuration of the prostitute, whether as victim or threat, was one way of making the unknown known, of representing something that was not only unspeakable for proper Victorians but also, in some sense, unsignifiable: the chain of contagion was rather like a sign without a stable referent, a signifier without a clear signified. It is not quite right to say, as Stallybrass and White do, that "the 'prostitute' . . . was *just* the privileged category in a metonymic chain of contagion which led back to the culture of the working classes."[130] She was this and more—the abject: her condition, as the Royal Commission put it, was one of "absolute rottenness," her body "falling to pieces" (366). Sympathy for these "wretched women who haunt[ed] the camps" (368) slid repeatedly into middle-class fear and disgust to produce the prostitute as the scapegoat for the haunting presence of the casual poor and, not least, for the disease that came back to haunt the bourgeoisie as the price for its ascendancy to power.

Indeed, the so-called provident marriages of the middle classes—which guaranteed capital accumulation and which Mill upheld as the model for the laboring masses—were themselves secured by the availability of poor women for whom prostitution was one way of surviving in an economy that put a low value on female labor. With the economic status of the middle classes at stake, such C.D.A. proponents as the industrialist W. R. Greg insisted that, inasmuch as male lust was spontaneous and ineradicable, and middle-class female virtue natural and sacred, prostitution was a necessary social evil.[131] As Mary Poovey writes, the object for Greg was simply to "remove infectious prostitutes temporarily from the free market system while leaving both the economic and moral dimensions of that system intact."[132]

For Mill, who advocated chastity for both sexes, such a solution enshrined the double standard, cast the state as the legal guardian and purveyor of vice, and failed to grasp the moral effects of the law of supply and demand. "Even if it is only by the fact that a considerable number of them [prostitutes] are withdrawn from their profession periodically," Mill told the commission, "the vacancy or gap that is thus made, as the demand calls forth a supply, has a natural tendency to be filled up . . . by healthy persons from other quarters," who will, in turn, become diseased as well. In fact, he held, "the law which produces it [that tendency] is as strong as any law in political economy" (364).

Suggesting that an insatiable and immoral male lust was the driving force behind prostitution, Mill neglected here, as throughout his testimony, to observe that the system of laissez-faire forced many working-class women to take to the streets. Suggesting that respectable women would soon join the army of seasoned prostitutes to make up the gap in supply, his remarks revealed middle-class anxieties about just how contaminating fallenness could be.[133] If the law of supply and demand could turn the modest woman into a prostitute, then the category of virtue itself was thrown into question: the respectable woman was subject to larger economic forces that could not be evaded through the simple exercise of moral choice. And if modest women were soon to be prostitutes, then the market economy too was doomed.

Inasmuch as female virtue was the very foundation of the gendered separation of spheres and of class distinctions, the attenuated autonomy of the prostitute had to be accounted for in ways that would dispel middle-class anxieties about an economic system run amok, about larger social determinations that could sweep up and finally ruin even those women—and everyone who came into sexual contact with them—who adhered to the code of proper femininity. Likewise, inasmuch as the desperate and commodified figure of the prostitute stood in radical political discourse, from at least the 1830s onward, as a metaphor for the social effects of the wage labor system, the prostitute had to be explained in terms that would diffuse the demands put forth by the urban working classes.[134] Both of these threats to bourgeois identity and power were managed through the cultural rhetoric of fallenness, which insisted on what Anderson calls the prostitute's "'determined' status, her unredeemable fall, her inevitable collapse."[135] Although it intimated the social effects of proletarianization, fallenness was largely a moral category that kept the prostitute at a safe (rhetorical) distance from polite society.

The rhetoric of fallenness performed yet another kind of cultural work in Victorian society: it dispelled the threatening aspects of a willful and public female sexuality. By representing the lower-class prostitute as degraded and demoralized, rather than as aggressive and sexualized, it could align her, in Poovey's words, "with—rather than in opposition to—the virtuous middle-class woman." On the one hand, this association risked blurring social distinctions between the middle and the working classes; on the other hand, it also upheld them, says Poovey, by translating a "class difference that might otherwise be seen as a *cause* of social unrest . . . into a gender similarity that can ideally serve as the *solution* to immorality."[136] What all women share as women, an asexual nature, is more important than what divides them along lines of social class.

This reformulation of the prostitute as a tragic and fallen figure, an "innocent magdalen" deserving of pity and charity,[137] was central to the Victorian idea of reclamation: the social rehabilitation of those led astray by a weak moral character and hard economic times—that is, by temporary crises in the market economy rather than by the structural inequality of the wage labor system. As Mill told the commission, it is "not beyond the proper function of the State to take means of making these persons [prostitutes] understand that they are not considered as totally unworthy of any kind of regard or consideration by the rest of their fellow-creatures, but that it is the object to reclaim them." One could contain vice and reduce suffering if they were "attended by those benevolent and excellent people [e.g., middle-class women] who undertake their reclamation." And the same ought to be done for "the criminal and vicious classes, the dangerous classes altogether" (365–366).

Although charitable work offered middle-class women a chance to move from the "little" sphere of the family to the "great" sphere of the social, it also contributed to the low value placed on women's work, which had propelled some women into prostitution. Thus, although the L.N.A. urged middle-class women to reclaim their fallen sisters, it maintained that prostitution was every woman's problem because the very same men who would police women were those who drove them into the streets in the first place. To solve the class problem of prostitution, one had to take up the sex-class cause of women's right to unrestricted industrial employment, to property, and to an equal wage.[138]

This was an argument to which Mill was highly sympathetic. Yet its conspicuous absence in his testimony and letters on the C.D.A. speaks to his tendency to translate the poverty that fueled prostitution into the moral poverty Mill blamed, more often than not, for class inequality. So, when asked whether he thought the medical examination of prostitutes to be degrading, Mill answered, "I dare say there are some of them to whom nothing is degrading, they are so degraded already; but there is reason to believe that there are many of them who have a considerable quantity of modesty left, and to whom therefore it is degrading." When pressed as to what is more degrading, the exam or the life the prostitute leads, Mill responded, "I think both are degrading, but degradation for degradation, that which is *compulsory* [the exam] seems to me always more degrading in its effects on the character than what is done *voluntarily* [self-prostitution]" (my emphasis). Concluding that the exam simply added more degradation to that "caused by [a freely chosen] debauched life," Mill's image of self-willed prostitution bore a not surprising resemblance to his notion of self-willed pauperism (367–368). What was missing in his defense of the Poor Laws was also missing in his opposition to the C.D.A.: a class analysis of inequality and a recognition that the severe restrictions placed on out-relief forced female paupers to take to the streets.

The logic at work in Mill's defense of the state's obligation to prevent death by starvation resurfaced in his defense of its duty to prevent death by syphilis. Asked whether relief would not encourage vice, Mill said that the same objection could be brought against "all poor laws . . . *since the people themselves are often very much to blame* for bringing themselves into a position in which they require relief, and no doubt the relief does in some not inconsiderable degree diminish the prudential motives for abstaining." Nevertheless, he added, society ought to help the destitute, "provided we do it in such a way as that it shall not provide facilities beforehand, but only deal with the evil when it has been incurred" (359, my emphasis).

Here we witness what Stephen Collini cites as the "moral psychology" that shaped Mill's objection to the C.D.A. and his discussion of related issues in *On Liberty*: "They interfere with the proper operation of the calculation of consequences upon the formation of the will."[139] Mill's insistence on, even obsession with, the need for self-discipline, however, was related to his profound fear that the will itself was threatened by the larger social forces of capitalism, which made a virtual mockery of the notion of moral choice as the basis for class differences. In the face of the massive destitution that characterized Victorian society in the 1840s and the seemingly ineradicable poverty that persisted to the end of the century, the idea of the autonomous individual was under siege. As Mill put this sense of attenuated autonomy in the *Autobiography*, "I felt as if I was . . . the helpless slave of antecedent circumstances; as if my character and that of all others had been formed for us by agencies beyond our control, and was wholly out of our own power."[140]

Far from being unique to his upbringing at the hands of a stern father, who held to "the doctrine of what is called Philosophical Necessity,"[141] Mill's "paralysing" sense that he was determined by his social environment bespoke the fear that haunted nineteenth-century English society at large. As the promise of a better world gave way to the nightmare of proletarianization, Mill and other social reformers became increasingly worried that, like syphilis, the attenuated autonomy of the working classes would spread to the middle classes and destroy, finally, Victorian culture. In many respects, the rhetoric of fallenness, the social criteria of moral difference, and, as Mill put it, the "ennobling . . . doctrine of freewill,"[142] can all be interpreted as part of a larger middle-class cultural and psychological strategy: to defend the bourgeois subject against an abject social other who came to figure as that which threatened one's own precarious social position, menaced one's own clean and proper self, and threw into question one's own capacity for agency and choice.

Inasmuch as the prostitute figured the political threat to middle-class power, the diseased threat to the social body, and the sexualized threat to the domestic ideal, she came to figure (like the female pauper) the tension in Mill's writings on gender, class, and personal liberty. So Mill had no quarrel with what the commission called the "interference with the liberty of the subject [by the police] to prevent solicitation in the streets to preserve the order of the streets" (369). But the Victorian order that required that the streets be kept clear of the woman who gave the lie to the ideology of self-help and the Malthusian logic of Poor Law reform was also that which required respectable women to remain respectable by respecting a gendered and classed public space.

When Mill's testimony on the C.D.A. is read in conjunction with *On Liberty*, then, it casts doubt on Himmelfarb's claim that the latter was "the case of women writ large" and therefore trivial.[143] For that claim neglects the far more ambiguous figure of woman in Mill's writings, a figure that cannot so easily be read into the seminal statement: "Over himself, over his own body and mind, the individual is sovereign."[144] The precarious sovereignty of that individual was shored up by insisting on his moral difference from those who failed to exercise self-restraint, and who must therefore be restrained by others. Insofar as Mill aligned the unruly passions with the female body (be it passive or active), his vision of a rational public sphere populated by sovereign subjects called for disciplining the bodies of those who would not discipline themselves. This not only compromised the liberty of poor women; it also, if often unwittingly and paradoxically, reinscribed all women in the Victorian domestic ideal.

CHAPTER FIVE

Resignifying the Woman Question in Political Theory

First we must ask: what is a woman?

—Simone de Beauvoir

The deceptively simple question that introduces this chapter opens the space of feminist criticism in *The Second Sex*.[1] I invoke it here to argue for the practice of a feminist political theory which, in the spirit of Beauvoir, refuses the woman question as it has been formulated in the Western tradition. Such a practice dislocates this familiar question by rearticulating it in a feminist frame of reference. In this frame, the woman question is itself called into question, defamiliarized; it is transformed from a question that secures the claims of political theory into one that unsettles them. The woman question, as Beauvoir inspires me to rephrase it, concerns political theory's *production* of, and investments in, woman *as* a question; it also concerns political theory's efforts to settle the meaning of the very riddle of femininity that both enables and undercuts its enunciative authority as a historical tradition of discourse.

The continued relevance of Beauvoir's question for feminist political theorists speaks to the tenacity of the woman question as it is posed in the classic texts; it speaks as well to the difficulty of dislodging that question from its masculinist frame of reference in contemporary criticism. Feminists have contested this frame by interrogating the woman question; but many have reproduced, albeit unwittingly, woman as a question—one that has a correct answer, so to speak. Traditional political theory does not get women right, argue a wide

138

array of feminist critics: its images of woman are so many misrepresentations of "real" women.[2] Informed by a referential model of language, such an approach to the canon divests the aforementioned, defamiliarized formulation of the woman question of its disruptive power: it searches for the right answer to the woman question instead of inquiring into that question's discursive function, namely, its part in the production of political meaning. Focusing on what woman signifies instead of on how she signifies, it neglects the semiotics of woman and politics and political theory as a signifying practice.

This focus on the what of signification is tied to the persistence, even in many of the more sophisticated feminist approaches to the canon, in reading images of women in terms of whether they do or do not add up to a coherent argument about politics and gender.[3] Although important, this approach may contribute, if unwittingly, to the further marginalization of feminist critiques: it implies that women are a problem for traditional political theory only once we insist that the case for their exclusion be logically sound, or once we try to add women back into the category of the citizen. I have attempted to demonstrate, on the contrary, that the figure of woman poses significant problems within and for a diverse group of political texts long before the modern reader tries to make the outsiders (women) insiders (citizens). This is so even in the case of one thinker (Mill) whom many feminists judge to be inclusive.

To argue this case I have read woman not as an image but rather as a sign, and less as a signified and more as a signifier. What is the difference between these two ways of reading?[4] The first approach compares competing images of woman (or women), shows that they are incompatible, and then demonstrates that the theorist's effort to resolve the tension often results in such oxymorons as Rousseau's "chaste coquette" or Mill's "innocent magdalen." I too make occasional use of this strategy, but with caution. It appears to me to be inadequate if not flawed for several reasons. First, because it assumes that the text, if it is to attain the status of an argument, ought to function as a unified whole, this strategy takes contradictory images of women as telling instances of a convoluted argument about gender and politics. The arbitrary and unstable character of language, its unruly differential structure, is thereby denied, opposed to the criterion of logical consistency.[5] And with that denial a powerful critical tool for feminist theory is lost. Second, in treating each discrete image as itself intrinsically coherent, such an approach neglects the extent to which the meaning of every image is constructed discursively in relation to other images. Third, it often assumes that the image has an intrinsic meaning that can be read off the page, as it were, quite apart from its narrative invocation in the text and, sometimes, apart from historical context.[6] These assumptions enable the production of a rather seamless tale about "women in the history of political thought" in which woman often appears as a static figure (associated with a disruptive sexuality, or a benevolent maternalism, or the private sphere) that recurs in all-too-familiar ways throughout time or, a more qualified version, throughout certain epochs.[7] Thinking we already know this figure, we reject it as "sexist" and leave it largely uninterrogated. We treat the image as if it were meaningful in itself, as if its meaning were not produced differentially through processes of signification and narration, and as if its production as meaning were successful, resistant to any strategic subversions or interrogations.

This approach, moreover, has the distinct disadvantage of positing woman as a category prior to its articulation and circulation in political texts; it occludes the fact that political theory, although not the inventor of this category, does code it in ways (as Elizabeth Cowie has written of filmic practices) that are "neither unique and independent of, nor simply reducible to, other practices defining the meaning of women in society."[8] I do not want to overstate the contribution made by canonical political theorists to this production of meaning, and yet it is important to take account of it. For one thing, if political theory is seen as merely reporting or importing existing, oppressive social definitions of woman into its discursive field, then, as Cowie observes, "the struggle over those definitions is placed elsewhere."[9] The function of political theory as a signifying practice, itself an active participant in the production of the "real," is occluded by the insistence that the political theory text is merely a (post hoc) legitimation of the material relations of women's lives and their exclusion from public life. The text is attacked for not showing "women as women," as human beings,[10] or as political beings, but not for *producing* woman. It is criticized for mirroring and lending further credence to preexisting social meanings of woman as mother, wife, worker, but its own investment in those social meanings is never analyzed. In short, if woman is assumed to already bear meanings that correspond to existing social codes of femininity, then the important question of how she comes to bear those meanings or comes to be coded in the political text is foreclosed. If that text is read as a reflection on or distortion of the oppressive meanings of woman (or women), it is dismissed as an ideological tract instead of interrogated for its part in the historical construction of sexual difference.

A large part of my quarrel with feminist approaches to the canon, then, centers on the uncritical assumption of the classical model of representation, which holds both that language is a transparent vehicle for communicating (a preexisting) meaning and that the text is a reflection or mystification of social reality. When language is conceptualized in this way (that is, as referential), it seems that the best way to contest political theory is to insist on a better fit between word and thing, sign and referent, women and "real" women—to get women right, after all.[11] This not only effaces the constitutive dimension of political theory as a signifying practice, it also betrays a yearning for an unmediated (and uncontaminated) representation that would show women as women—as fully human and political beings. Is such a representation possible? Is it desirable? Could it be that the longing itself, the wish for a true and unmediated representation of flesh-and-blood women, is itself a product of political theory's symbolic work?

In posing these questions, I suggest interpretive pathways for moving beyond a feminist critique that takes images of women to be a matrix of misrepresentations characterizing the workings of canonical political theory. Rather than condemn political theory as a tradition of deception that produces, among other illusions, woman as masculinist fantasy, I have tried throughout this study to interrogate the cultural work performed by the figure of woman in the context of larger questions about signification, subjectivity, and politics. Rather than demand a more adequate or inclusive representation of "real" women from political theory, I have focused on the symbolic role played by its unruly sexual(ized) other, the disorderly and disorder-

ing woman, in the construction of the unified citizen-subject, in
the discursive elaboration of naturalized sexual difference, and, not
least, in the figuration and containment of politics.

What is at stake, then, for contemporary interpretation and politics in questioning the classical model that gives the referent priority
over the sign, the signified over the signifier, meaning over articulation? Nothing less than the recasting of the woman question and its
effective refiguration of the political; nothing less than how we read
political theory and theorize politics. When the classical model remains unchallenged, woman appears as a natural entity (to be accepted or rejected) rather than the fragile product of symbolization
and political theorizing. When language is thought of as representation, it is difficult to recognize the processes of figuration and signification that produce, not only woman qua woman but also woman as
the complex site of political stabilization and destabilization, consolidation and contestation. It becomes impossible, in fact, to think
about the figure of woman as signifying (whether truly or falsely, it
matters not) anything *but* women. It becomes impossible to think
through the ways woman figures and signifies the political. The
result? Woman is of interest only for those "interested" special-
ists called feminists who concern themselves with what is quaintly
termed "the woman question."

The referential model of language, then, conceals several problems faced by readers concerned to establish as politically significant
the symbolic figures, such as the disorderly and disordering woman,
which inhabit the territorial edge of political theory. It conceals,
among other things, the processes of symbolic displacement that
figure woman as the site of the dissonant (i.e., unsettled, uncertain,
unfinished) features of both the citizen-subject as a speaking being
and politics as a realm of speech. Without wishing to reduce these
issues to the arbitrary and differential structure of the sign, I have
argued that, in the texts of Rousseau, Burke, and Mill, the linguistic
ambiguity that characterizes language understood as articulation
(i.e., as an infinite play of differences, of signifiers that only belatedly
and retroactively produce meanings and identities) finds expression
in the figuration of woman as bearer of culture and chaos. The
disorderly woman is, in part, a way of encoding the unruly character

of language itself, its resistance to unified and unitary meaning. She figures and is figured as the excess or residue of signification, the play of differences or signifiers that both elicits and defies the theorist's efforts to bring order to the social qua semiotic chaos. Indeed, woman functions as the scapegoat for semiotic discontinuities, for the very failure of language to produce and maintain clear and distinct meanings. When read in this way and against the grain, however, the disorderly woman is indeed *dis*-ordering—albeit not in ways anticipated by the theorist: she disrupts the whole structure of binary oppositions (e.g., private/public, feminine/masculine, nature/culture) that political theorists articulate in their frantic efforts to contain the play of signification; she interrupts and animates the longing for closure and coherence, unity and commonality, which characterizes, finally, the work of Rousseau, Burke, and Mill.

But the chaos to which these theorists would bring order and which they figure as the disorderly woman is not simply a semiotic chaos that inheres in the differential structure of language. It is also, and in very specific ways, as I have argued, a disorder produced through multiple and historical political contestations. Sometimes woman is put into discourse to encode these contestations in ways that make the unfamiliar familiar, the unknown known. Political theory works on a heterogeneous field of social phenomena that demands and often elides the writer's understanding; as Hayden White points out, it assimilates those phenomena by analogy "to those areas of experience felt to be *already* understood as to *their* essential natures."[12] If woman is figured as both culture and chaos in the political texts I have examined, it is partly because woman is the term whose essence is taken for granted, sometimes questioned and then reconstructed as in Mill, but always thought to be understood and reassuringly represented in an existing cultural vocabulary. The political theorist as writing subject does not already fully comprehend such things as revolution or the threat of it. But he does already "know" what a woman is: she is a saint or a devil, a mother or a prostitute, a moral angel or a carnal magdalen. Nothing surprising in those cultural tags. Just reassurance.

Or so it would seem. Because the so-called real essence of woman is, in fact, precisely what Rousseau, Burke, and Mill do not know.

They make a claim to know it through the use of the term itself: by putting woman into discourse, by trying to fix the meaning of woman in language. But, as Locke said long ago, "we in vain pretend to range Things into sorts, and dispose them into certain Classes, under Names, by their real Essences, that are so far from our discovery or comprehension."[13] The term "woman" is the site of immense ambiguity and anxiety in political theory precisely because it resists the efforts of theorists to fix woman as the ground or essence of meanings. Jacques Derrida explains that woman, too, is a signified that "is always already in the position of the signifier," always in flux, always dependent for its meaning on its difference to every other signifier.[14] All one can do is to pretend, with deadly seriousness perhaps but in vain, that woman is a stable meaning, a foundation or ground, a real essence. The pretense is costly. The insistence that the meanings of woman precede their discursive inscription in the political text requires constant work to keep the term "woman" from unraveling within the linguistic play of the text itself.

Consider Burke's *Reflections on a Revolution in France*. At stake in the meaning of woman as beauty, order, and submission is nothing less than the ancien régime. Although the gender binarism of the feminine beautiful and the masculine sublime is confused by the incursion of women into public space, it remains in play in the text to account precisely for that other unknown—public women who confound the essential meaning of woman and, with it, all other Burkean political meanings. The idea of the sublime is called on to account for and represent something that by its essential nature cannot be sublime (woman) but that must be accounted for and represented—that is, if the abyss of signification ("a king is but a man, a queen is but a woman . . .") is to be kept at bay. Once woman is sublime, however, the sublime itself spins out of control because it has lost its mooring in the binary relation just mentioned. This is why the sublime no longer holds the same privileged position in the *Reflections* that it held in the *Enquiry into the Sublime and the Beautiful*; it also explains why beauty is then assigned a far more important symbolic role in representing social order: beauty must be amplified if the unnatural feminine sublime is to be tamed.

The symbolic work of the "furies of hell," however, entails less a misrepresentation of the women of the sansculottes than the creation of the illusion of a referent that exists in unmediated relation to the sign. Political women are the raw material, so to speak, of Burke's tale of horror, but whatever meanings they come to have in his narrative are produced through signifying processes that fully transfigure the referent precisely by figuring it as sublime, or rather uncanny, such that the referent (political women) is all but indistinguishable from the sign (the furies). The ideological work of the *Reflections* aims precisely *to hide* this symbolic work. It makes the furies appear as if they were the referent, the Revolution as if it were an intrinsically tragic event, and political women as if they were monsters.

One could counter this reading, of course, and say that Burke's hysterical prose is itself proof that those furies are not the referent but rather creatures of the writer's pen. But isn't the illusion of referentiality reproduced by that counter, by its denial that the symbolic figure of the furies bears any relation whatsoever to the women of the sansculottes? Isn't it rather a question of how the relation between the sign and the referent is produced in Burke's texts, and thus of how Burkean political meaning is produced? a question of how an interpretive code is produced which then determines what counts as real, as extradiscursive? a question of how the sign signifies rather than what it signifies? or better, a question of how that very what is itself constituted through the how, the process of signification? A critical feminist practice of reading ought not simply reject those furies as a blatant instance of Burke's conservatism, as nothing but a misrepresentation of political women. It should analyze rather how and why this trope is produced and disseminated in the text to generate the interrelated meanings of gender and class. And it should examine how the margins of the Burkean political are constituted and unsettled by the uncanny figure of woman. Burke's horrific feminine trope, I have shown, can be pushed to its limit, and there those furies are not distinct from, but contiguous with, their symbolic opposite: the feminine beautiful figured as Marie Antoinette; there the space of the writer's figuration of revolution dissipates into the semiotic play of the text, and there the masculine identity of the writing subject collapses in a frenzied but illicit identification with his endangered feminine object, the "Queen of France."

There is, needless to say, nothing intrinsically political to the areferential model of language employed in this study, and a feminist critical practice that attends to it clearly must do more than celebrate linguistic ambiguity and semiotic arbitrariness. What I am arguing for is not the practice of deconstruction per se (even as I acknowledge its powerful uses for feminism) but, rather, a feminist reading that would radically defamiliarize one of the fundamental terms that grounds representation in the political text—woman. Woman is the term and the category that must be called into question—destabilized and defamiliarized rather than simply rejected out of hand or corrected. If the theorist deploys woman to make the unknown known, feminists might redeploy woman to make the known unknown, fully strange and alien, not the least bit reassuring. As unauthorized readers, they might even take serious and illicit delight in assuming the part of political theory's disorderly qua disordering woman; often enough this will take the form of a critical analysis that theory celebrates in other settings.

The kind of critical intervention I am calling for here, then, consists not in a rejection of woman as a misrepresentation of women but rather in a tenacious interrogation of the relation between the two as it is discursively constituted and rhetorically deployed in the political text. The stakes of that interrogation are not only scholarly, they are also political. The relation between woman as masculinist construct and women as social beings may be, as Teresa de Lauretis tells us, "an arbitrary and symbolic one," but it structures the subject positions and social spaces that can be occupied by those persons called women.[15] That is to say, women are socially constructed through the figure of woman, and to contest woman is not to affirm the existence of "real" women but rather to question women (and by extension man) as a category of social existence and as a way of organizing social difference.[16] This is not to deny that (the social beings called) women exist, for that would be to efface gender as indeed a very real, lived relation to the symbolic terms of sexual difference. We need to think the gendered subject (both masculine and feminine) as a social and discursive production, as an ongoing process that has everything to do with how gender is symbolized, which is to say how gender is socially constructed, daily.

If political theory, for its part, plays a role in that construction, then the question arises of how best to contest woman without falling into the trap of validating the existence of "real" women and thus affirming the category of sex. I have suggested that feminists adopt the strategy of defamiliarization as it is practiced in *The Second Sex*. Now I examine how we might further denaturalize sexual difference by disarticulating not only the woman/women connection but also the binary opposition of masculinity and femininity. Rather than working with unified entities like the categories of women and men, femininity and masculinity, we should explore and exploit the ways these categories are, as Cora Kaplan writes, "always, already, ordered and broken up through other social and cultural terms, other categories of difference."[17]

That is one reason I have made class central to my analysis. Attending to class, we reduce the danger of treating the figure of woman in the political text as if it were a signifier that has a singular, foundational, fundamental signified. When class differences are accounted for in the works of Mill, for instance, woman cannot be read as a unified category. There is no woman in Mill's texts; there are rather figurations of middle-class women, of working-class women, and of pauper women. Woman, in other words, is a meaning that is constructed in relation not only to a sexual other but also to a series of class others. At the same time, I have tried to avoid the simplistic reduction of woman to a signifier of class. Thus the figure of Marie Antoinette does not stand simply for the aristocratic world in the Burkean text; nor is that world represented by the salonnière in the Rousseauean text. To assume as much, one would need to explain, among other things, why it is that the king cannot be substituted for the queen in the *Reflections*, the gallant for the aristocratic idol in the *Letter to D'Alembert*. Such substitutions are impossible because woman and man signify meanings in the political text that are themselves contingent on (though never simply reducible to) social definitions of sexual difference. Even as the timeless beauty of the queen or the sumptuous body of the salonnière symbolize two very different perspectives on the class order of the ancien régime, they depend for their meaning on a symbolic and cultural order in which woman is associated with beauty and vulnerability, luxury and commerce. According to Rousseau, then, men may actively promote or fall victim to luxury. But luxury is not a man, it is a woman. The courtier, in fact, does not even count as a member of his own "sex" but rather betrays it and, in the process, loses his relation to it: practicing luxury he becomes what luxury is—a woman. The citizen is he who takes up his place in the sociosymbolic order as a man by casting off that which is coded at once as aristocratic and feminine.

Another reason woman is never simply a signifier of either class difference or gender difference concerns the crucial matter of the discursive construction of sexuality as class- and gender-specific.[18] Just as I have tried to unpack what appears to be the recurring association of woman with a disruptive sexuality by showing that the sexualized woman is figured in shifting class terms, so have I endeavored to unpack the term "sexuality" itself by showing that it is articulated and organized along lines of sexual difference. Part of my concern has been to disclose that sex is no more the biological referent of political theory than are women the social referent of woman.[19] My readings of Rousseau, Burke, and Mill complicate the familiar image of the theorist as the tamer of eros, usually treated as "natural heterosexual instinct": Before he can tame it, he has to name or rather constitute it as instinct and as a threat to the good society. Rousseau's texts reveal sexual desire to be just that—a desire rather than an instinct, wholly imaginary rather than hormonal. Moreover, those texts do not merely assume or take up preexisting cultural representations of feminine sexuality. Instead, they rework them to produce the menacing figure of the carnal woman as a political meaning to justify, among other things, her domestication, and to underwrite the need for a fraternal social contract. Likewise, Mill's texts rework the Victorian idea of sex as an archaic drive to account for poverty and class conflict within the framework of utilitarianism.

The historical construction of sexuality has been crucial to my effort to complicate what is too often assumed to be political theory's timeless refrain about the disorderly woman. Do not feminist readers re-produce the very thing to be critiqued when they narrate it as if it were to be found throughout the history of political thought? In the texts we have examined, not all women are disorderly and, what is more, not all "count fully" as women—particularly if to be women, as Beauvoir remarks, they have to "share in that mysterious and threatened reality known as femininity."[20] Moreover, femininity itself is inscribed, in the texts of Rousseau, Burke, and Mill, along historical lines of gender and class, and in accordance with shifting conceptions of masculine and feminine sexuality. In their works, proper femininity is constructed differentially and deployed discursively to unify the category of women, to articulate changing social relations, and to mitigate class conflict.

To think about proper femininity in this way—as a form of political artifice akin, say, to a social contract—enables a more complicated reading of woman in the classic texts. Attending to the multiple and historical significations of woman points up the enormous cultural work necessary to sustain the fiction of a naturalized sexual difference as the ground of other sociopolitical oppositions, such as class relations. The symbolic economy figured around woman (and especially around the domestic ideal), however, turns out to be unstable partly because, despite increasingly urgent if not desperate historical efforts to the contrary, female sexual difference itself was figured in the eighteenth and nineteenth centuries in terms of class difference. So in Mill's works, for instance, the pauper and the prostitute ought to participate in the domestic ideal but they do not; one kind of woman threatens the other kind of woman and everything the right kind of woman stands for: civilization and self-restraint, economic productivity and class harmony. Mill criticizes Victorian femininity, but he then produces his own version of it to unite all women—including women who do not "act like women" and thus threaten the category of women—under the banner of the asexual woman.

Mill is of particular importance to my argument that the meaning of woman is produced discursively in the political text because it was he who insisted that no one knows the essence of woman. Rather than accuse Mill of a lack of feminist commitment, I have tried to show that the pursuit of authorial intention is an interpretive dead end. It is not a matter of what Mill really wanted to say but rather of how his texts said what they said and how the saying constituted the meaning and, finally, undermined his challenge to Victorian woman-hood and his critique of capitalism. His texts begin with representa-tions of women (of all classes) and of the laboring population as the victims of larger social and cultural forces, then go on to figure both of these as the cause of the problems for which they were seen at first to be the effect. But it is especially women (and also men) of the working classes who come to figure the very forces Mill initially saw as responsible for their victimization. This slippage, I have argued, is largely tropological: metaphoric associations between subjects and their socioeconomic world replace metynomic ones.

Even as Mill produces a narrative account of class difference as moral difference, we have also seen that he produces the menacing image of the abyss. In linguistic terms, the abyss marks the place in Mill's texts, as it does in those of Rousseau and Burke, where the signifier is unleashed from its purported social referent, where it fails to produce a clear signified and, indeed, extends into a space devoid of internal boundaries, of clear lines of difference—a space of sym-bolic chaos. In historical terms, there is an increasing association of the abyss with the masses, yet in each of these theorists it is woman who figures the abyss (albeit not exclusively; it is also figured by the masses in Burke and Mill). This persistent association of woman with a chaos that is at once social and symbolic is figured—to the extent that it can be figured at all—in class terms (the salon woman in Rousseau, the revolutionary woman in Burke, the pauper woman in Mill). The woman whose proper femininity ought to serve as a screen over the abyss (Sophie in Rousseau, Marie Antoinette in Burke, the middle-class woman in Mill), however, also recedes, within the linguistic play of the texts, into that very chaos.

To explain this aspect of the political text, I have drawn on the work of Julia Kristeva, who argues that woman stands as a kind of frontier figure, an internal limit or borderline of the sociosymbolic order. Coded as maternal, woman is abject, that which "does not succeed in differentiating itself as *other* but threatens one's *own and clean self*"[21]—it is the writing subject's clean and proper self. What comes to be figured as woman, as other, is inside the always (and therefore) unstable writing subject who tries to stabilize himself by exteriorizing woman and domesticating her as a stable, referential signifier of the other of masculinity, better known as proper femininity.

Yet, no matter how proper, how domesticated, woman always retains her connection with the abyss, the abject, both of which connote the fragile limit of identity and of meaning proper. More exactly, the abyss is where identity and meaning are not. Although the abyss image usually emerges, so to speak, in passages that depict class conflict and gender inversion, it is characterized by an accelerating disintegration of such lines of demarcation as feminine/masculine, nature/culture, and, with them, of the oppositions that structure gender and class relations. So, in the *Reflections*, the recognizable topos of the woman on top gives way first to the prostitute, then to unmarried mothers, then to the Women's March on Versailles, then to the attack on the almost naked queen, then to the furies of hell, and finally to a confusion or mingling of genders and classes that is almost unsignifiable, incapable of representation in terms of gender inversion—like the woman on top that formed the first link in this signifying chain.

There are several reasons for political theorists to attend to this image of the abyss. First, it shows just what is at stake in maintaining the figure of woman as proper femininity, however it is defined. One woman is the abyss and that other woman, the screen woman, is the defense against it.[22] Insisting that this screen of proper femininity is a form of political artifice, I have situated woman at the charged intersection of a virtual battle of social languages in the text, at the site where the theorist endeavors to articulate, mediate, and, all too often, settle political contestation. Indeed woman, we have seen, is deployed discursively not only to figure the abyss but also to contain politics; in Rousseau, Burke, and Mill, her domestication is imbricated in the larger domestication of the political.

Here emerges another reason for attending to the abyss. Woman as she figures culture and chaos complements and complicates much of what has been said of late about the containment or displacement of politics which characterizes a large part of Western political theory.[23] The absence of fixity or certitude that is the catalyst behind the political theory enterprise has been met, more often than not, with a call for order. But when political theorists understand their task to be one that eliminates dissonance, settles conflict, and consolidates community, there is a danger that those aspects of the self and society that refuse to be so ordered will be displaced onto an externalized other, who comes to figure all that one denies or fears in oneself and one's culture. Does it matter that this other is often (although not exclusively) figured as feminine, if not as woman?

Kristeva suggests that it does. She gives us a language for thinking about why that is so, highlighting the human costs of abjection and the costs of refusing to recognize the irreducible alterity that inhabits the speaking subject. Her work prompts me to conclude that woman is to the political theories of Rousseau, Burke, and Mill what the hysteric is to psychoanalysis: an unruly other produced by the discourse that purports merely to describe if not to contain it; an unruly other that is absolutely necessary to the functioning of the theory itself. To put the same point even more sharply: no woman, no social contract in Rousseau; no constitutional monarchy in Burke; no representative government in Mill. Just as psychoanalysis needed and produced the hysteric to justify its own claims to knowledge, so these three great figures of modern political thought need and produce woman as bearer of culture and chaos to justify the necessity of their distinct political visions. Those visions not only exclude women from full participation in the public sphere but also deeply impoverish the public sphere itself. In the perpetual if unacknowledged struggle against an other that is not, in fact, outside but rather inside the borders of his own identity, each theorist is driven, even against what is best in his own theory, to build a fortress around the public sphere and the citizen-subject, to pursue, finally, politics as an achievement of unity, order, and coherence, and, consequently, to depreciate politics as diversity, conflict, and dissonance.

If I am correct in arguing that this holds even for a theorist as hostile to conformity and attuned to diversity as John Stuart Mill, we should not underestimate the magnitude of the problem posed by Kristeva's account of abjection. Indeed if politics has consisted in large measure of abjection—that is, the denial, expulsion, and containment of a (feminized) other—then surely a different politics, a different political theory, must entail something more than a polite discussion of the woman question as it has been traditionally posed by the classic theorists and contested by feminists. The woman question effaces subjectivity as a legitimate question for political theory precisely by perpetuating a fantasy of the unified and stable masculine subjectivity that Kristeva exposes as just that. Could it be that political theory's obsession with the woman question belies its anxiety about another kind of question, what Kathy Ferguson calls "the man question"?[24] Could it be that the woman question as well as political theory's belief—our belief?—in woman (be she madonna or magdalen, savior or scapegoat, culture or chaos) is nothing but a desire for solace in the face of the uncertainty and fragility that characterizes our all-too-human condition? a desire, that is, for a place beyond signification, beyond ambiguity, beyond alterity—in a word, beyond politics? These questions demand answers, and certain kinds of answers demand the practice of a new political theory.

Notes

1. Political Theory as a Signifying Practice

1. I refer here to the important work of the following feminist theorists: Susan Moller Okin, *Women in Western Political Thought* (Princeton: Princeton University Press, 1979); Jean Bethke Elshtain, *Public Man, Private Woman: Women in Social and Political Thought* (Princeton: Princeton University Press, 1979); Zillah Eisenstein, *The Radical Future of Liberal Feminism* (New York: Longman, 1981); Hanna Pitkin, *Fortune Is a Woman: Gender and Politics in the Thought of Niccolò Machiavelli* (Berkeley: University of California Press, 1984); Arlene Saxonhouse, *Women in the History of Political Thought: Ancient Greece to Machiavelli* (New York: Praeger, 1985); Judith Evans, ed., *Feminism and Political Theory* (London: Sage, 1986); Carole Pateman, *The Sexual Contract* (Stanford: Stanford University Press, 1988), and *The Disorder of Women: Democracy, Feminism, and Political Theory* (Stanford: Stanford University Press, 1989); Wendy Brown, *Manhood and Politics: A Feminist Reading in Political Theory* (Totowa, N.J.: Rowman & Littlefield, 1988); Joan B. Landes, *Women and the Public Sphere in the Age of the French Revolution* (Ithaca: Cornell University Press, 1988); Tamasin E. Lorraine, *Gender, Identity, and the Production of Meaning* (Boulder: Westview, 1990); Mary Lyndon Shanley and Pateman, eds., *Feminist Interpretations and Political Theory* (Princeton: Princeton University Press, 1991); Christine Di Stefano, *Configurations of Masculinity: A Feminist Perspective on Modern Political Theory* (Ithaca: Cornell University Press, 1991). I emphasize that feminist political theorists are not a monolithic group of commentators on the Western tradition but a highly diverse group of cultural critics. In the chapters that follow, especially Chapter Five, I try to specify more precisely the differences among these critics and the extent of my differences from those whose work is of particular relevance to this study.

2. Obviously women have attained the status of citizens. What feminist theorists argue, however, is that they remain second-class citizens. To explain why that is so, many have turned to the canonical texts, where they find that woman as noncitizen is the condition for the man-citizen. For women to become equal members of the public sphere, feminists maintain, the very category of the citizen itself must be radically rethought rather than merely enlarged. See especially Okin, *Women in Western Political Thought*; Pateman, *The Sexual Contract*; Shanley and Pateman, "Introduction" to *Feminist Interpretations*; Di Stefano, *Configurations of Masculinity*; Joan Landes, *Women and the Public Sphere*; Eisenstein, *The Radical Future of Liberal Feminism*.

3. On this point, see Di Stefano, *Configurations of Masculinity*; Brown, *Manhood and Politics*; Lorraine, *Gender and the Production of Meaning*; Pateman, *The Sexual Contract*.

4. I borrow William E. Connolly's adoption of W. B. Gallie's famous phrase. See William E. Connolly, *The Terms of Political Discourse*, 2d ed. (Princeton: Princeton University Press, 1983), 10.

5. See Norman Jacobson, *Pride and Solace: The Functions and Limits of Political Theory* (Berkeley: University of California Press, 1978); Judith Shklar, *Men and Citizens: A Study of Rousseau's Social and Political Thought* (Cambridge: Cambridge University Press, 1969); Sheldon Wolin, *Politics and Vision: Continuity and Innovation in Western Political Thought* (Boston: Little, Brown, 1960).

6. For a useful critique of the referential model that holds language to be transparent and reduces signification to the process of naming, the word-object relationship, see Michael Shapiro, *The Politics of Representation: Writing Practices in Biography, Photography, and Policy Analysis* (Madison: University of Wisconsin Press, 1988), esp. chap. 1; Samuel Weber, *Return to Freud: Jacques Lacan's Dislocation of Psychoanalysis* (Cambridge: Cambridge University Press, 1991), chaps. 3–4.

7. I do not mean to imply that woman is the only figure onto which arbitrariness, dissonance, and the like are displaced. As we see in the works of Burke and Mill, the lower classes are also figured as disorderly and disordering. A similar argument could be made as well about the colonial other in their writings. That would be the subject of another study.

Several of these points about language and politics have been made by others, whose work I am pleased to acknowledge here and to take up in Chapter 5. See especially William Corlett, *Community without Unity: A Politics of Derridean Extravagance* (Durham, N.C.: Duke University Press, 1989); William E. Connolly, *Identity/Difference: Democratic Negotiations of Political Paradox* (Ithaca: Cornell University Press, 1991); Bonnie Honig,

Political Theory and the Displacement of Politics (Ithaca: Cornell University Press, 1993); Anne Norton, *Reflections on Political Identity* (Baltimore: Johns Hopkins University Press, 1988); Michael Shapiro, *Language and Political Understanding: The Politics of Discursive Practices* (New Haven: Yale University Press, 1981).

8. Ferdinand de Saussure, *Course in General Linguistics* (New York: McGraw Hill, 1966), 120. As Samuel Weber argues, Saussure's fundamental contribution to linguistics resides not in the notion of semiotic arbitrariness (which is as old as Plato's *Cratylus* and entirely compatible with the metaphysical concept of the sign) but rather in the claim that the principle of the linguistic sign is difference. Meaning is an effect of the differential, relational structure of language. "A sound [or acoustical image] can only operate as a signifier insofar as it is distinguishable from other sounds; a thought [or concept] can only be signified insofar as it is distinguishable from other thoughts. Thought of in this way, signification is no longer conceived of as a process of representation, but as one of *articulation*. . . . [Language is thus] determined and defined by a difference that produces identities only belatedly and retroactively: as concrete and individual signifiers and signifieds." Weber, *Return to Freud*, 27. For a critique of Saussure's retreat from his own radical theory of the sign, see Jacques Derrida, *Of Grammatology*, trans. Gayatri Chakravorty Spivak (Baltimore: Johns Hopkins University Press, 1976), 263–267.

9. On the difference between language as representation and language as articulation, see Weber, *Return to Freud*, chaps. 2–3. I discuss the stakes of this difference for political and feminist theorists in Chapter 5.

10. It is crucial to recognize that "woman," as a meaning or signified, emerges in relation not only to the signifier "man" but also to all other signifiers. To define woman in relation strictly to man is to locate both in a binary opposition the better to stabilize their meanings. This is precisely the kind of theoretical move that Derrida, in *Of Grammatology*, locates in Saussure's efforts to stabilize the very linguistic sign he radically destabilized. Still, even as Saussure betrays his own insight, he demonstrates that signification entails a play of differences that is not, in fact, reducible to such opposition. See Weber, *Return to Freud*, chap. 3.

11. Feminist works that focus explicitly on the discursive construction of gender in the political text include Di Stefano, *Configurations of Masculinity*; Lorraine, *Gender and the Production of Meaning*; Pateman, *The Sexual Contract*; Brown, *Manhood and Politics*. For insightful and clear accounts of poststructuralist approaches to gender and language, see Zillah R. Eisenstein, *The Female Body and the Law* (Berkeley: University of California Press, 1988);

Joan Wallach Scott, *Gender and the Politics of History* (New York: Columbia University Press, 1988); Jane Flax, *Thinking Fragments: Psychoanalysis, Feminism, and Postmodernism in the Contemporary West* (Berkeley: University of California Press, 1988).

12. "Political theory begins precisely at the moment when things become, so to speak, unglued." Jacobson, *Pride and Solace*, 10. See also Wolin, *Politics and Vision*, 8. Although I do not want to occlude the fact that a number of political theorists are women, I retain the masculine pronoun here and elsewhere in the text to emphasize the masculinist character of the canon of political theory. The contributions of women to historical political theory are rarely acknowledged or cited in the scholarly literature. And, as I have argued elsewhere, the Western tradition itself denies women the status of speaking subjects. My use of the masculine pronoun, then, serves as a marker of women's absence as subjects and their difficult relationship with figurations of woman in political theory. See Linda M. G. Zerilli, "Machiavelli's Sisters: Women and 'the Conversation' of Political Theory," *Political Theory* 19 (May 1991): 252–276.

13. There is a world of difference, for instance, between the "French Revolution" of Edmund Burke and that of Thomas Paine or Mary Wollstonecraft.

14. Jacobson, *Pride and Solace*, esp. 58.

15. That is one reason why the figuration of woman as bearer of chaos ought to be of interest to scholars who are concerned to delineate and complicate what Wolin calls the "relationship between the disorder of the actual world and the role of the political philosopher as the encompasser of disorder." For disorder, to restate Jacobson's thesis, is never simply an empirical fact; it is always also a symbolic meaning created in and through the language of a political theory, including its figuration of woman. *Politics and Vision*, 8.

16. The phrase is John Locke's. *An Essay Concerning Human Understanding*, ed. Peter Nidditch (Oxford: Clarendon Press, 1975), 3.10.490.

17. As we see in the chapters that follow, feminist theorists as diverse as Lorenne Clark and Lynda Lange (*The Sexism of Social and Political Theory*), Carole Pateman (*The Sexual Contract; The Disorder of Women*), Zillah Eisenstein (*The Radical Future of Liberal Feminism*), and Susan Okin (*Women in Western Political Thought*) have argued persuasively that the Western tradition is riddled with contradictory images of women. Through close and tenacious critical readings of the canonical texts, they have exposed not only the androcentricism of political theory but also the logical inconsistencies that undercut the so-called arguments for women's political exclusion. I agree

with Wendy Brown, however, that this approach, although invaluable, "tends to reduce texts in political theory to systems of definitions that either add up to a coherent and persuasive case or fail to do so." *Manhood and Politics*, 12. Brown may overstate the extent to which the feminists just mentioned neglect the rhetorical dimensions of political theory, but she is right to emphasize the need to develop an approach to texts that takes specific account of the multiple and contradictory symbolic meanings of figurative language.

18. Connolly, *The Terms of Political Discourse*, 236.

19. See, especially, Paul de Man, "The Epistemology of Metaphor," in *Language and Politics*, ed. Michael Shapiro (New York: New York University Press, 1984), 193–214, and *Allegories of Reading: Figural Language in Rousseau, Nietzsche, Rilke, and Proust* (New Haven: Yale University Press, 1979). From a slightly different angle, Michèle Le Doeuff has argued that philosophical discourse relies on the very marginal tropes and figures that appear at first glance to be expendable to meaning. Philosophy claims to be a meta-discourse, wholly rational and logical, yet it is absolutely dependent on images. It denies this dependence, which is, in the last analysis, its dependence on language, by projecting its need for images onto nonphilosophical readers. *The Philosophical Imaginary*, trans. Colin Gordon (Stanford: Stanford University Press, 1989).

20. Quotation from Shklar, *Men and Citizens*, 226. That the Western tradition's arguments for keeping women out of the public sphere have been shown quite clearly by feminist readers to be fatally flawed at best, blatant ideological pleas at worst, suggests that the criterion of logical consistency is important but insufficient. "The conventional technique for assessing the validity of prose discourses," as Hayden White observes, "is to check, first, for their fidelity to the facts of the subject being discussed and, then, for their adherence to logical consistency." This critical approach to texts, says White, "flies in the face of the practice of discourse, if not some theory of it, because the discourse is intended to constitute the ground whereon to decide what shall count as a fact in the matters under consideration and to determine what mode of comprehension is best suited to the understanding of the facts thus constituted." This whole process, he argues, is fundamentally "tropological." *Tropics of Discourse: Essays in Cultural Criticism* (Baltimore: Johns Hopkins University Press, 1978), 3.

21. Feminist political theorists have been rightfully frustrated, as Shanley and Pateman have written, by the fact that "remarkably little attention has been paid to the implications of feminist arguments in the ever-increasing volume of commentary on the famous texts." *Feminist Interpretations and*

Political Theory, 1. It has been all too easy, for instance, for political theory scholars to take account of the feminist critique of gendered imagery and then to dismiss that imagery either as an unfortunate expression of the theorist's "personal problem" with women or as a mere rhetorical flourish that is marginal to the substantive political matter at hand. I wish, at the very least, to show how that dismissal must entail a loss of political meaning inasmuch as I show woman to be the ground of such meaning.

22. For this point I am indebted to Peter Stallybrass and Allon White, *The Politics and Poetics of Transgression* (Ithaca: Cornell University Press, 1986), 23.

23. Shklar, *Men and Citizens*, 225.

24. See especially, Mikhail M. Bakhtin, "Discourse in the Novel," in *The Dialogic Imagination: Four Essays*, ed. Michael Holquist, trans. Caryl Emerson and Michael Holquist (Austin: University of Texas Press, 1981). On this point, see Teresa de Lauretis, *Alice Doesn't: Feminism, Semiotics, Cinema* (Bloomington: Indiana University Press, 1984), 1, 3.

25. Julia Kristeva, "The System and the Speaking Subject," in *The Kristeva Reader*, ed. Toril Moi (New York: Columbia University Press, 1986), 27. Kristeva's theory of the speaking subject is heavily indebted to the work of Emile Benviniste, who holds that "language is possible only because each speaker sets himself up as subject by referring to himself as I in his discourse." Emile Benviniste, *Problems in General Linguistics* (Coral Gables, Fla.: University of Miami Press, 1971), 47. Kristeva draws on Benviniste to argue for the importance of attending to the social context of the utterance and to the construction of subjectivity in language. Although Benviniste was caught up in the structuralist tendency to treat language as a universal and rule-governed system, says Kristeva, he "nevertheless opened this object called language to practices in which it realizes itself, which go beyond it, and on the basis of which its very existence as monolithic object is either made relative or appears as problematic." Julia Kristeva, *Revolution in Poetic Language*, trans. Margaret Waller (New York: Columbia University Press, 1984), 5. Kristeva refers here to the tendency of the structuralist approach to "eliminate from its field of inquiry everything that cannot be systematized, structured, or logicized into a formal entity" (4).

26. Kristeva heralds Bakhtin for "situat[ing] the text within history and society, which are then seen as texts read by the writer, and into which he inserts himself by re-writing them" (a process she calls "intertextuality"). Kristeva, "Word, Dialogue, and Novel," in *The Kristeva Reader*, 36.

27. Julia Kristeva, "The Ruin of a Poetics," in *Russian Formalism*, ed. Stephen Bann and John E. Bowlt (New York: Harper and Row, 1973), 109.

For a useful interpretation of Kristeva's appropriation of Bakhtin's notion of the dialogic, see Carol Mastrangelo Bovè, "The Text as Dialogue in Bakhtin and Kristeva," *University of Ottawa Quarterly* 53, no. 1 (1982): 117–125.

28. Mikhail M. Bakhtin, *Rabelais and His World*, trans. Hélène Iswolsky (Bloomington: Indiana University Press, 1984). See Stallybrass and White, *The Politics and Poetics of Transgression*, 8.

29. Kristeva, "Word, Dialogue, and Novel," 36.

30. Kristeva, *Revolution in Poetic Language*, 23–24.

31. Julia Kristeva, "From One Identity to Another," in *Desire in Language*, ed. Leon S. Roudiez, trans. Thomas Gora, Alice Jardine, and Leon S. Roudiez (New York: Columbia University Press, 1980), 136, and *Revolution in Poetic Language*, 41.

32. For a lucid discussion of this point, see Cynthia Chase, Review of Kristeva, *Criticism* 26 (1984): 194.

33. Julia Kristeva, *Powers of Horror: An Essay on Abjection*, trans. Leon S. Roudiez (New York: Columbia University Press, 1982), 1.

34. Ibid., 9–10.

35. Ibid., 2. See Sigmund Freud, "The Uncanny," *The Complete Psychological Works of Sigmund Freud*, vol. 17 (London: Hogarth, 1971), esp. 245. I discuss Freud's idea of the uncanny in Chapter 2.

36. Kristeva, *Powers of Horror*, 2, 4, 74, 10. Indeed "the abject," as Elizabeth Grosz puts this point, "attests to the impossibility of clear borders, lines of demarcation or divisions between the proper and the improper, the clean and the unclean, order and disorder, as required by the symbolic." *Sexual Subversions: Three French Feminists* (North Sydney, Australia: Allen & Unwin, 1989), 73.

37. In important respects, my approach to political texts builds on the fundamental work of Di Stefano and Pateman, both of whom have called our attention, albeit in diverse ways, to the unspoken elements of political theory discourse. Taking up the absent maternal presence that goes under the name of the primal mother of the state of nature (Pateman) or the archaic (m)other of infantile fantasy (Di Stefano), each has shown that the masculine subject as a political subject is produced through a form of violence against the feminine or maternal. Whereas Pateman excavates the sexual contract beneath the fraternal social contract, Di Stefano adopts object relations theory to account for the production of modern masculinity. For related readings of modern masculinity which employ object relations theory, see Jane Flax, "Political Philosophy and the Patriarchal Unconscious," in *Discovering Reality*, ed. Sandra Harding and Merrill B. Hintinka (Boston: Reidel, 1983), 245–281; Dorothy Dinnerstein, *The Mermaid and the Minotaur:*

Sexual Arrangements and Human Malaise (New York: Harper, 1976). Although Dinnerstein is not occupied with the linguistic matters that concern Kristeva, she does advance a powerful and original reading of woman as scapegoat in Western culture.

On the one hand, I share Di Stefano's concern that Lacanian accounts of gender identity treat both the subject "simply as an 'effect' of signification, and signification itself . . . [as being] constituted in relation to the always phallic signifier." *Configurations of Masculinity*, xv. On the other, I find object relations theory inadequate for theorizing language as the basis of subjectivity. Here I have found the recent work of Lorraine (*Gender, Identity, and the Production of Meaning*) especially helpful. Lorraine uses Lacan to argue for a psycholinguistic approach to the philosophical texts of Hegel, Nietzsche, and Heidegger. I have also found helpful the work of the literary theorist Juliet Flower MacCannell, who employs Lacan to read Rousseau. *The Regime of the Brother: After the Patriarchy* (New York: Routledge, 1991).

38. Kristeva, *Revolution in Poetic Language*, 37.

39. That Rousseau, for instance, lost his mother in early childhood would be, in Kristeva's view, irrelevant for understanding his ambivalent attitude toward women. To employ a Kristevan approach to Rousseau's texts, then, is not to cast light on the historical personage named Jean-Jacques Rousseau. It is, rather, to work on the language through which he produces specific social and political meanings and himself as writerly subject.

40. As Michèle Barrett has written, when the text is wrested out of social context one "simply privileges the artifact itself, divorced from its conditions of production and existence, and claims that it alone provides the means of its own analysis." "Ideology and the Cultural Production of Gender," in *Feminist Criticism and Social Change: Sex, Class, and Race in Literature and Culture*, ed. Judith Newton and Deborah Rosenfelt (New York: Methuen, 1985), 75.

41. Kristeva, *Powers of Horror*, 68.

2. "Une Maitresse Imperieuse": Woman in Rousseau's Semiotic Republic

1. Jean-Jacques Rousseau, *Discourse on the Origin and Foundations of Inequality among Men*, in *The First and Second Discourses*, ed. Roger D. Masters, trans. Roger D. Masters and Judith R. Masters (New York: St. Martin's Press, 1964), 135.

2. Jean Jacques Rousseau, *Politics and the Arts: Letter to M. D'Alembert on the Theatre*, ed. and trans. Allan Bloom (Ithaca: Cornell University Press, 1977), 101, my emphasis. As Paul Thomas interprets this passage, "the eroticism of female idleness is unmistakable and implies that women are at all costs to be kept busy. The alternative is too horrible to contemplate." "Jean-Jacques Rousseau, Sexist?" *Feminist Studies* 17 (Summer 1991): 213.

3. Jean-Jacques Rousseau, *The Confessions*, trans. J. M. Cohen (Harmondsworth: Penguin Books, 1953), 27–28. There are variations on this figure of a masterful mistress throughout Rousseau's work. Following Gilles Deleuze's study of masochism, one could argue that it is not the father but rather the mother who gives the law in Rousseau's thought. The masochist, argues Deleuze, aligns himself with the mother against the father. He "experiences the symbolic order as an intermaternal order in which the mother represents the law under certain prescribed conditions," whence the notion of the contract that is crucial to the masochism. *Masochism*, trans. Jean McNeil (New York: Zone Books, 1991), 63. For a study of Rousseau's masochism from within the political theory tradition, see William H. Blanchard, *Rousseau and the Spirit of Revolt* (Ann Arbor: University of Michigan Press, 1967). Blanchard argues convincingly that Rousseau's desire to give himself over to a masterful mistress shaped his entire social thought. For a psychobiography of Rousseau's personal relations to women, see Maurice Cranston, *Jean-Jacques Rousseau: The Prophetic Voice, 1758–1778*, vol. 2 (New York: Macmillan, 1973), and *Jean-Jacques: The Early Life and Work of Jean-Jacques Rousseau, 1712–1754* (New York: Norton, 1982). Whereas these works focus on the writing self, Huntington Williams has treated Rousseau's autobiographical writings as constructions of the written self. *Rousseau and Romantic Autobiography* (Oxford: Oxford University Press, 1983). For a convincing reading of the *Confessions* as a work of political theory, see Christopher Kelly, *Rousseau's Exemplary Life: The Confessions as Political Philosophy* (Ithaca: Cornell University Press, 1987).

4. The reading I advance draws on and departs from those offered by Joel Schwartz and Penny Weiss, both of whom have done much to situate gender at the center of the scholarly debate on Rousseau. Although Schwartz rightly argues that sexual difference is a political issue, he errs in asserting that Rousseau is a "materialist" who believes that "the bodily differences between men and women unalterably differentiate women from men." *The Sexual Politics of Jean-Jacques Rousseau* (Chicago: University of Chicago Press, 1984), 85. For a similar, if somewhat more qualified and critical, version of this argument, see Jean Bethke Elshtain, *Public Man, Private Woman* (Princeton: Princeton University Press, 1979), 160–161. On

the contrary, for Rousseau anatomical difference is nothing apart from the signifiers of sexual difference, from linguistic and sartorial signifiers. In contrast to Schwartz, Penny Weiss has shown that for Rousseau gender difference is not in any way natural but rather "should be created, encouraged, and enforced because of what he considers to be their necessary and beneficial consequences." She correctly insists, moreover, that "Rousseau's rhetoric [about "natural" sexual difference] is consistently undercut by his theoretical argument." "Rousseau, Antifeminism, and Woman's Nature," *Political Theory* 15 (February 1987): 83, 94. His rhetoric is undercut as well, I argue, by the vicissitudes of male desire and by his own claim that gender is performative: nothing more than a way of speaking and of dressing, simply a cultural matter of words and clothes.

5. Shoshana Felman, "Rereading Femininity," *Yale French Studies* 62 (1981): 42.

6. Rousseau, *Letter to D'Alembert*, 109.

7. The best-known example of this argument is given by Judith Shklar, who maintains that Rousseau presents us with the man and the citizen as two possible models for living, "and the two were meant to stand in polar opposition to each other." The citizen is the radically denatured man. *Men and Citizens: A Study of Rousseau's Social Theory* (Cambridge: Cambridge University Press, 1969), 3. Shklar's thesis has been accepted (or has remained uncontested) throughout most of the scholarly literature. Susan Okin has suggested that in *Emile* Rousseau tries to create the man and the citizen at once. *Women in Western Political Thought* (Princeton: Princeton University Press, 1979), 168–169. In the pages that follow, I take up and complicate this insight.

8. Julia Kristeva, "Women's Time," in *The Kristeva Reader*, ed. Toril Moi (New York: Columbia University Press, 1986), 202.

9. Julia Kristeva, *Powers of Horror: An Essay on Abjection*, trans. Leon S. Roudiez (New York: Columbia University Press, 1982), 63.

10. Rousseau, *Discourse on Inequality*, p. 76. Further page references are cited in the text.

11. "I have no intention of courting the favor of women; I accept their honoring me with the epithet Pedant, so dreaded by all our gallant philosophers. I am crude, sullen, impolite on principle; and I want no one [no woman] to fawn on me; so I will speak the truth quite unhampered." Jean-Jacques Rousseau, "Last Reply [to critics of the *Discourse on the Sciences and Arts*]," in *The First and Second Discourses, Replies to Critics, and Essay on the Origin of Languages*, trans. and ed. Victor Gourevitch (New York: Harper and Row, 1986), 68. On Rousseau's rhetorical deployment of the maternal

voice of Nature against the speaking women of the salon, see Sarah Kofman, "Rousseau's Phallocratic Ends," *Hypatia* 3 (Winter 1989): 123–136.

12. I discuss Lacan's notion of the "mirror stage" later in this chapter. Because the maternal voice is a lost primordial object "whose 'otherness' is never strongly marked," says Silverman, it comes later to stand, on the one hand, for what promises to restore to the masculine subject an imaginary wholeness, on the other, for what threatens to throw him back into the chaos of his "infantile babble." In its utopic Rousseauist version, it is the voice of mother Nature; in its dystopic, it is the voice of the actress or salonniere. Kaja Silverman, *The Acoustic Mirror: The Female Voice in Psychoanalysis and Cinema* (Bloomington: Indiana University Press, 1988), 85, 81.

13. Jean-Jacques Rousseau, *Discourse on the Sciences and the Arts*, in *The First and Second Discourses*, ed. Masters, 46–47, my emphasis.

14. I am indebted here to Sarah Kofman's reading of Freud, in whose writings the veil functions as a screen over the truth of the mother, Mother Nature. *The Enigma of Woman: Woman in Freud's Writings*, trans. Catherine Porter (Ithaca: Cornell University Press, 1985), 94–95.

15. Jean Starobinski, *Jean-Jacques Rousseau: Transparency and Obstruction*, trans. Arthur Goldhammer (Chicago: University of Chicago Press, 1988). Starobinski's thesis is that Rousseau's writings are a long meditation on the obstacle of the veil. He accuses Rousseau of blaming everyone but himself for the failure of human communication. So, he argues, even as Rousseau seeks to lift the veil, he also preserves it in order to protect himself against the other, that is, a radical other consciousness. As I have suggested, the veil has yet another function, namely, to screen over the abyss which is, in the last analysis, the unmediated relation to the maternal, where the distinction between subject and object ceases to exist. As we see, in Rousseau's texts woman must always be veiled.

16. Jean-Jacques Rousseau, Letter to M. de Franquières, *Oeuvres Complètes* (Paris: Bibliothèque de la Pléiade, 1959), 4:1137. Translated in Starobinski, *Jean-Jacques Rousseau*, 76.

17. Third Letter to Malesherbes, *Oeuvres Complètes*, 1:1141 (my translation).

18. "Are we destined then to die fixed to the edge of the pit where the truth has hidden?" asks Rousseau. "This reflection alone should rebuff, from the outset, any man who would seriously seek to educate himself by the study of philosophy." *Discourse on the Science and Arts*, 48. Of course, as Rousseau tells us elsewhere, there are a "few sublime geniuses capable of piercing the veils in which the truth wraps itself," a few almost mythical heros who are able to wrest from the very womb of Mother Nature her most

intimate secrets—for instance, Socrates. But we all know what happened to the Athenian on his return to the cave: "It cost Socrates his life to have said exactly the same things I am saying," declares Rousseau. *The First and Second Discourses, Replies to Critics, and Essay on the Origin of Languages*, 107, 66. Then again, even if (like the Genevan) one ends up being "buried alive" by one's society for seeking and speaking the truth, it is still somewhat better than being "born dead"; and still somewhat better to seek endlessly than to know intimately the truth of the mother, better to be active than passive, better to be "perverse" than to be "born learned," better "to emerge from [one's] happy ignorance" than to be stillborn in carnal knowledge.

19. As Rousseau put it in a letter to Malesherbes: "Had I unveiled all nature's mysteries, I think I should have found myself in a state less delightful than the dizzying ecstacy to which my mind gave itself over unreservedly, and which in my agitated excitement made me sometimes cry out, O! Great Being! O! Great Being!, unable to say or to think anything more." Third Letter to Malesherbes, *Oeuvres Complètes*, 1:1141. Translated in Starobinski, *Jean-Jacques Rousseau*, 77.

20. Jean-Jacques Rousseau, *Les Reveries du Promeneur Solitaire*, Septieme Promenade, *Oeuvres Complètes*, 1:1067.

21. Rousseau, *Essay on the Origin of Languages*, ed. Gourevitch, 243.

22. Ibid., 241.

23. Ibid., 260–262.

24. Ferdinand de Saussure, *Course in General Linguistics* (New York: McGraw Hill, 1966), 120.

25. This point, discussed in detail later in this chapter, is persuasively argued by Jacques Derrida in *Of Grammatology*, trans. Gayatri Chakravorty Spivak (Baltimore: Johns Hopkins University Press, 1976).

26. Rousseau, *Essay on the Origin of Languages*, 272.

27. Ibid.; see Derrida, *Of Grammatology*, 263–267.

28. Rousseau, *Essay on the Origin of Languages*, 272.

29. Ibid., 271.

30. Claude Lévi-Strauss, *The Elementary Structures of Kinship*, ed. Rodney Needham, trans. James Harle Bell and John von Sturmer (Boston: Beacon Press, 1969), 493.

31. See Carole Pateman, *The Sexual Contract* (Stanford: Stanford University Press, 1988). Drawing on the work of Freud and Lévi-Strauss, Pateman maintains that a sexual contract, male sex-right, subtends the social contract. In *Totem and Taboo*, Freud wrote, "In the beginning was the deed": the murder of the primal father, which established a kind of contract among the sons. But Freud, Pateman argues, glossed over the first violent deed, the

rape of the primal mother. This rape is the "original deed" (107). She then reconstructs the "primal scene" in the social contract narratives of Hobbes, Locke, and Rousseau. After the murder of the father, the sons appropriate his patriarchal right and distribute it in an orderly fashion among themselves. "That is, the brothers *make a sexual contract.* They establish a law [exogamy] which confirms masculine sex-right and ensures that there is an orderly access by each man to a woman" (109). Pateman argues that women cannot enter into the social contract because they "are purely objects of exchange and signs" (112). As to the marriage contract, these theorists must maintain that women enter into it, lest the entire edifice of social contract theory collapse (112). Male sex-right gives the lie to the marriage contract, says Pateman, and both give the lie to the ideas of freedom and consent that underwrite social contract theory. I find Pateman's substantive thesis persuasive, but it overlooks the extent to which, as I argue later, the scene of the sexual contract is characterized by forms of gratification that exceed their containment by law.

32. Lévi-Strauss, *Structures of Kinship*, 496–497.

33. Rousseau, *Essay On the Origin of Languages*, 258, and *Rousseau juge de Jean Jaques—Dialogues II*, *Oeuvres Complètes*, 1:825.

34. Catherine Clément, "The Guilty One," in *The Newly Born Woman*, by Clément and Hélène Cixous, trans. Betsy Wing (Minneapolis: University of Minnesota Press, 1986), 28.

35. It is not quite right to say, as Derrida does, that the "nonprohibition is interrupted *after the festival.*" *Of Grammatology*, 263. The festival, rather, as both Clément ("The Guilty One," 30) and Lévi-Strauss show, is site of both incestuous pleasure and its prohibition.

36. Lévi-Strauss, *Structures of Kinship*, 495–496.

37. Rousseau, *Essay on the Origin Languages*, 271.

38. Lévi-Strauss, *Structures of Kinship*, 491. Lévi-Strauss interprets the festival through Freud's notion of the feast, whereby the sons, having killed the primal father, then eat him. The festival, writes Freud, is characterized by "gaiety accompanied by the unchaining of every impulse and the permission of every gratification," including sexual gratification. Both incest and the taboo on incest take root in the festival, both the unrestricted access to women and the renunciation of it. *Totem and Taboo*, trans. A. A. Brill (New York: Vintage, 1946 [1918]), 183, 181.

39. Rousseau, *Essay On the Origin of Languages*, 272, my emphasis.

40. Derrida, *Of Grammatology*, 266.

41. Julia Kristeva, *Tales of Love*, trans. Leon S. Roudiez (New York: Columbia University Press, 1987), 42.

42. Kristeva, *Powers of Horror*, 64.

43. William E. Connolly makes a similar point when he argues that, in Rousseau, the law creates the very evil it is supposed to contain. "Rousseau's polity loads the counterself with illicit desires. It doubles pleasure by adding the pleasure of transgression to the original desire, and the world of virtue produces perfect human objects for the realization of its intensified pleasures." *Politics and Ambiguity* (Madison: University of Wisconsin Press, 1987), 90. Likewise, Georges Batailles argues that there is "a profound complicity of law and the violation of law." That complicity turns on desire and pleasure. *Eroticism: Death and Sensuality*, trans. Mary Dalwood (San Francisco: City Lights, 1986), 36.

44. For a critique of Lévi-Strauss on this point, see Elizabeth Cowie, "Woman as Sign," in *The Woman in Question*, ed. Parveen Adams and Elizabeth Cowie (Cambridge: MIT Press, 1990).

45. Jacques Lacan, *The Four Fundamental Concepts of Psychoanalysis*, trans. Alan Sheridan (New York: Norton, 1978), 106.

46. On the mirror stage, see Jacques Lacan, *Écrits*, trans. Alan Sheridan (New York: Norton, 1977), 1–7. What is more, as Kaja Silverman reminds us, the "look of the mother articulates the mirror image, and facilitates the child's alignment with it." "Fragments of a Fashionable Discourse," in *Studies in Entertainment: Critical Approaches to Mass Culture*, ed. Tania Modeleski (Bloomington: Indiana University Press, 1986), 142–143.

47. J. C. Flugel, *The Psychology of Clothes* (New York: International Universities Press, 1930), 18–20.

48. Ibid., 34.

49. Ibid., 110–111.

50. Rousseau, *Discourse on the Sciences and the Arts*, 37.

51. Flugel, *The Psychology of Clothes*, 113.

52. Rousseau, *Essay on the Origin of Languages*, 242, 243.

53. Ibid.

54. Women are blamed for the degeneration of "natural" language, "the plain tongue of common sense," as Norman Jacobson puts it, into "metaphysical double-talk." *Pride and Solace: The Functions and Limits of Political Theory* (Berkeley: University of California Press, 1978), 107. Paul Thomas argues that, for Rousseau, "women, in their capacity as bearers or agents of civilization, are also necessarily the bearers or agents of corruption too." Thomas shows that women are "in effect stand-ins or surrogates for civilization and [human] perfectibility." "Jean-Jacques Rousseau, Sexist?" 212.

55. Rousseau, *Letter to D'Alembert*, 48. Further page references are cited in the text.

56. Jean-Jacques Rousseau, *Emile, or On Education*, trans. Allan Bloom (New York: Basic Books, 1979), 322.

57. "It is on this principle that a Spartan, hearing a foreigner singing the praises of a lady of his acquaintance, interrupted him in anger: 'Won't you stop,' he said to him, 'slandering a virtuous woman?'" *Letter to D'Alembert*, 48.

58. As Elshtain rightly notes, "The depth of Rousseau's mistrust of women is apparent in the fact that those closer to original nature, by his own logic, are not allowed to speak in the always-to-be trusted voice of that nature." The result is an attempt to shut up not only salon women and actresses but also the natural woman par excellence, Sophie. *Public Man, Private Woman*, 164.

59. Joan Landes, *Women and the Public Sphere in the Age of the French Revolution* (Ithaca: Cornell University Press, 1988), 24–25. On gender inversion and the masquerade, see Terry Castle, *Masquerade and Civilization: The Carnivalesque in Eighteenth-Century English Culture and Fiction* (Stanford: Stanford University Press, 1986).

60. Rousseau, *Rousseau juge de Jean Jaques—Dialogues*, *Oeuvres Complètes*, 1:815 (my translation).

61. Rousseau, *Emile*, 359.

62. See Landes, *Women and the Public Sphere*, 30; Domna Stanton, "The Fiction of Préciosité and the Fear of Women," *Yale French Studies* 62 (1981): 129. On women's place in the public spaces of the theater and the salon, see Barbara G. Mittman, "Women and the Theater Arts," in *French Women and the Age of Enlightenment*, ed. Samia I. Spencer (Bloomington: Indiana University Press, 1984), 155–169. On public debates about actresses as agents of cultural chaos, see Kristina Straub, *Sexual Suspects: Eighteenth-Century Players and Sexual Ideology* (Princeton: Princeton University Press, 1992).

63. Thomas Crow, "The Oath of the Horatii in 1785: Painting and Pre-Revolutionary Radicalism in France," *Art History* 1 (December 1978), 442.

64. Derrida, *Of Grammatology*, 240.

65. Rousseau, *Emile*, 42. Further page references are cited in the text.

66. Mary Jacobus, *Romanticism, Writing, and Sexual Difference* (Oxford: Oxford University Press, 1989), 242.

67. Rousseau's critique of wet-nursing was neither wholly novel nor accurate. As George Sussman has shown, the overwhelming majority of the children who were given over to wet nurses came not from the nobility (that is, not, as Rousseau would have it, from families in which the mothers "devote themselves gaily to the entertainments of the city"; *Emile*, 44) but rather from the preindustrial urban class of independent artisans and shop-

keepers. It was, moreover, especially poor but not indigent urban families who were most affected by "the polemical campaign against wet-nursing that began around 1760." *Selling Mother's Milk: The Wet-Nursing Business in France, 1715–1914* (Urbana: University of Illinois Press, 1982), 24, 30.

68. The result of such cruel mothering? Nothing less than the chaos of intermingling or intermixture which opens *Emile*: "Everything is good as it leaves the hands of the Author of our being; everything degenerates in the hands of man. He forces one soil to nourish the products of another, one tree to bear the fruit of another. He mixes and confuses the climates, the elements, the seasons. He mutilates his dog, his horse, his slave. He turns everything upside down; he disfigures everything; he loves deformity, monsters" (37).

69. The peasant child, in contrast, is kept at a distance from, and therefore does not imitate the voice of, the mother, who is hard at work in the fields. Peasant children, says Rousseau, speak in a clear and accented voice, their speech is that of "sentiment and truth." *Emile*, 71, 72.

70. Jacobus, *Romanticism, Writing, and Sexual Difference*, 246.

71. Starobinski, *Jean-Jacques Rousseau*, 146.

72. Rousseau's first masterful mistress was his childhood governess, Mlle Lambercier. *Confessions*, 26.

73. Kristeva, *Tales of Love*, 107, 116. Kristeva observes further that primary narcissism (what Rousseau calls *l'amour de soi*), "being far from originary," is rather a "supplement" to the "autoeroticism of the mother-child dyad" (22). It therefore marks the very first stage of primal differentiation. Narcissism, she argues, is necessary to maintain that space of "emptiness" between self and mother, "lest chaos prevail and borders dissolve" (24). Rousseau, in his own way, knows this too, which is why distancing the child from the nurse/mother and strengthening his love of self are the pedagogical goals of Books I–III, indeed, why *l'amour de soi* is for Rousseau the very source of man's strength.

74. See especially Kristeva, *Powers of Horror*, 62–63.

75. Kristeva, *Tales of Love*, 109–110.

76. On the frontispiece to Book V of *Emile*, see Patricia Parker, *Literary Fat Ladies: Rhetoric, Gender, Property* (New York: Methuen, 1987), 207.

77. Allan Bloom, Introduction to *Emile*, 15–16. Even though Bloom recognizes that the imagination plays a large part in Rousseau's discussion of sexuality, he also assumes that sexual desire is merely a rechanneling of sexual instinct. Bloom's reading of Rousseau fits the familiar image of the political theorist as the tamer of eros. Once so-called heterosexual instinct is posited as just that, an instinct, it can be treated as if it were a universal and

potential chaos that has to be contained in the interests of social order (I discuss this point further in Chapter 5). Rousseau himself shows that all sexual desire, indeed any form of desire, is culturally created through the boundless play of the imagination; it has nothing to do with instinct. "I am persuaded that a solitary man raised in a desert, without books, without instruction, and without women, would die there a virgin at whatever age he had reached" (*Emile*, 333).

78. Rousseau, *Confessions*, 109.

79. Writes Binet: "Amorous fetishism has a tendency to detach completely, to isolate (the object) from anything separating it from its cult-worship, and when the object is part of a living person, the fetishist tries to render this part an independent entity." "La Fetichisme dans l'amour" [1887], quoted in Emily Apter, *Feminizing the Fetish: Psychoanalysis and Narrative Obsession in Turn-of-the-Century France* (Ithaca: Cornell University Press, 1991), 21. Deleuze observes that "fetishism, as defined by the process of disavowal and suspension of belief, belongs esentially to masochism. . . . There can be no masochism without fetishism in the primary sense." The masochist employs the fetish to preserve the masterful mistress, the phallic mother, the mother who lacks nothing. The fetish is also crucial to the world of reverie and the art of delay that characterize Rousseau's amorous accounts. See *Masochism*, 32.

80. The citation from Rousseau is quoted by Binet. See Apter, *Feminizing the Fetish*, 21.

81. Mary Wollstonecraft, *A Vindication of the Rights of Woman*, ed. Miriam Brody Kramnick (Harmondsworth: Penguin, 1975), 107.

82. Rousseau's strict semiotics for female adornment relate to the place of the fetish in his thought. The purpose of the fetish, on the psychoanalytic account, is to disavow female sexual difference. See Apter, *Feminizing the Fetish*, esp. 13; Deleuze, *Masochism*, 31. Even though woman in Rousseau's texts is duty-bound to conceal her lack (with the adornment he prescribes), she is also duty-bound to reveal it (in ways that uphold rather than undercut the masculine subject, of course). The trick is to find the right quality and quantity of adornment: a disguise that signifies that woman lacks, in order for the masculine subject to deny his own symbolic castration and affirm symbolic wholeness; but also a disguise that does not signify that she lacks too much, in order not to confront the masculine subject with castration (the sin of the "ugly woman").

83. Rousseau's logic yields such mind-boggling statements as the following: "We are told that women are false. They become so. Their particular gift is skill and not falseness. According to the true inclinations of their sex, even when they are lying they are not false." *Emile*, 385.

84. Flugel, *The Psychology of Clothes*, 119. On Rousseau's penchant for self-display and exhibitionism, see Starobinski, *Jean-Jacques Rousseau*, 170–177.

85. As Nannerl O. Keohane puts it, "In fitting Sophie for her fate, Rousseau employs a panoply of artifices indistinguishable from those he excoriated in the second *Discourse*: dissimulation, dependence, reliance on the opinions of others as a guide for behavior and as a source for one's very own sense of self." "'But for Her Sex . . .': The Domestication of Sophie," *University of Ottawa Quarterly* 49, nos. 3–4 (1979): 397. Wollstonecraft argued the same point in the *Vindication*.

86. This is one reason the natural woman must remain, as Clément argued and as Rousseau himself says, a child all her life (*Emile*, 211)—speaking little but causing men's talk.

87. For another example of woman's duty to efface the trace of her own artifice, see Rousseau's description of Julie's garden in the novel *La nouvelle Heloise, Oeuvres Complètes*, 2:472.

88. "The moral of Sophie's education," as Jacobus puts it, "is that women must be the guarantors and safe-keepers, not only of masculinity, but of language made chaste, naturalized, and brought into imaginary correspondence with reality." *Romanticism, Writing, and Sexual Difference*, 249.

89. Schwartz argues that Rousseau creates Sophie as a complement to Emile and as a subject in her own right. Contrasting Emile with the hero (Valere) of Rousseau's play *Narcisse, ou l'amant de lui-même*, Schwartz writes that, whereas Valere "falls in love with a girl whom he can only imagine," Emile falls in love with a girl who "actually *is* a girl, and not Emile's male self dressed to resemble a girl." It is Emile who, when he does love, "loves another." *The Sexual Politics of Jean-Jacques Rousseau*, 81. On the contrary, I maintain that, inasmuch as Sophie is the scapegoat of the masculine desire to dress like a girl (not to mention to play with "jewels, mirrors, and dolls"), she is not Emile's sexual other but his specular double.

90. The "whole art [of coquetry] depend[s] . . . on sharp and continuous observations which make her [woman] see what is going on in men's hearts at every instant, and which dispose her to bring to each secret movement that she notices the force needed to suspend or accelerate it." *Emile*, 385.

91. Luce Irigaray, *Speculum of the Other Woman*, trans. Gillian C. Gill (Ithaca: Cornell University Press, 1985), 54. If it is true that Sophie or the woman is the specular double of Emile or the man, then the argument advanced, albeit in different ways, by Weiss and Schwartz (i.e., that Rousseau aims to create interdependence between the sexes) seems highly debatable to say the least.

92. Kristeva, *Powers of Horror*, 98, 99.

93. Like uncleanliness, "extreme ugliness" in a woman is "disgusting," and both are at bottom the relation with the abject, that is, with death: "Ugliness which produces disgust is the greatest of misfortunes. This sentiment, far from fading away, increases constantly and turns into hatred. Such a marriage is hell. It would be better to be dead than to be thus united." *Emile*, 409. On the subject of Sophie's cleanliness, see Keohane, " 'But for Her Sex,' " 396.

94. Flugel writes, "In the case of the [male] exhibitionistic desires connected with self-display, a particularly easy form of conversion may be found in a change from (passive) exhibitionism to (active) scoptophilia (erotic pleasure in the use of vision)—the desire to be seen being transformed into the desire to see. This desire to see may itself remain unsublimated and find its appropriate satisfaction in the contemplation of the other sex, or it may be sublimated and find expression in the more general desire to see and know." *The Psychology of Clothes*, 118. That it is the powerful and dangerous desire to be seen that subtends the masculine subject's desire to see helps to explain the character of Wolmar, in *La Nouvelle Héloïse*, who wanted to "become a living eye," seeing without being seen; *Oeuvres Complètes*, 2:491. It also explains why Rousseau, in the *Reveries*, expressed his wish to own the magic ring of Gyges, which would have given him the power to render himself invisible at will; ibid., 1:1057–1058.

95. Flugel again: "In such cases there is clearly some element of identification with the woman. . . . We incline in general to identify ourselves with such persons as we admire or envy [for their opportunity for bodily and sartorial display]." This identification is obviously dangerous for the masculine subject, but not nearly as threatening as the following: if the woman does not accept her role as adorned object, then the man's desire for exhibitionism could seek satisfaction in transvestitism, whereby "the man may consciously seek to identify himself with a woman by wearing feminine attire." *The Psychology of Clothes*, 118–119.

96. Shklar reads *Emile* as the model for making a man and associates it with Rousseau's ideal of the Golden Age. See *Men and Citizens*, esp. 11, 147–148. Okin argues, "Rousseau clearly tries to make of Emile a citizen, as well as a natural and independent man." *Women in Western Political Thought*, 168.

97. If Emile has to travel to avoid becoming his sexual other, why does he have to fall in love before he travels? This question is answered by Rousseau himself, who tells us that he got the idea while visiting the governor of a young Englishman. The governor was reading a letter to his pupil (Lord John) when suddenly, says Rousseau, "I saw the young man tear off the very

fine lace cuffs he was wearing and throw them one after the other into the fire." *Emile*, 470. It turned out that the cuffs were a present given to Lord John by a "city lady," and that the letter described his country fiancée hard at work making him a quite different set of cuffs with her own hands. This incident reveals, once again, the place of Sophie or the woman in the masculine renunciation of aristocratic finery, not to mention his own femininity.

98. Okin argues that Rousseau places incompatible demands on his female characters. The chaste coquette is doomed right from the start because she must excite and restrain male desire. What is more, "no woman educated and confined as Julie [of *La Nouvelle Héloïse*] and Sophie are would ever be able to behave like the Spartan mother whose patriotism Rousseau so much admired." These women are "even more vulnerable than men to the conflicts of loyalties" that Rousseau showed to exist between the state and the family. And thus women as mothers become a problem for men as citizens. *Women in Western Political Thought*, 193. Likewise, Zillah Eisenstein maintains that, in *Emile*, the dependent woman creates significant problems for the independent man. *The Radical Future of Liberal Feminism* (New York: Longman, 1981), 80–83.

99. Okin (*Women in Western Political Thought*), Elshtain (*Public Man, Private Woman*), and Pateman (*The Sexual Contract*) have shown quite clearly that women cannot be added to the social contract. As Landes puts it, "the very generality of the [general] will is predicated on the silent but tacit consent of women." *Women and the Public Sphere*, 66. Schwartz, for his part, has tried to track women down in the supplement to written law: the morals, customs, and public opinion that form the basis of the impersonal authority Rousseau seems to credit as the ultimate source of social stability. "Because Rousseau acknowledges the necessity of hidden and personal rule, he can also acknowledge and admire the political power of women (even as he advocates their formal political powerlessness)." *Rousseau's Sexual Politics*, 43–44. On the contrary, as we see in this section, this informal power is not the good to be preserved but rather the problem to be solved by the social contract.

100. Jean-Jacques Rousseau, *On the Social Contract*, published together with *Geneva Manuscript and Political Economy*, ed. Roger D. Masters, trans. Judith R. Masters (New York: St. Martin's Press, 1978). Further page references are cited in the text. Actually, it is not the word "woman" but "women" that appears three times in Rousseau's text: twice in connection with the fecundity of a people (73, 74) and once in connection with "foreigners," "children," and "slaves" (99).

101. Rousseau, *Emile*, 43.

102. Hilail Gilden, *Rousseau's Social Contract: The Design of the Argument* (Chicago: University of Chicago Press, 1983), 27.

103. Ibid., 23.

104. Rousseau, *Geneva Manuscript*, 171, see also 158.

105. See Shklar, *Men and Citizens*, 155.

106. Rousseau, *Geneva Manuscript*, 177.

107. On this point, see Derrida, *Of Grammatology*, 264–265.

108. Rousseau, *Geneva Manuscript*, 180. "Qu'il mutile en quelque sorte la constitution de l'homme pour la renforcer." *Oeuvres Complètes*, 3:313.

109. Jean-Jacques Rousseau, *The Government of Poland*, trans. and ed. Willmoore Kendall (New York: Bobbs-Merrill, 1972), 6, my emphasis.

110. Kristeva writes: "Circumcision would thus separate one from maternal, feminine impurity and defilement; it stands instead of sacrifice, meaning not only that it [circumcision] replaces it [sacrifice] but is its equivalent—a sign of the alliance with God. . . . [What] circumcision carves out on his [the masculine subject's] very sex, is the other sex, impure, defiled." *Powers of Horror*, 99–100.

111. Ibid., 94.

112. Rousseau, *Emile*, 321.

113. Rousseau, *Essay on the Origin Languages*, 242. Rousseau gives a particularly telling example from the Old Testament, which reveals the use of woman as Sign, the Sign that transforms a fleeting bond into something durable, the oath into a people, the voices of the many into that of the one: "When the Levite of Ephraim wanted to avenge the death of his wife he did not write to the Tribes of Israel; he divided her body into twelve pieces which he sent to them. At this ghastly sight they rushed to arms, crying with one voice: *No, never has anything like this happened in Israel, from the day when our fathers left Egypt until this day!* And the Tribe of Benjamin was exterminated. Nowadays it would have been turned into lawsuits, debates, perhaps even jokes; it would have dragged on, and the most ghastly crime would finally have remained unpunished" (ibid.).

Actually—and this must have been known to Rousseau—what spurred the eleven tribes of Israel to revenge against the twelfth (the Benjamites) was the mutilated body of the concubine (the second or third wife) of the polygamous Levite, who had given her over to a mob of Benjamite men to save himself from being sodomized. It was her raped and brutalized corpse that the Levite then cut into pieces and sent to the other tribes, who promptly put aside their differences and united as a people to avenge her murder. Out of the Benjamite tribe, as Rousseau says, "only six hundred of its men, without any women or children, were left" (ibid.). These men fled into the desert and, in time, were called back by the Israelite elders, who grieved deeply for them and felt duty bound to ensure their continued existence. Fratricide led to mourning and then to reparation through another bloody act: having vowed never to give their daughters to any of the Benjamites, the elders sent an army to Jabash-gilead, which seized four hundred virgins and slaughtered the rest of the population. Then, because there were still not enough women for the Benjamites, the elders advised the remaining bachelors to go to the town of Shiloh where each should abduct a girl at the annual festival. This they did and were thus saved from extinction (see Judges 19:2–21:25).

The Book of Judges, which concludes with the line, "In those days Israel had no King; everyone did as he saw fit" (21:25), points up the moral depravity, intertribal disputes, and pagan ways into which the Israelites had fallen since the deaths of Moses and Joshua. The story Rousseau cites also shows that woman is the visible sacrifice that recalls to the Israelites the fading memory of their covenant with an invisible God. One could read the rape of the concubine, not to mention the abduction of women at the festival, as confirming Pateman's thesis that violence and male sex-right subtend the fraternal social contract. One could read the woman's dismembered body as sign as confirming Kristeva's thesis that the sociosymbolic contract is a sacrificial contract. And one could confirm both with Rousseau's claim that, at the sight of a piece of the woman's corpse, the Israelites all began "crying in one voice," the "celestial voice" of the general will.

114. Rousseau, *Emile*, 323.

115. Rousseau, *The Government of Poland*, 15. One must see always and everywhere the image of the fatherland, beginning at birth: "The newly-born infant, upon first opening his eyes, must gaze upon the fatherland, and until his dying day should behold nothing else" (19). Needless to say, the very first gaze he beholds is that of the mother.

116. Rousseau, *Emile*, 322.

117. Ibid.

118. Rousseau, *The Government of Poland*, 14.

119. Ibid., 72.

120. Michel Foucault, "The Eye of Power," in *Power/Knowledge: Selected Interviews and Other Writings, 1972–1977*, ed. Collin Gordon (New York: Pantheon Books, 1980), 152.

121. Rousseau, *The Government of Poland*, 89.

122. Ibid., 15–16. For a thoughtful discussion of how Rousseau's critique of inherited property intersects with his attack on idleness, see Eisenstein, *The Radical Future of Liberal Feminism*, 68–71.

123. That spectacular display is constitutive of masculinity suggests that Rousseau does not depart from what Landes calls "the iconic spectacularity of the Old Regime." *Women and the Public Sphere*, 67. In fact, Rousseau is much closer to that mode of self-representation than Landes allows.

124. Rousseau, *The Government of Poland*, 18.

125. Ibid., 14. "One does not stamp out luxury with sumptuary laws. You must reach deep into men's hearts and uproot it by implanting there healthier and nobler tastes" (18).

126. Benjamin R. Barber, *Supermen and Common Men* (New York: Praeger, 1972), 61. As Thomas puts this point, "The articulation of the general will may depend upon an overcoming of distinctions among the (male) citizenry, but these distinctions have first to exist if they are to be overcome." "Jean-Jacques Rousseau, Sexist?" 202.

127. Compare my argument with Marshall Berman's thesis that the social contract is a "maternal state" in which child-citizens bask in the warmth of an unmediated "flow of nourishment, affection, [and] love." *The Politics of Authenticity: Radical Individualism and the Emergence of Modern Society* (New York: Atheneum, 1970), 204. Berman draws largely on Rousseau's maternal images of the state in *Discourse on Political Economy*.

128. Rousseau, *The Government of Poland*, 69.

129. Derrida, *Of Grammatology*, 136.

130. Kristeva, *Powers of Horror*, 104.

131. Rousseau, *Emile*, 372.

132. Felman, "Rereading Femininity," 28.

3. The "Furies of Hell": Woman in Burke's "French Revolution"

1. Edmund Burke, *Reflections on the Revolution in France*, published together with Thomas Paine's *The Rights of Man* (New York: Anchor Books, 1973 [1790]), 93, 84 (hereafter, *Reflections*).

2. Isaac Kramnick, *The Rage of Edmund Burke* (New York: Basic Books, 1977), 137. Kramnick argues that Burke coped with his own feelings of sexual and political "ambivalence" toward the sublime experience of the French Revolution by exposing "the horror inflicted by unleashed masculinity" and by pleading "the feminine cause" (152).

3. Apart from the writings on France, I have in mind here Burke's impassioned defense of the princesses of Oudi in his protracted legal crusade against Warren Hastings. See "The Speeches of Edmund Burke on the Impeachment of Warren Hastings," *Works*, vols. 1–2, Bohn's Standard

Library (London: George Bell & Sons, 1902). See also Kramnick on Burke's detailed account of the sexual humiliation of the princesses. *The Rage of Edmund Burke*, 137.

4. C. B. Macpherson, *Burke* (New York: Hill and Wang, 1980), 34. Although Macpherson is aware of the power of Burke's dramatic style, he treats it as a curious digression that distracts both author and reader from the political economic issues of the French Revolution. Michael Freeman argues that Burke's chivalric themes are part of his "medievalism," in *Edmund Burke and the Critique of Political Radicalism* (Chicago: University of Chicago Press, 1980), 100. For related eighteenth-century views of Burke's style, see James Mackintosh, *Vindiciae Gallicae*, 3d ed., 1791; Mary Wollstonecraft, *Vindication of the Rights of Men* (Gainesville, Fla.: Scholar's Facsimiles & Reprints, 1960); Thomas Paine, *The Rights of Man*, published together with Burke's *Reflections* (New York: Anchor Books, 1973). Nineteenth-century critics, such as John Morley and the historian Henry Thomas Buckle, for whom Burke was a liberal constitutionalist, insisted that Burke's writings on the French Revolution were to be treated cautiously. In Burke's French period, wrote Buckle, "the proportions of that gigantic intellect were disturbed." Quoted in Macpherson, *Burke*, 4.

5. John Morley quoted in Macpherson, *Burke*, 36. Yet Morley writes that "it was reverence rather than sensibility, a noble and philosophic conservatism . . . which raised the storm in Burke's breast." John Morley, *Edmund Burke, a Historical Study* (London: Macmillan, 1880), 131.

6. Paine, *The Rights of Man*, 296. In contrast to eighteenth-century radicals, however, the recent efforts of such well-known scholars as Macpherson and J. G. A. Pocock to locate Burke squarely in the modern era have been directed at salvaging his political theory by rescuing the author from the nostalgic impulses and figurative excesses of his own pen. See, for instance, Pocock's reading of the assault on the queen in "The Political Economy of Burke's Analysis of the French Revolution," in *Virtue, Commerce, and History: Essays in Political Thought and History, Chiefly in the Eighteenth Century* (Cambridge: Cambridge University Press, 1985), 198.

7. W. J. T. Mitchell, "Eye and Ear: Edmund Burke and the Politics of Sensibility," in *Iconology: Image, Text, Ideology* (Chicago: University of Chicago Press, 1986), 116–150.

8. Frans De Bruyn, "Edmund Burke's Gothic Romance: The Portrayal of Warren Hastings in Burke's Writings and Speeches on India," *Criticism* 29 (Fall 1987): 435. See also Carol Kay, *Political Constructions* (Ithaca: Cornell University Press, 1988), 265–278; Neal Wood, "The Aesthetic Dimension

of Burke's Political Thought," *Journal of British Studies* 4 (November 1964): 41–64.

9. Edmund Burke, *A Philosophical Enquiry into the Origin of Our Ideas of the Sublime and the Beautiful*, ed. James T. Boulton (Notre Dame, Ind.: Notre Dame Press, 1958), 172, 175 (hereafter, *Enquiry*). On Burke's theory of language, see Mitchell, "Eye and Ear"; Gordon McKenzie, *Critical Responsiveness* (Berkeley: University of California Press, 1949); Dixon Wecter, "Burke's Theory Concerning Words, Images, and Emotion," *PMLA* 55 (1940): 167–181. In addition to an analysis of Burke's linguistic theory, Wecter provides an interesting historical commentary on the *Enquiry*'s roots in the ideas of Locke and Berkeley.

10. De Bruyn draws interesting parallels between Burke's political narratives and eighteenth-century archetypal plots, for instance, those found in such novels as *Clarissa* and *The Mysteries of Udolopho*. See "Edmund Burke's Gothic Romance," esp. 421, 430–433.

11. Ronald Paulson, *Representations of Revolution: 1789–1820* (New Haven: Yale University Press, 1983), 217.

12. On this point, see Peter Hughes, "Originality and Allusion in the Writings of Edmund Burke," *Centrum* 4, no. 1 (1976): 32–43.

13. Burke, *Reflections*, 90.

14. De Bruyn, "Edmund Burke's Gothic Romance," 424.

15. Burke, *Enquiry*, 1. Further page references are cited in the text.

16. See Michael Mosher, "The Skeptic's Burke: Reflections on the Revolution in France, 1790–1990," *Political Theory* 19 (August 1991): 395.

17. The gendered poles of the Burkean aesthetic have been noted before, but what most readings of the *Enquiry* miss is how Burke constructs, through language, the feminine beautiful/masculine sublime dichotomy. See Kramnick, *The Rage of Edmund Burke*, 93–98; Terry Eagleton, "The Ideology of the Aesthetic," in *The Rhetoric of Interpretation and the Interpretation of Rhetoric*, ed. Paul Hernadi (Durham, N.C.: Duke University Press, 1989), 78; Wood, "The Aesthetic Dimensions of Burke's Political Thought," 48–51.

18. Sigmund Freud, "The Uncanny," in *The Complete Psychological Works of Sigmund Freud*, vol. 17 (London: Hogarth, 1971), 219.

19. Ibid.

20. This delight, says Burke, is not the same as pleasure—a positive feeling that is not simply the absence of pain, which is likewise positive (35–36)—but rather is "the sensation which accompanies the removal of pain or danger." *Enquiry*, 37.

21. H. J. Rose, *A Handbook of Greek Mythology* (New York: Penguin, 1991 [1959]), 85. See also Jean-Pierre Vernant and Pierre Vidal-Naquet, *Myth and*

Tragedy in Ancient Greece, trans. Janet Lloyd (New York: Zone Books, 1988), 156. In the *Enquiry*, the section titled "Terror," which immediately precedes Milton's obscure image of Death, cites "serpents" as an example of what both terrifies and delights the subject in the field not of the invisible but of the visible—that is, "with regard to sight" (57). Although not Gorgons like the famed Medusa—who, on Freud's all too familiar psychoanalytic account "makes the [male] spectator stiff with terror, turns him to stone" (i.e., produces at once "the terror of castration" and its phallic resolution: "I am not afraid of you. I defy you. I have a penis")—the Erinyes are nevertheless ferocious. Freud, "Medusa's Head," in *Sexuality and the Psychology of Love*, ed. Philip Rieff (New York: Collier, 1963), 212–213.

22. Agents of blood vengeance, the Erinyes were born of the blood of the castrated Ouranos (the male sky). As the myth goes, Gaia (mother earth)— who stands opposed to Chaos, an undifferentiated void that existed in the beginning of the world—creates from her own self her male opposite: Ouranos. Gaia becomes angry with her mate, for he covers her and prevents their offspring from developing. She sends their son Kronos to mutilate him; this he does and from the bloody member of Ouranos are born the Erinyes, the Melian nymphs, and the Giants. For an excellent account of this myth which challenges traditional Oedipal readings, see Vernant and Vidal-Naquet, *Myth and Tragedy in Ancient Greece*, 95–98.

23. Quoted in Vernant and Vidal-Naquet, *Myth and Tragedy in Ancient Greece*, 157. The Erinyes, argue Vernant and Vidal-Naquet, confound the pure/impure, raw/cooked, nature/culture distinctions. "They can claim both extremes: What is 'pure' and 'natural' is also what is raw. They do not drink wine but they do eat men." Their nature "is not altered when they become the Eumenides. As goddesses of the night, they are the focus of the nocturnal festival with which the trilogy ends. They usually receive their victims, their sacrificial offerings . . . with their throats cut" (156).

24. Ibid., 62.

25. Freud, "The Uncanny," 224–226, 241.

26. Ibid., 233.

27. Ibid., 245.

28. Ibid., 225, 224.

29. Although intriguing, "something is not quite right with Freud's 'Das Unheimliche'," writes Jane Marie Todd. For Freud "preferred to remain *abseits*, a bit to one side, of the central problems of literary theory—the beautiful and the sublime." In Todd's reading of Freud's essay, two motifs are developed only to be pushed aside: "the central figure of woman . . . and the related theme of being and not being seen." Freud's account of "The

Sandman" as an oedipal narrative, she argues, represses the male subject's terror of female sexual difference and maternal power, both of which Freud denies when he aligns the uncanny with the fear of castration. By pushing the problem of the maternal *Heim* off to the side, Freud's language situates and contains the more terrifying because diffuse character of preoedipal anxiety within a father-son conflict of more reassuring dimensions. Jane Marie Todd, "The Veiled Woman in Freud's 'Das Unheimliche'," *Signs: Journal of Women in Culture and Society* 11 (Spring 1986): 519, 521.

30. Thomas Weiskel, *The Romantic Sublime: Studies in the Structure and Psychology of Transcendence* (Baltimore: Johns Hopkins University Press, [1976] 1986), 92. On Weiskel's provocative reading of a key passage from Homer's *Iliad* quoted in the *Enquiry* (34), the sense of astonishment and the accompanying feeling of delight both express the unconscious thought: "'I am not going to be punished, I am home free'." Further, the awe experienced by Burke as a reader of such sublime literature represents an "identification with the Father, an identification which both presupposes the renunciation of parricidal aggression and facilitates an escape from the imagined consequences of a murder" (91).

31. Julia Kristeva, *Powers of Horror*, trans. Leon S. Roudiez (New York: Columbia University Press, 1982), 11, 8, 2.

32. Ibid., 12.

33. In certain respects this passage iterates those cultural representations of femininity as delicate and endangered found in the eighteenth-century literary texts and conduct manuals that shaped some aspects of the domestic ideology of the English middle classes. See Nancy Armstrong and Leonard Tennenhouse, eds., *The Ideology of Conduct: Essays in Literature and the History of Sexuality* (New York: Methuen, 1987); Keith Thomas, "The Double Standard," *Journal of the History of Ideas* 20 (1959): 195–216; Ian Watt, *The Rise of the Novel: Studies in Defoe, Richardson, and Fielding* (London: Chatto and Windus, 1957); Marlene LeGates, "The Cult of Womanhood in Eighteenth-Century Thought," *Eighteenth-Century Studies* 10, no. 1 (1976): 21–39.

34. Frances Ferguson, "A Commentary on Suzanne Guerlac's 'Longinus and the Subject of the Sublime'," *New Literary History* 16 (Winter 1985): 294. Burke credits women with the conscious deployment of feminine artifice, but in so doing, writes Ferguson, he raises "a kind of uncertainty principle about the degree to which one can read weakness as weakness rather than strength." The Burkean solution to the dissimulative art of women is to recuperate it entirely as the product of masculine sensibility. Femininity "flatters" men into compliance; it sustains the illusion of the masculine ego through a gesture of submission: women need men to rescue them from

their mistakes. But within the subject-oriented aesthetic, feminine beauty must give evidence of itself on the masculine viewer, who reads those mistakes not as a kind of semiotic ambiguity, and certainly not as feminine power, but as a sign of his own potency. Thus, Ferguson concludes, Burke suppresses "an intentional, initiatory consciousness" (women's) and promotes "an affective, responsive consciousness" (men's) (296).

35. Kristeva, *Powers of Horror*, 16.

36. The full title is *Reflections on The Revolution in France, and on the proceedings in certain societies in London relative to that event: in a letter intended to have been sent to a gentleman in Paris*. Further page references are cited in the text.

37. Burke, *Enquiry*, 46.

38. The phrase is from Milton's *Paradise Lost* (3.23). Burke cites it as an example of how words move us without raising any clear ideas of the things for which custom has appointed them to stand. *Enquiry*, 175.

39. On how the writer might assume a persona other than that of the moralist, see Terry Castle, "The Carnivalization of Eighteenth-Century English Narrative," *PMLA* 99 (October 1984): 903–916.

40. When Burke draws on the masquerade he draws on a rich symbolic domain of English culture. Castle argues that one finds a "spectacular rise of carnivalesque activity in England in the second and third decades of the eighteenth century." Ibid., 903. The pleasure with which Burke read the novels of Fanny Burney, who makes powerful if didactic use of the masquerade, suggests his awareness of the narrative uses of the carnival in scenes of seduction. On Burney, see Castle, *Masquerade and Civilization* (Stanford: Stanford University Press, 1986), chap. 6.

41. Compare, for instance, Freeman's "Natural Law" Burke (*Edmund Burke and the Critique of Political Radicalism*), Kramnick's "ambivalent conservative" (*The Rage of Edmund Burke*), Macpherson's "political economist" (*Burke*), and Morley's "heir to Locke" (*Edmund Burke, a Historical Study*).

42. See Mikhail Bakhtin, *Rabelais and His World*," trans. Hélène Iswolsky (Bloomington: Indiana University Press, 1984), and "Discourse in the Novel," in *The Dialogic Imagination*, trans. Caryl Emerson and Michael Holquist (Austin: University of Texas Press, 1981).

43. Julia Kristeva, "The Ruin of a Poetics," in *Russian Formalism*, ed. Stephen Bann and John E. Bowlt (New York: Harper & Row, 1973), 109.

44. *The Correspondence of Edmund Burke*, 9 vols. (Cambridge: 1958–1971), Burke to Depont (November 1789), 6:41.

45. John Locke, *An Essay Concerning Human Understanding*, ed. Peter H. Nidditch (Oxford: Oxford University Press, 1975), 105 (2.1.28).

46. Weiskel, *The Romantic Sublime*, 17–18, 15.

47. See Harold Perkin, *The Origins of Modern English Society, 1780–1880* (London: Routledge & Kegan Paul, 1969), 24; Nancy Armstrong, "The Rise of the Domestic Woman," in *The Ideology of Conduct*, 96–141.

48. As John Gillis argues, Hardwicke's Marriage Act sought to put an end to the popular tradition of "self-marriage and self-divorce." The act "mandated that valid marriages be celebrated at established churches, but the truth is that there was massive noncompliance everywhere." Among other reasons for such noncompliance, the poor as well as dissenters resented paying marriage fees to the church. John Gillis, "Married but Not Churched: Plebeian Sexual Relations and Marital Nonconformity in Eighteenth-Century Britian," in *'Tis Nature's Fault': Unauthorized Sexuality during the Enlightenment*, ed. Robert Purks Maccubbin (Cambridge: Cambridge University Press, 1985): 34.

49. Edmund Burke, "Speech on a Bill for the Repeal of the Marriage Act, June 15, 1781," *The Works of the Right Honorable Edmund Burke* (Boston: Little, Brown, 1894), 7:135 (hereafter, *Works*).

50. See Burke, "Speech on Divorce Bill" (29 April 1771), in *The Writings and Speeches of Edmund Burke*, ed. Paul Langford (Oxford: Clarendon Press, 1981), 2:357.

51. J. G. A. Pocock, "Burke and the Ancient Constitution: A Problem in the History of Ideas," *Historical Journal* 3, no. 2 (1960): 125–143, 131.

52. Consider Burke's quarrel with those "gentlemen of the Society for Revolutions [i.e., Price and company]" who claimed to find a precedent for their Jacobinism in the Glorious Revolution of 1688. How then, asks Burke, are they to explain why the English "searched in strange lands for a foreign princess, from whose womb the line of our future rulers were to derive their title to govern millions of men through a series of the ages?

The Princess Sophia was named in the act of settlement of the 12th and 13th of King William, for a *stock* and root of *inheritance* to our kings, and not for her merits as a temporary administratrix of . . . power. . . . She was adopted for one reason, and for one only, because, says the act, 'the most excellent Princess Sophia, Electress and Dutchess Dowager of Hanover, is *daughter* of the most excellent Princess Elizabeth, late Queen of Bohemia, *daughter* of our late *sovereign lord* King James the First . . ." Burke argues the "kind of succession which is to preclude a choice of the people for ever" by inscribing the generative power of the female body in a fiction of paternity (e.g., "stock," "inheritance") which is also a *persona ficta*. Sophia's womb connects future monarchs with the "old [Protestant] stock of inheritance in King James the First" and thus ensures that the monarchy remain unbroken throughout the ages *Reflections*, 34–36. A hardly novel argument, but nonetheless interesting because, like Burke's argument about aristocratic blood, the stability of paternity and *persona ficta* turns on the stability of their representations.

53. "Letter to a Member of the National Assembly," *Works*, 4:29–30, my emphasis.

54. Ibid., 4:31.

55. Ibid.

56. Rose, *Handbook of Ancient Mythology*, 28, 29. See the *Aeneid*, 3:242–277.

57. Natalie Zemon Davis, "Women on Top," in *Society and Culture in Early Modern France* (Stanford: Stanford University Press, 1965), 129.

58. Edmund Burke, "Letters on a Regicide Peace," Letter I, *Works*, 5:312–314.

59. Thomas, "The Double Standard," 201.

60. See Jane Abray, "Feminism in the French Revolution," *American Historical Review* 80 (February 1975): 47–48.

61. "Letters on a Regicide Peace," Letter I, *Works*, 5:315.

62. Kristeva, *Powers of Horror*, 85.

63. Burke, "Letters on a Regicide Peace," Letter I, *Works*, 5:313.

64. Pocock, "The Political Economy of Burke's Analysis of the French Revolution," 197. On disorganized reproduction as a threat to social order in the revolutionary period, see Catherine Gallagher, "Response to Neil Hertz," *Representations* 4 (1983): 55–57.

65. Burke, "Letters on a Regicide Peace," Letter I, *Works*, 5:313.

66. Hughes, "Originality and Allusion in the Writings of Edmund Burke," 32.

67. The Women's October 5 March on Versailles led the municiple government to send the National Guard, under the leadership of the Marquis de Lafayette, to try to prevent a counterrevolution by bringing the king to Paris. After the assault on the palace on the morning of the sixth, the king agreed to return to Paris with the royal family. See Ruth Graham, "Loaves and Liberty: Women in the French Revolution," in *Becoming Visible: Women in European History*, ed. Renate Bridenthal and Claudia Koonz (New York: Houghton Mifflin, 1977), 241; D. G. Levy, H. B. Applewhite, and M. D. Johnson, eds., *Women in Revolutionary Paris 1789–1795: Selected Documents* (Urbana: University of Illinois Press, 1979), 15.

68. Graham, "Loaves and Liberty," 241 (my emphasis). On women's political activism in the October Days, see Abray, "Feminism in the French Revolution"; Olwen Hufton, "Women in Revolution, 1789–1796," *Past and Present* 53 (1971): 90–108; Levy et al., eds., *Women in Revolutionary Paris*; Lynn Hunt, *Politics, Culture, and Class in the French Revolution* (Berkeley:

University of California Press, 1984); Joan Landes, *Women and the Public Sphere in the Age of the French Revolution* (Ithaca: Cornell University Press, 1988).

69. To contemplate the naked queen was to "penetrate all the mystery of the aristocratic principle," to discover the "principle of equality." Kramnick, *The Rage of Edmund Burke*, 153.

70. "For Burke," writes Terry Eagleton, "the revolutionaries who seek to 'strip all the decent drapery of life' from political power, de-aestheticize it, are in danger of exposing the phallus of this transvestite law, which decks itself out as a woman." "The Ideology of the Aesthetic," in *The Rhetoric of Interpretation and the Interpretation of Rhetoric*, ed. Paul Hernadi (Durham, N.C.: Duke University Press, 1989), 79. But this reading neglects the possibility that Jacobin frenzy is tied, not to resentment of the phallus, that master signifier, but rather to the search for origins that leads back to the maternal.

71. Burke, "Letters on a Regicide Peace," Letter III, *Works*, 5:400.

72. Burke to Philip Francis, 20 February 1790, *Correspondence*, 6:91.

73. Here I am indebted to Thomas Weiskel's reading of Wordsworth. *The Romantic Sublime*, 29.

74. Paul de Man, *The Rhetoric of Romanticism* (New York: Columbia University Press, 1984), 7.

75. Burke, "Letters on a Regicide Peace," Letter I, *Works*, 5:284.

76. Burke, "Letters on a Regicide Peace," Letter IV, *Works*, 6:52–53.

77. Burke, "Letters on a Regicide Peace," Letter III, *Works*, 5:443.

78. Ibid., 5:360.

79. Burke, "Letters on a Regicide Peace," Letter IV, *Works*, 6:100–101.

80. Burke, "Letters on a Regicide Peace," Letter I, *Works*, 5:239; *Reflections*, 90.

81. Burke, "Remarks on the Policy of the Allies," in *Writings and Speeches of Edmund Burke*, 8:480.

82. Mosher, "The Skeptic's Burke," 413–414. The phrase "holy war" is from Don Herzog, "Puzzling through Burke," *Political Theory* 19 (August 1991): 360.

83. Mosher, "The Skeptic's Burke," 413.

84. Herzog, "Puzzling through Burke," 359.

85. Burke, "Letter to a Noble Lord," *Works*, 5:187–188, my emphasis. The translation is from *The Aeneid*, trans. L. R. Lind (Bloomington: Indiana University Press, 1962), 3.242–248.

86. Kristeva, *Powers of Horror*, 7.

87. Burke, "Letters on a Regicide Peace," Letter II, *Works*, 5:358–359.

88. Burke, "Letter to a Member of the National Assembly," *Works*, 4:38–40.

89. Burke, "Letters on a Regicide Peace," Letter III, *Works*, 5:404.

90. Burke, *Enquiry*, 37.

4. The "Innocent Magdalen": Woman in Mill's Symbolic Economy

1. The dream description is Mill's. John Stuart Mill to Harriet Taylor Mill, 17 February 1857, *The Later Letters of John Stuart Mill*, ed. F. E. Mineka and David N. Lindley, vols. 14–17 of *The Collected Works of John Stuart Mill*, 33 vols., ed. John M. Robson (Toronto: University of Toronto Press, 1963–1991), 17:523–524 (hereafter *LL*). For accounts of Mill's dream, see Bernard Semmel, *John Stuart Mill and the Pursuit of Virtue* (New Haven: Yale University Press, 1984), chap. 2; Bruce Mazlish, *James and John Stuart Mill: Father and Son in the Nineteenth Century* (New York: Basic Books, 1975), 302–303.

2. Mary Poovey, *Uneven Developments: The Ideological Work of Gender in Mid-Victorian England* (Chicago: University of Chicago Press, 1988), 11.

3. John Stuart Mill, *The Subjection of Women*, in *Essays on Sex Equality*, ed. Alice Rossi (Chicago: University of Chicago Press, 1970), 137.

4. John Stuart Mill, "Early Essays on Marriage and Divorce," in *Essays on Sex Equality*, 76.

5. Zillah Eisenstein, *The Radical Future of Liberal Feminism* (New York: Longman, 1981), 113–144; Jean Bethke Elshtain, *Public Man, Private Woman* (Princeton: Princeton University Press, 1981), 132–146; Susan Moller Okin, *Women in Western Political Thought* (Princeton: Princeton University Press, 1979), 197–230. For an analysis of how Mill's empiricist method in *The System of Logic* created problems for his feminism, see Jennifer Ring, *Modern Political Theory and Contemporary Feminism: A Dialectical Analysis* (Albany: State University of New York Press, 1991), 59–106. For an analysis of the tension between reformism and radicalism in Mill's essay, see Julia Annas, "Mill and the Subjection of Women," *Philosophy* 52 (1977): 179–194.

6. Mary Lyndon Shanley, "Marital Slavery and Friendship: John Stuart Mill's *The Subjection of Women*," in *Feminist Interpretations and Political Theory*, ed. Shanley and Carole Pateman (University Park: Pennsylvania State University Press, 1991), 176, 175.

7. There is evidence that Mill understood quite clearly that women's responsibility for "the superintendence of a household" was an impediment to their self-development. See, for example, *The Subjection of Women*, 209.

8. John Stuart Mill, *Principles of Political Economy*, vols. 2–3 of *Collected Works*, 2: 370, 368, 367 (hereafter, *Principles*).

9. See Graeme Duncan, *Marx and Mill: Two Views of Social Conflict and Social Change* (Cambridge: Cambridge University Press, 1973); Semmel, *John Stuart Mill and the Pursuit of Virtue*; Alan Ryan, *J. S. Mill* (London: Routledge and Kegan Paul, 1974).

10. See Duncan, *Marx and Mill*, 230.

11. John Stuart Mill, *On Liberty*, in *Mill: Three Essays*, ed. Richard Wollheim (Oxford: Oxford University Press, 1975), 5.

12. As Lynda Nead writes, "The term 'magdalen' was commonly used in [Victorian] religious and medical publications as a euphemism for the prostitute." *Myths of Sexuality: Representations of Women in Victorian Britain* (Oxford: Basil Blackwell, 1988), 69.

13. Mill, *Principles*, xci. Further page references are cited in the text.

14. On Mill's quarrel with Smith's "general law of the remuneration of labor," see *Principles*, 380–385.

15. On Owenism and women, see Sally Alexander, "Women, Class, and Sexual Difference in the 1830s and 1840s: Some Reflections on the Writing of a Feminist History," *History Workshop* 17 (Spring 1984): 125–149; Barbara Taylor, *Eve and the New Jerusalem: Socialism and Feminism in the Nineteenth Century* (New York: Pantheon Books, 1983).

16. On the debate between the Owenites and the utilitarians over the question of free will, see Catherine Gallagher, *The Industrial Reformation of English Fiction: Social Discourse and Narrative Form, 1832–1867* (Chicago: University of Chicago Press, 1985), 3–35.

17. See also *Principles*, 208. As C. B. Macpherson argues, Mill "found the actual prevailing distribution of the produce of labour wholly unjust. He found the explanation of that unjust distribution in an historical accident, not in the capitalist principle itself." *The Life and Times of Liberal Democracy* (Oxford: Oxford University Press, 1980), 55. See also Duncan, *Marx and Mill*, 244. For a critique of Mill's perspective on questions of economic distribution from within the liberal tradition, see Amy Gutman, *Liberal Equality* (Cambridge: Cambridge University Press, 1980).

18. Mill to Lord Amberly, 2 February 1870, *LL*, 1693.

19. John Stuart Mill, *Considerations on Representative Government*, in *Mill: Three Essays*, 187 (hereafter, *Considerations*).

20. Christine Di Stefano, *Configurations of Masculinity: A Feminist Perspective on Modern Political Theory* (Ithaca: Cornell University Press, 1991), 154, 152.

21. John Stuart Mill, "Nature," *Collected Works*, 10:393.

22. Ibid.

23. Di Stefano, *Configurations of Masculinity*, 155, 154.

24. "Discipline and self-control, which figure prominently throughout Mill's work, represent the harnessing of nature at the level of the individual. Civilization can proceed only by means of constant self-control and self-discipline on the part of the human species." Ibid., 155.

25. Mill, "Nature," 394.

26. I am indebted here to Peter Stallybrass and Allon White, who locate a similar slippage in both Henry Mayhew's *London Labour and the London Poor* (1861) and Edwin Chadwick's *Report . . . on and Inquiry into the Sanitary Conditions of the Labouring Population of Great Britain* (1842). *The Politics and Poetics of Transgression* (Ithaca: Cornell University Press, 1986), 129–130.

27. Mill, "Nature," 395.

28. Amanda Anderson, "Prostitution's Artful Guise," *Diacritics* 2–3 (Summer–Fall 1991): 117n. See also Stallybrass and White, *The Politics and Poetics of Transgression*, 197.

29. Gareth Stedman Jones, *Outcast London: A Study in the Relationship between Social Classes in Victorian Society* (Oxford: Clarendon, 1971), 14. See also Stallybrass and White, *The Politics and Poetics of Transgression*, chap. 3. Middle-class anxieties about the poor were tied to the breakdown of traditional relations of authority. As Stedman Jones writes, "In the course of the nineteenth century, the social distance between rich and poor expressed itself in an ever sharper geographical segregation of the city. Merchants and employers no longer lived above their places of work. The old methods of social control based on the model of the squire, the parson, face to face relations, deference, and paternalism, found less and less reflection in the urban reality. Vast tracts of working-class housing were left to themselves, virtually bereft of any contact with authority except in the form of the policeman or the bailiff" (13–14).

30. See Stallybrass and White, *The Politics and Poetics of Transgression*, chap. 4.

31. "Interview with Julia Kristeva," in *Women Analyze Women*, ed. Elaine Hoffman Baruch and Lucienne J. Serrano (New York: New York University Press, 1988), 135–136.

32. For a thoughtful critique of Mill's Malthusianism, see Duncan, *Marx and Mill*, chap. 7. Di Stefano rightly argues that Mill stresses moral choice because his view of "nature is so dreadful that if human nature were not malleable, all would be lost." *Configurations of Masculinity*, 158.

33. As Ryan explains, this theory held that "at any given time there was a fixed quantity of wage-goods available to be given to the suppliers of labour,

hence that the average wage rate was rigidly determined by that total divided by the number of workers among whom it was to be distributed." *J. S. Mill*, 166.

34. In contrast to Mill, however, Owen had insisted that, as slaves of necessity, workers were too poor and too ignorant to be morally responsible. Their rapid multiplication was indeed antithetical to their distant social interests, but it was caused less by the irrational forces of animal instinct than by those of the market. Workers could not be expected to improve morally until their situation improved economically. See Gallagher, *The Industrial Reformation of English Fiction*, 13–16.

35. As Mill wrote to Edward Herford, "A sounder morality on the subject of overpopulation . . . , even if it were not necessary to prevent the evils of poverty, would equally be requisite in order to put an end to the slavery to which the existing state of things condemns women." 22 January 1850, *LL*, 45.

36. Mill's analysis of the differences between Continental peasant proprietors and English hired agricultural workers shows that he understood that the rapid rise in population was attributable to proletarianization. See *Principles*, 252–296. Yet Mill does not advocate a return to an agricultural economy partly because it comprises "single families, each ruled internally . . . by a patriarchal despot, and having scarcely any community of interest, or necessary mental communion, with other human beings" (768).

37. As Angus McLaren argues, "The unusual high fertility of workers in general was 'rational' given the particular conditions of high infant mortality and the fact that children raised frugally and put to work early could be valuable assets." "Women's Work and Regulation of Family Size: The Question of Abortion in the Nineteenth Century," *History Workshop* 4 (Autumn 1977): 70–71.

38. "My own opinion is that when productive employment can be claimed by every one from the public as a right, it can only be rendered undesirable by being made virtually slave labor." Mill to Edward Herford, 22 January 1850, *LL*, 44.

39. "Remove the regulation of their [workers'] wages from their own control; guarantee to them a certain payment; . . . and no amount of comfort that you can give them will make either them or their descendants look to their own self-restraint as the proper means of preserving them in that state." *Principles*, 359.

40. Catherine Gallagher, "The Body versus the Social Body in the Works of Thomas Malthus and Henry Mayhew," *Representations* 14 (Spring 1986): 86.

41. Malthus, writes Gallagher, poses as "the vindicator of the rights of the body." Thus he disputes William Godwin's hypothesis—advanced as well by Mill—that "the passion between the sexes will become extinct." Malthus "denies this hypothesis . . . on the grounds that the instincts are not base," and "he presents all of Godwin's schemes for self-discipline, for the exercise of the 'power of the mind over the body,' as so many recipes for enfeeblement." Ibid., 88, 89.

42. Mill, "Nature," 398.

43. According to Foucault, "*bio-power* . . . brought life and its mechanisms into the realm of explicit calculations." Michel Foucault, *The History of Sexuality*, vol. 1, trans. Robert Hurley (New York: Vintage, 1978), 143.

44. Ibid., 114. One of the figures to have emerged from "this preoccupation with sex," argues Foucault, was "the Malthusian couple," who were to regulate their bodies out of sense of obligation to the social body as a whole. *History of Sexuality*, 105. As Jeffrey Weeks writes, Foucault shows how "an obsessive concern with the sexuality of the working class, the social other, displac[ed] in the end the acute social crisis [of the 1840s] from the area of exploitation and class conflict, . . . into the framework of . . . 'morality.'" *Sex, Politics, and Society: The Regulation of Sexuality since 1800* (London: Longman, 1989), 20.

45. See Mill to Reverend Henry William Carr, 7 January 1852, *LL*, 81.

46. Working-class antipathy to Malthus developed out of what were seen as conservative social applications of his theory. Reformers who focused on the problem of overpopulation in the 1830s and 1840s were viewed with suspicion by the laboring classes and their advocates. See Weeks, *Sex, Politics, and Society*, 68–69.

47. Ryan quoted in T. Walter Herbert, Jr., "The Erotics of Purity: *The Marble Faun* and the Victorian Construction of Sexuality," *Representations* 36 (Fall 1991): 116. Studies on the working-class family suggest that the female wage laborer had more control over her sexuality than Mill allows, partly because she had access to contraceptive information in the workplace, and partly because of the family's dependence on her wages. McLaren argues that in the middle classes the decision about family size was primarily the man's "because he was the sole bread-winner, because the main method of contraception—withdrawal—was a male technique, and because the middle-class woman . . . was cut off from both the economic and sexual knowledge on which choice would finally depend." Working women had more say in economic matters, and abortion, condemned by the middle-class, was one means of their exercising control over reproductive matters. "Women's Work and Regulation of Family Size," 71. On the same point, see

Patricia Knight, "Women and Abortion in Victorian and Edwardian England," *History Workshop* 4 (Autumn 1977): 57–68.

48. Mill to Professor Green, 8 April 1852, *LL*, 89.

49. Nina Auerbach argues that beneath the familiar Victorian image of woman as victim was a more disturbing image of woman as a figure of irrepressible mobility and awesome power of self-creation, a figure she locates as well in the writings of John Stuart Mill. *Woman and the Demon: The Life of a Victorian Myth* (Cambridge: Harvard University Press, 1982), 56–58.

50. Fred R. Berger, *Happiness, Justice, and Freedom: The Moral and Political Philosophy of John Stuart Mill* (Berkeley: University of California Press, 1984), 184. Mill argued that "guardians and overseers are not fit to be trusted to give or withhold other people's money according to their verdict on the morality of the person soliciting it." *Principles*, 962.

51. For a list of the commissioners appointed in 1832 to study the Poor Laws, see Anne P. Robson's and John M. Robson's editorial note to the *Principles*, 744.

52. See Pat Thane, "Women and the Poor Law in Victorian and Edwardian England," *History Workshop* 6 (Autumn 1978): 29–51.

53. John Stuart Mill, "The Poor Laws," from the *Examiner*, 9 March 1835, *Collected Works*, 23:687. See also "First Report of the Poor Law Commissioners," *Globe and Traveller*, 8 September 1835, *Collected Works*, 24:776–778.

54. Mill, "The Poor Laws," 687.

55. Thane, "Women and the Poor Law," 29. Further, writes Thane: "If the husband entered the workhouse, the wife would have no choice but to follow. A destitute wife could be refused entry to the workhouse if her husband would not enter, or permission to leave if he would not leave. If a male pauper was officially classified 'not able-bodied', so was his wife, whatever her personal physical condition" (31).

56. Quoted in U. R. Q. Henriques, "Bastardy and the New Poor Law," *Past and Present*, no. 37 (July 1967): 103–129, 109.

57. See ibid., 108, 117. The church denounced the double standard on moral, and ratepayers on financial, grounds. The latter argued that because destitute unmarried mothers were entitled to relief, if the father could not be made to pay, then they would have to pay. As a result, the Bastardy Clauses were dropped in the 1844 Poor Law Act Amendment. On the same point, see Thane, "Women and the Poor Law," 32.

58. The commissioners who framed the Bastardy Clauses of the 1834 act cited testimony to the effect that "loose women would swear not to the real father of the child, but to the wealthiest man against whom the charge could

stick. There were cases of women blackmailing the men around with threats of bringing affiliation actions against them. Any woman could use these laws [the Poor Laws before the 1834 act] to provide herself with 'what every woman looks upon as the greatest prize—a husband,'" and a well-to-do one at that. Henriques, "Bastardy and the New Poor Law," 106.

59. As to the separation of the sexes, Mill wrote to Edward Herford: "I am sorry to see in your Circular the ignorant & immoral doctrine that the 'separation' enforced in the workhouse is among the sources of 'degradation' & diminished 'self-respect' for the pauper. I consider it an essential part of the moral training, which, in many ways (but in none more important) the reception of public relief affords an opportunity of administering." 22 January 1850, *LL*, 45. As to imposing restrictions on improvident marriages, Mill wrote to Dr. Henry MacCormac, "I would say, that restrictions on marriage, or on any other human action when so conducted as to be directly injurious to others than the agents themselves, do not appear to me objectionable on the principles of Liberty." 4 December 1865, *LL*, 1124. For a similar argument, see *On Liberty*, 132; *Principles*, 346–348. As we see shortly, Mill also feared such an extension of state power, and he sought other means of promoting "spontaneous motives of restraint," including wage labor, woman's suffrage, and moral motherhood.

60. As Henriques writes, "The Commissioners were not concerned wholly with morality, nor even with bastardy. They were concerned with the multiplication of an impoverished population." "Bastardy and the New Poor Law," 111. But if the commissioners put forth domesticity and female chastity as partial solutions to social immiseration, the able-bodied female pauper posed a problem for guardians, who were undecided as to whether pauper mothers belonged in the home or in the workplace. Although the emerging assumptions about female dependence and the nuclear family in the 1830s and 1840s entailed an increasing condemnation of women's work outside the home, not all guardians were convinced that out-door relief for women was the answer because many remained unconvinced that poor women made the best of mothers and, thus, uncertain as to whether children's welfare was best secured by keeping them out of the workhouse. Moreover, the central argument of Poor Law reform (that restrictions on out-door relief would reduce pauperism by giving the able-bodied an incentive to find work) was even less persuasive when it came to women, because female labor outside the home—as well as the sweating out of work within it—was seen by state officials (as well as by many labor activists) as a primary cause of low wages, thus of poverty among those "willing" to work. See Thane, "Women and the Poor Law," 36.

61. Even Mill, who recognized that women qua women were paid less than men for comparable work, tended to elide the relationship of sexual inequality and class exploitation—indeed, blamed "custom," rather than capitalist patriarchy, for enabling male workers to take from female workers their fair share of the wages fund. See *Principles*, 395.

62. See Gallagher, *The Industrial Reformation of English Fiction*, 123–124. Poovey argues that, in the 1844 parliamentary debate about factory conditions, Lord Ashley, like many other advocates of protective legislation, expressed concerns about "female promiscuity" in the workplace. *Uneven Developments*, 131.

63. See Herbert, "The Erotics of Purity," 115. See especially Poovey, *Uneven Developments*, 77–80.

64. Mill had not always advocated women's right to compete. In an 1832 article in the *Examiner*, he proposed a law that would interdict "the employment of . . . *females of any age*, in manufactories," citing the "obvious" reason that no "mother . . . should be employed in any gainful occupation which withdraws her from the midst of her family." "Employment of Children in Manufactories," *Collected Works*, 23:399. Responding to a letter received from the "female operatives of [Todmoren]," who had expressed "no little anxiety for your [Mill's] opinion on the Factory Bill," Mill advised first, that "the interdiction might be confined to married females," who have "no legitimate claim on any male relative for support"; and second, that the operatives might consider seriously the possibility of emigration, for independent women "are exactly the persons to whom emigration holds out the greatest advantages." "Female Emigrants," *Examiner*, 26 February 1832, *Collected Works*, 23:419–420.

65. Stallybrass and White, *The Politics and Poetics of Transgression*, 126. "Chadwick," write Stallybrass and White, "worked in Benthamite circles in the 1820s and from 1830–2 worked closely with Bentham himself" (139). Furthermore, they observe, "as Foucault has argued, nineteenth-century policing found its privileged form in Bentham's Panopticon, which ensured the 'permanent visibility' of the inmate." Like most proposals for reform, it spoke to the higher classes' intense fear of the " 'invisibility' of the poor" and to the belief that to be under the gaze of others, preferably one's moral and social betters, would prevent wrongdoing" (134). See also Michel Foucault, *Discipline and Punish: The Birth of the Prison*, trans. Alan Sheridan (New York: Random House, 1979), 201; and Stedman Jones, *Outcast London*, 13–16.

66. Quoted in Stallybrass and White, *The Politics and Poetics of Transgression*, 131. Mill heralds Chadwick's report for showing that the demoralizing conditions of factories were nothing in comparison to "the private dwellings

of a large part of the labouring population." Moreover, factories—even though they lacked "proper ventilation and other important requisites"— were instrumental in teaching habits of self-discipline and thus in curtailing population growth. "Report on the Sanitary Condition of the Labouring Population of Great Britain," *Examiner*, 20 August 1842, *Collected Works*, 24:829. See also, in the same volume, "The Poor Rates as a Burden on Agriculture," 862–864. For a significantly different picture of the scope of industrial reform, see Friedrich Engels, *The Condition of the Working Class in England in 1844*.

67. One of the paradoxes of Mill's attack on familial patriarchy, as Jacques Donzelot has argued of other Victorian social reformers, was that it significantly increased the power of the patriarchal state over the lower-class family. *The Policing of Families*, trans. Robert Hurley (New York: Pantheon, 1979), 103.

68. The report of the Handloom Weavers' Commission reflected growing male union agitation over female labor, the struggle for a family wage, and an increasing sense among skilled workers that a dependent wife at home was a sign of respectability.

69. Likewise, Mill writes: "In an otherwise just state of things, it is not, therefore, I think, a desirable custom, that the wife should contribute by her labour to the income of the family. In an unjust state of things, her doing so may be useful to her, by making her of more value in the eyes of the man who is legally her master." She should have, but not necessarily exercise, "the power of earning." *The Subjection of Women*, 179.

70. According to Poovey, "The scope of the [redundant women] 'problem' had been widely publicized by the 1851 Census, which calculated that 42 percent of the women between the ages of twenty and forty were unmarried and that two million out of Britain's six million women were self-supporting." Further, "the proportion of women to men within the marriageable age-group of fifteen to forty-nine years was 107 percent." *Uneven Developments*, 4, 14. See also 158.

71. "It does not follow that a woman should *actually* support herself because she should be *capable* of doing so: in the natural course of events she will *not*. It is not desirable to burthen the labour market with a double number of competitors." Mill, "Early Essays on Marriage and Divorce," 74–75.

72. Julia Kristeva, *Powers of Horror*, trans. Leon S. Roudiez (New York: Columbia University Press, 1982), 77–79. It seems appropriate here to note as well Mill's documented contempt for his mother, who bore his father (a self-proclaimed Malthusian and man of reason) nine children. See John

Stuart Mill, *Autobiography*, ed. Jack Stillinger (Houghton Mifflin, 1969), 33. For a reading of Mill's representation of his sexualized mother in relation to his asexual wife, see Linda M. G. Zerilli, "Constructing 'Harriet Taylor': Another Look at J. S. Mill's *Autobiography*," in *Constructions of the Self*, ed. George Levine (New Brunswick: Rutgers University Press, 1992), 191–212; Christine Di Stefano, "Rereading J. S. Mill: Interpretations from the (M)Otherworld," in *Discontented Discourses*, ed. Marleen S. Barr and Richard Feldstein (Urbana: University of Illinois Press, 1989), 160–172.

73. "I think it most probable that this particular passion will become with men, as it is already with a large number of women, completely under the control of reason. It has become so with women because its becoming so has been the condition upon which women hoped to obtain the strongest love and admiration of men." Mill to Lord Amberly, 2 February 1870, *LL*, 1692–1693.

74. See, Poovey, *Uneven Developments*, 160.

75. Kristeva, *Powers of Horror*, 102, 72. Mill argued that the mother teaches the child the habits of industry, manual labor, and abstinence. See *LL*, 1469.

76. Page references to the *Considerations* are cited in the text.

77. John Stuart Mill, "Thoughts on Parliamentary Reform," *Collected Works*, 19:327.

78. Gallagher, *The Industrial Reformation of English Fiction*, 229. See also what Dennis Thompson calls "the principle of competence," which calls for the greatest influence of the most qualified citizens. *John Stuart Mill and Representative Government* (Princeton: Princeton University Press), 9–10, 54–90.

79. The First Reform Bill had left workers cynical and distrustful of middle-class leadership. These sentiments were expressed succinctly in 1841 by the Chartist P. M. McDougall: "Promised plenty came in the shape of the accursed Poor Law Bastilles, promised security in the shape of a Russian Police, promised economy in additional taxation." Quoted in Gallagher, *The Industrial Reformation of English Fiction*, 29.

80. Adopting Bentham's phrase, Mill defines "sinister interests" as those which conflict "more or less with the general good of the community." *Considerations*, 237.

81. The descriptive model held that political rights are necessary to guard against misgovernment, and that different representatives should resemble their respective constituencies by sharing their social and economic interests. On the split that developed within the utilitarian camp in the 1850s and 1860s over this model, see Gallagher, *The Industrial Reformation of English Fiction*, 222–226.

82. Mill, as Gallagher writes, wants to "make a sharp distinction between the empirical self, encumbered by personal and class interests, mere social facts, and the disinterested political self, laden with values." Ibid., 232.

83. "Though everyone ought to have a voice—that everyone should have an equal voice is a totally different proposition." *Considerations*, 232. On Mill's suggestions for developing a test of mental superiority, see ibid., 284–285. What Mill really wants to measure is "moral worth," but for that, he concedes, "it is not so easy to find an available test." "Thoughts on Parliamentary Reform," 323. Fully aware that his plurality scheme stood little chance of being adopted, Mill wanted to redefine the symbolic terms of citizenship. See *Considerations*, 286.

84. So dangerous is the selfishness of the average voter that, even after "all men and women are admitted to vote in virtue of their fitness," "the control of publicity [afforded by open-voting] would be as needful as ever." *Considerations*, 310.

85. See Michael Foucault, "The Eye of Power," in *Power/Knowledge: Selected Interviews and Other Writings, 1972–1977*, ed. Colin Gordon (New York: Pantheon, 1980), 153–155.

86. This well-known argument is elaborated as well in *The Subjection of Women*, 172, 174, 220.

87. See John Stuart Mill, "Women's Suffrage [3]," 12 January 1871, *Collected Works*, 29:402. Mill held the doctrine of natural equality to be culturally pernicious for at least two reasons: first, it denied the important moral and intellectual differences between human beings which ought to count in any theory of political representation; second, all appeals to nature are immoral inasmuch as they encourage an abandonment to brute instincts. See "Thoughts on Parliamentary Reform," 323; *Principles*, 768; "Nature," 365.

88. Mill to Florence Nightingale, 31 December 1867, *LL*, 1344. Even if one were to remove tomorrow all the miseries under which women suffer, Mill told Nightingale, "in ten years new forms of suffering would have arisen; for no earthly power can ever prevent the constant unceasing unsleeping elastic pressure of human egotism from weighing down and thrusting aside those who have not the power to resist it" (ibid.). See James Mill, "Essay on Government" (1820), cited in Okin, *Women in Western Political Thought*, 201.

89. See John Stuart Mill, "Remarks on Mr. Fitzroy's Bill for the More Efficient Prevention of Assaults on Women and Children," *Collected Works*, 21:101–108. In proposing an amendment to the Reform Bill on 20 May 1867, Mill contested the notion that "the interests of all women are safe in

the hands of their fathers, husbands, and brothers," reminding his parliamentary colleagues "of the number of women who are annually beaten to death, kicked to death, or trampled to death by their male protectors." Just as "workmen need other protection than that of their employers," Mill argued, so too did women "need other protection than that of their men." "Proposed Amendment to the Reform Bill," in *The Woman Question: Society and Literature in Britain and America, 1837–1883*, vol. 2, ed. Elizabeth K. Helsinger, Robin Lauterbach Sheets, and William Veeder (Chicago: University of Chicago Press, 1983), 44.

90. Mill, *Principles*, 765–766. See the full citation for the rhetorical connection between domestic violence and the working class's present incapacity to exercise the suffrage properly. See also the class distinctions Mill draws in "Mr. Fitzroy's Act," 105.

91. Eisenstein, *The Radical Future of Liberal Feminism*, 113–144.

92. See Denise Riley, *"Am I That Name?": Feminism and the Category of Women in History* (Minneapolis: University of Minnesota Press, 1988), 70–72.

93. Quoted in *The Woman Question*, 45.

94. To extend the franchise to single women (with property) would encourage those other nine women out of ten to adopt the willful posture of that one "unnatural woman"; it would then snowball into a movement for sexual equality: married women's property reform and women's right to unrestricted industrial employment and equal wages. See ibid., 44–46.

95. Mill to Mrs. Peter Alfred Taylor, *LL*, 1649.

96. See especially Julia Annas, "Mill and the Subjection of Women"; Okin, *Women in Western Political Thought*, 213; Di Stefano, *Configurations of Masculinity*, 182–183.

97. Mill, *The Subjection of Women*, 228. Di Stefano finds "striking parallels between Mill's rendition of nature's drag effect on rationality, progress, and civilization . . . and the wife's retardation of her husband's noble aspirations." *Configurations of Masculinity*, 183. In other words, the domestic ideal herself stands in an ever uneasy relation to the forces of destruction—animal instinct. As Poovey argues, the Victorian figure of the moral mother was highly ambivalent, since "conceptualizing women's reproductive capacity as *the* basis of femininity inevitably (if inadvertently) foregrounded women's sexuality alongside their moralized maternal nature." Thus, "when it was given one emphasis, woman's reproductive capacity equaled her maternal instinct; when given another, it equaled her sexuality." *Uneven Developments*, 11. On a similar point, see Lucy Bland, "The Domain of the Sexual: A Response," *Screen Education* 39 (Summer 1981): 58–59.

98. On the same point, see Mill, *The Subjection of Women*, 168.

99. This was the same problem faced by working-class radicals, who argued that workers were "wage slaves" yet insisted they were ready for the franchise. See Gallagher, *The Industrial Reformation of English Fiction*, 3–33.

100. Mill to Charles Eliot Norton, 24 September 1868, *LL*, 1442. Diffusing the specter of increased class strife, Mill argued that, since the women's vote would "probably be about equally shared among all classes, no harm will be done." "Proposed Amendment to the Reform Bill," in *The Woman Question*, 43. As to sex-class war, Mill wrote to Richard Russell, "There is a more even balance between men and women than between any other two classes and therefore the attainment of justice through equal representation may be more easily trusted to the reason & right feeling of the best among each acting as a check to violence or party feeling on either side." 6 March 1867, *LL*, 1252.

101. Mill to Florence Nightingale, *LL*, 1345.

102. John Stuart Mill, "Women's Suffrage [1]," 18 July 1869, *Collected Works*, 29:377.

103. Riley, *"Am I That Name?"* 46.

104. Mill, "Women's Suffrage [1]," 375–378.

105. As Nead observes, "Although to work for money transgressed the boundaries of respectability, charitable work actually became a means of defining respectable femininity." *Myths of Sexuality*, 201.

106. The 1869 Poor Law Board set out to draw clearer lines between the "deserving" and the "undeserving." The former were to be directed to private charities—which had grown considerably since 1834—so that the latter could be dealt with in the workhouses and workhospitals, as Thane puts it, "with full deterrent rigour." Further, the problems were articulated in terms of the longstanding conflict between central policy and local practice, and the Poor Board redoubled pressure on local guardians to refuse outdoor relief to the able-bodied. By 1870, central policymakers declared "that out-relief should in no circumstances be given to able-bodied single women, except on a labour test." Like men, women were to be treated as "potentially recalcitrant members of the labour force." "Women and the Poor Law," 38.

107. See Nead, *Myths of Sexuality*, 204.

108. Mill, "Women's Suffrage [3]," 405–406, To see that "I am now speaking, not of women as they might be," Mill told his audience, "but of women as they now are," one need only look at "the Sanitary Commission in the late American War," which, from beginning to end, "was women's work" (406).

109. Mill was not alone in recommending that women take up the duties of workhouse supervisors. In *Workhouses and Women's Work* (1858), Louisa Twining argued a similar point: women supervisors would provide "other influences that may impart some feeling and sympathy into the system. It is not an alteration of the system itself that is demanded but rather the introduction of the law of love into it." Quoted in Nead, *Myths of Sexuality*, 199.

110. Mill, "Women's Suffrage [2]," 387.

111. Mill, *The Subjection of Women*, 226.

112. Mill, "Women's Suffrage [2]," 387–388.

113. Educated in the sentiments, women are "unable to see, and unwilling to admit, the ultimate evil tendency of any form of charity or philanthropy which commends itself to their sympathetic feelings. The great and continually increasing mass of unenlightened . . . benevolence," Mill writes, "saps the very foundations of the [poor's] self-respect, self-help, and self-control." And this "waste of resources and of benevolent feelings," he adds, "is immensely swelled by women's contributions, and stimulated by their influence." *The Subjection of Women*, 227.

114. Mill, *On Liberty*, 5.

115. Ibid., 15.

116. There are numerous qualifications in *On Liberty* which relate to the casual poor. For example, Mill argues that the state has no right to punish "idleness, except in a person receiving support from the public" (120). Taking up the matter of the centralized state, Mill argues the national Poor Law Board is absolutely justified in exerting power over "the administrators of the Poor Rate throughout the country" because "no locality has a moral right to make itself by mismanagement a nest of pauperism, necessarily overflowing into other localities, and impairing the moral and physical condition of the whole labouring community" (14). This was the position Mill defended in all his writings on the Poor Laws. And it was a response not only to mismanagement at the local level but also to the unwillingness of many local guardians to impose the regulations devised by the national Poor Law Board to restrict out-door relief.

117. Gertrude Himmelfarb, *On Liberty and Liberalism: The Case of John Stuart Mill* (New York: Knopf, 1974), 168. Maintaining that the issue of liberty was not pressing in Mill's time, Himmelfarb's object is really twofold: one, to rescue "the other Mill, who belongs to the older liberal tradition of Montesquieu, Burke, [etc.]" from the Mill of *On Liberty*; two, to discredit the latter text (or rather feminism and Harriet Taylor). *On Liberty* "was somehow connected with the trivial cause of women" (169–170).

118. Nancy Woods, "Prostitution and Feminism in Nineteenth-Century Britain," *m/f* 7 (1982): 61–77. As Linda Mahood argues, the regulation of prostitution was part of the more general "moral regulation of working-class female sexuality. . . . working-class women were overwhelmingly the targets of legislation designed to clean up street disorders, which the bourgeoisie perceived as plaguing their cities' streets." *The Magdalenes: Prostitution in the Nineteenth Century* (New York: Routledge, 1990), 3.

119. Woods, "Prostitution and Feminism," 64.

120. Ibid., 66; Judy Walkowitz, *Prostitution and Victorian Society: Class and the State* (Cambridge: Cambridge University Press, 1980), 46.

121. As John Robson notes, the London National Society for Women's Suffrage split on the issue of C.D.A. agitation, with Mill leading the ranks of those who wanted at all costs to avoid linking the suffrage to the repeal of the acts. *LL*, 1818, n. 2. Mill shared that concern with another defender of women's suffrage, Charles Kingsley, who wrote Mill: "Unmarried women will damage the cause of woman by speaking out on an issue about which they are supposed to be innocent." *The Woman Question*, 2:159. Kingsley, as Leonore Davidoff notes, was "an active sanitary reformer who was constantly preoccupied with personal cleanliness and cold baths." "Class and Gender in Victorian England," in *Sex and Class in Women's History*, ed. Judith L. Newton, Mary P. Ryan, and Judith R. Walkowitz (London: Routledge & Kegan Paul, 1983), 25.

122. Quoted in *The Woman Question*, 159.

123. Mill to George Croom Robertson, 15 November 1871, *LL*, 1854.

124. Mill to George Croom Robertson, 20 September 1871, *LL*, 1835; 15 November 1871, *LL*, 1854.

125. John Stuart Mill, "The Contagious Diseases Acts," *Collected Works*, 21:351–352. Further page references are given in the text.

126. Quoted in *The Woman Question*, 2:161. Shanley is right to argue that Mill, like Butler, "saw in the Contagious Diseases Acts not only a threat to 'fallen women' or those likely to be mistaken as such, but to *all* women, and not only to women on the streets but to those properly married." *Feminism, Marriage, and the Law in Victorian England, 1850–1895* (Princeton: Princeton University Press, 1989), 85. But for Mill, I would add, the threat was also that posed by the prostitute to the middle-class woman.

127. Anderson, "Prostitution's Artful Guise," 108.

128. As William Acton wrote in 1857, "Prostitution is a transitory state, through which an untold number of British women are ever on their passage" to other jobs and to an improved social position. Quoted in *The Woman Question*, 156.

129. "If the object is to protect those who are not unchaste," said Mill, "the way to do that is to bring motives to bear on the man and not on the woman" (354). One such motive would be to allow the wife to dissolve the marriage tie—divorce *a vinculo*.

130. Stallybrass and White, *The Politics and Poetics of Transgression*, 138, my emphasis.

131. Defenders of the acts like Greg saw prostitution as a necessary institution "which acted as a giant sewer, drawing away the distasteful but inevitable waste products of male lustfulness, leaving the middle-class household and middle-class ladies pure and unsullied." Davidoff, "Class and Gender in Victorian England," 19. As Mill remarked in a letter to Lord Amberly, "prostitution seems the only resource to those . . . who look upon the problem to be solved to be, how to allow the greatest license to men consistently with retaining a sufficient reserve or nursery of chaste women for wives." 2 February 1870, *LL*, 1693.

132. Mary Poovey, "Speaking of the Body: Mid-Victorian Constructions of Female Desire," in *Body/Politics: Women and the Discourses of Science*, ed. Mary Jacobus, Evelyn Fox Keller, and Sally Shuttleworth (New York: Routledge, 1990), 37.

133. See Anderson, "Prostitute's Artful Guise," 117. Mill's remarks also reworked the more threatening possibility that, in political-economic parlance, if demand was either steady or on the increase, then, as Nead argues, it was really the prostitute who had, at least to some degree, the power of supply. *Myths of Sexuality*, 99.

134. See Joan Scott, *Gender and the Politics of History* (New York: Columbia University Press, 1988), 146.

135. Anderson, "Prostitution's Artful Guise," 106.

136. Poovey, "Speaking of the Body," 33. Inasmuch as the prostitute threatened a Victorian symbolic economy organized around an aggressive masculinity and a passive femininity, quite a bit was at stake in recasting the carnal magdalen as the innocent magdalen. Natural female virtue could be preserved even in the face of the rampant prostitution industry, the asexual woman as a justification for the separation of spheres, the domestic ideal as the prize for abstinence and thrift.

137. Ibid., 32. The image of the demoralized woman was related as well, as Davidoff writes, to "a hardening of the [moral and social] lines between professional and casual prostitution." "Class and Gender in Victorian England," 20. Among other things, this entailed the separation of different kinds of prostitutes in the workhouses and workhospitals.

138. As Butler told the Royal Commission in 1870, "so long as men are

vicious and women have no employment, this evil [prostitution] will go on."
Quoted in Shanley, *Feminism, Marriage, and the Law*, 86.

139. Stephen Collini, "Introduction" to *Collected Words*, 21:xxxviii.

140. Mill, *Autobiography*, 101. Seeking an alternative to this "paralysing"
feeling, Mill continues: "What is really inspiriting and ennobling in the
doctrine of freewill, is the conviction that we have real power over the
formation of our own character; that our will, by influencing some of our
circumstances, can modify our future habits or capabilities of willing" (102).

141. Ibid.

142. Mill, *Autobiography*, 102.

143. Himmelfarb, *On Liberty and Liberalism*, 181. Himmelfarb's argument is linked to her claim that Mill's feminist case in *On Liberty* had little to
do with "such other matters as the distribution of wealth, . . . the nature of
representative government, [or] the utilitarian foundation of ethics" (206).

144. Mill, *On Liberty*, 15.

5. Resignifying the Woman Question in Political Theory

1. For a closer look at Beauvoir's rhetorical strategy in *The Second Sex*, see
Linda M. G. Zerilli, "'I Am a Woman': Voice and Ambiguity in *The Second
Sex*," *Women and Politics* 11, no. 1 (1991): 93–107, and "A Process without a
Subject: Simone de Beauvoir and Julia Kristeva on Maternity," *Signs: Jour-
nal of Women in Culture and Society* 18 (Autumn 1992): 111–135.

2. The major breakthrough in recent feminist political theory has been
to shift the debate from an exclusive focus on positive or (usually) negative
images of woman (or women) in the Western tradition and to advance instead critical, interrogative rereadings of these images that show the political
exclusion of women to be not incidental to but constitutive of the very
category of the citizen. This shift entailed a complication of feminist critiques in which representations of woman had been read, as Lorenne Clark
and Lynda Lange put it, as little more than "window dressing" over the
social reality of male power. *The Sexism of Social and Political Theory* (Toronto:
University of Toronto Press, 1979), x, xvii. See also Eva Figes, *Patriarchal
Attitudes* (Greenwich, Conn.: Fawcett, 1970); Mary Mahowald, *Philosophy of
Women: Classical to Current Concepts* (Indianapolis: Hacket, 1978); Teresa
Brennan and Carole Pateman, "Mere Auxiliaries to the Commonwealth:
Women and the Origins of Liberalism," *Political Studies* 27, no. 2 (1979): 183–
200. Rather than simply condemn such images, in other words, feminists
began to reflect on how they continue to delineate and delimit the positions

from which women can participate in the public sphere, as well as how the public sphere itself is defined in terms of those positions. See Pateman, "The Public/Private Dichotomy," in *The Disorder of Women: Democracy, Feminism, and Political Theory* (Stanford: Stanford University Press, 1989); Joan Landes, *Women and the Public Sphere in the Age of the French Revolution* (Ithaca: Cornell University Press, 1988), 202. Still, as I argue in detail in this chapter, most feminist political theorists retain the referential model of language, according to which an image is viewed as either true or false.

3. Susan Moller Okin (*Women in Western Political Thought*) and the early work of Pateman (*The Disorder of Women*), for example, sought to prove that women, as Wendy Brown writes, "cannot be added to a theorist's conception of man [or the citizen] without rendering other parts of the theory incoherent." *Manhood and Politics: A Feminist Reading in Political Theory* (Totowa, N.J.: Rowman & Littlefield, 1988), 12. In accordance with this critical approach to the canon, Okin and Pateman treat competing images of women as evidence of a failure of logical coherence, as telling instances of a flawed argument about gender and politics. They are right. Yet they do not take proper account of the symbolic field of meaning, in which the figure of woman is not reducible to matters of logic and argument. Other feminist commentators, including Hanna Pitkin, Brown, and Christine Di Stefano, have approached the canonical texts from a different angle. Rather than treat woman as the site of a failure of logic or argument, they pursue the intimations of this figure as it gives meaning to and unsettles the masculine citizen subject and the space of the political. See Pitkin, *Fortune Is a Woman: Gender and Politics in the Thought of Niccolò Machiavelli* (Berkeley: University of California Press, 1984); Brown, *Manhood and Politics*; Di Stefano, *Configurations of Masculinity: A Feminist Perspective on Modern Political Theory* (Ithaca: Cornell University Press, 1991).

4. For a useful introduction to these critical strategies, see Griselda Pollock, "What's Wrong with Images of Women?" *Screen Education* 24 (Autumn 1977), 25–33; Elizabeth Cowie, "Woman as Sign," in *The Woman in Question*, ed. Parveen Adams and Elizabeth Cowie (Cambridge: MIT Press, 1990), 117–133.

5. I am not arguing that this criterion is useless, but only that it not be used in such a way that it forecloses the important question of the ambiguity of language. As I have said, there are figurative elements to the text that do not meet this criterion yet nevertheless function to generate the symbolic space of political meaning. Here I have found Zillah Eisenstein, *The Female Body and the Law* (Berkeley: University of California Press, 1988), especially useful. Eisenstein does not focus simply on the question of logical contradic-

tions in legal discourse but rather on the symbolic construction of the female body. She redeploys the pregnant body as it has been constituted discursively in terms of sameness/difference to undercut this opposition among others.

6. This is true of the "patriarchal attitudes" approach of Figes, but also, if to a lesser extent, of the "women and reproduction" approach of the authors of *The Sexism of Social and Political Theory*. Likewise, Mary O'Brien's argument that Western political and philosophical thought has been a running commentary on the universal male anxiety about the fiction of paternity and about women's natural connectedness to the species seems to make equally universalistic claims. *The Politics of Reproduction* (Boston: Routledge & Kegan Paul, 1981), 53. The work of Mary Lyndon Shanley offers a sobering alternative to ahistorical readings of the political text. She has advanced our understanding of how definitions of woman (and maternity) are produced in specific social contexts. See especially her *Feminism, Marriage, and the Law in Victorian England, 1850–1895* (Princeton: Princeton University Press, 1989).

7. Consider Okin's argument that women have been defined in functionalist terms throughout history. Although original in its conceptualization, the thesis itself creates a sense that the significant differences among theorists, which Okin herself outlines quite clearly, are not nearly as important as the fact that all have seen women in terms of "what they are for." A similar difficulty arises in, and is symbolized by the title of, Jean Elshtain's *Public Man, Private Woman*. Once again, although Elshtain recognizes that the meaning of the public/private distinction has been historically varied, the very category itself is re-produced through its repeated invocation and association with the man/woman distinction. The problem in both texts is that the category of women is assumed to exist prior to its representation in the political text. The text becomes at best the site of a misrepresentation. Women are not represented as fully human or political beings. And even in Pateman's stunning work, *The Sexual Contract*, the thesis (that male sex-right subtends the social contract) suppresses, finally, the differences among Hobbes, Locke, and Rousseau. Pateman too rightly criticizes the exclusion of women from the making of political meaning, yet she assumes, to some extent, the very category she wants to critique: women. The very act of narrating the "other story" of the sexual contract has the unintended effect of reproducing the story of the social contract as if it were a fairly seamless tale of woman's subjection.

Even as acute a critic as Pateman, who rightly insists that the figure of the disorderly woman is a modern one (*The Disorder of Women*, 17), produces a narrative in which Rousseau and Freud are found to be not very different on the matter of woman's disruptive nature and incapacity for justice. In her lead essay, "The Disorder of Women," the problem, it seems to me, lies in the way Pateman's feminist prose works. She restates the statements made about women in Rousseau and Freud, all of which confirm the modern notion: "Women, it is held, are a source of disorder because their very being, or their nature, is such that it necessarily leads them to exert a disruptive influence in social and political life" (18). We do not see how the texts of Rousseau and Freud construct the disorderly woman, or how unstable that representation is, or how other categories of difference, such as class, figure in it (all the more curious because Pateman is a persistent critic of class relations). Consequently, the disorderly woman is re-produced as a monolithic and stable image.

8. Cowie, "Woman as Sign," 18.

9. Ibid.

10. As Beverly Thiele puts it, "what is missing from social and political theory is, to use Clark and Lange's phrase, women qua women." Once again, the monolith of "male-stream" thought is re-produced in the feminist account: "It is common knowledge among feminists that social and political theory was, and for the most part still is, written by men, for men and about men." "Vanishing Acts in Social and Political Thought: Tricks of the Trade," in *Feminist Challenges: Social and Political Theory*, ed. Pateman and Elizabeth Gross (Boston: Northeastern University Press, 1986), 30.

11. On this point, see Parveen Adams, who argues that feminists ought to advance "an alternative position where what is represented must be considered to be an effect of the action of the means of representation." "A Note on the Distinction between Sexual Division and Sexual Differences," in *The Woman in Question*, 106; Paul Hirst, "Althusser and the Theory of Ideology," *Economy and Society* 5, no. 4 (1976): 385–412.

12. Hayden White, *The Tropics of Discourse: Essays in Cultural Criticism* (Baltimore: Johns Hopkins University Press, 1978), 5.

13. John Locke, *An Essay Concerning Human Understanding*, ed. Peter H. Nidditch (Oxford: Clarendon Press, 1975), 444 (3.6.9). Woman (or women) is such a name; it is not a real but rather a nominal essence that "the Mind makes" (3.6.11). What is in a name according to Locke? Everything as far as human knowledge is concerned, including the meaning of the real essence which is itself a name, a nominal essence. Locke did not attend to the instability of the nominal essence; that is he did not claim, as Saussure would, that every term is constructed negatively through differences or, as Derrida later would, that those differences are so infinite that meaning itself

is a constant deferral of meaning. Nor did he advance a theory of language as constitutive of the subject. But Locke did show that the sign stands in a perfectly arbitrary relation to the referent, and that the referent is figured by the sign. He showed, in other words, that whatever we claim to know of real essences is nothing, we know only the nominal essences we create through language. Although limited by the empiricist understanding of language as naming, Locke's insight provides the basis from which one can examine the production of the illusion of referential knowledge in the political text and challenge the classical model of representation that assumes the transparency of language and thus the natural link between the referent and the sign, the world and the word.

14. Jacques Derrida, *Of Grammatology*, trans. Gayatri Chakravorty Spivak (Baltimore: Johns Hopkins University Press, 1976), 73.

15. Teresa de Lauretis, *Alice Doesn't: Feminism, Semiotics, Cinema* (Bloomington: Indiana University Press, 1984), 6. I take this to be de Lauretis's point when she writes that women "cannot as yet be defined outside of those discursive formations [which have produced woman]" (5).

16. Here I must take issue with what appears to be an implicit acceptance of the categories of men and women (male and female) in many feminist readings of the canon. Arlene Saxonhouse argues "the theoretical importance of recognizing the differences between the sexes and the need for a self-conscious understanding of the implications of such a division in the human species." Intimating that sexual difference is not only social but biological, she condemns liberal theorists for ignoring it, admires the ancients for taking account of it, and thus uncritically re-produces it as the ontological ground of politics. *Women in the History of Political Thought: Ancient Greece to Machiavelli* (New York: Praeger, 1975), 16. See also Moira Gatens, "A Critique of the Sex/Gender Distinction," in *Beyond Marxism? Interventions after Marx*, ed. Judith Allen and Paul Patton (Sydney: Intervention Publications, 1983), 143–63. A related problem is evident in Elshtain's *Public Man, Private Woman*, which retains women as women to protect the family against the state, against radical feminists, and against androgyny. Okin, who is intensely critical of biologism in political theory, concludes *Women in Western Political Thought* by saying that women "cannot become equal citizens . . . until the functionalist perception of their sex is dead" (304). But the problem, as Monique Wittig has argued, is not simply a functionalist conception of (the female) sex; it is the very category of sex, the very idea of "the female." See Monique Wittig, "One Is Not Born a Woman," *Feminist Issues* 1, no. 2 (1981): 47–68, and "The Straight Mind," *Feminist Issues* 1, no. 2 (1980): 103–11.

17. Cora Kaplan, "Pandora's Box: Subjectivity, Class, and Sexuality in Socialist Feminist Criticism," in *Sea Changes: Culture and Feminism* (London: Verso Press, 1986), 149. A similar point is made by Adams, "Distinction between Sexual Division and Sexual Differences," 108.

18. Joan Scott's recent work is especially insightful on these issues. *Gender and the Politics of History* (New York: Columbia University Press, 1988). See also Denise Riley, *Am I That Name?: Feminism and the Category of 'Women' in History* (Minneapolis: University of Minnesota Press, 1988).

19. Here I have found the work of Michel Foucault and Thomas Laqueur important. Foucault, *The History of Sexuality*, vol. 1: *An Introduction*, trans. Robert Hurley (New York: Vintage, 1980). Thomas Laqueur, *Making Sex: Body and Gender from the Greeks to Freud* (Cambridge: Harvard University Press, 1990).

20. Simone de Beauvoir, *The Second Sex*, ed. and trans. H. M. Parshley (New York: Vintage, 1974), xvi.

21. Julia Kristeva, *Powers of Horror: An Essay on Abjection*, trans. Leon S. Roudiez (New York: Columbia University Press, 1982), 65.

22. I borrow the phrase "screen woman" from Shoshana Felman, "Rereading Femininity," *Yale French Studies*, no. 62 (1981): 19–44, 29. The modern reader cannot reject this figure of woman as "sexist" yet retain other aspects of the theory if woman is the ground of political meaning. I am not trying to prove that woman cannot be added to canonical conceptions of the political. Nor am I calling for a wholesale rejection of the theories examined in this study (although I am tempted in the case of Burke). My objective, rather, is to bring out certain contradictions and ambivalences within the Western tradition and, especially, to advance a more nuanced reading that attends to the symbolic borderland of the classic texts and thus to woman as a central because marginal figure in political theory.

23. I have in mind here the following works, which have done much to highlight how the concern for order in political theory produces an other who must then be disciplined by the community. See William Corlett, *Community without Unity: A Politics of Derridean Extravagance* (Durham, N.C.: Duke University Press, 1989); William E. Connolly, *Identity\Difference: Democratic Negotiations of Political Paradox* (Ithaca: Cornell University Press, 1991); Bonnie Honig, *Political Theory and the Displacement of Politics* (Ithaca: Cornell University Press, 1993); Anne Norton, *Reflections on Political Identity* (Baltimore: Johns Hopkins University Press, 1988).

24. Kathy E. Ferguson, *The Man Question: Visions of Subjectivity in Feminist Theory* (Berkeley: University of California Press), 1993.

Index

158n, 164n, 173n, 174n, 186n, 203n, 204n, 206n
Owen, Robert, 100, 101, 104, 189n

Paine, Thomas, 61, 76
Parker, Patricia, 170n
Pateman, Carole, 11, 25, 155n, 156n, 157n, 158n, 159n, 161n, 166n, 167n, 174n, 176n, 202n, 203n, 204n
Paulson, Ronald, 62
Perkin, Harold, 183n
Pitkin, Hanna, 155n, 203n
Pocock, J. G. A., 78, 84, 178n
political theorist: psychobiographical accounts of, 8, 12, 145, 194n–195n; as subject in process/on trial, 12; as writing subject, 2, 8, 11, 12, 62, 63, 74, 76, 83, 85, 89, 93, 142, 150, 163n
political theory: and authorial intention, 8, 12, 74–75, 149; and language, 3, 4, 7, 15, 22, 61, 141, 142, 143, 179n; masculinist, 138, 148, 151, 153, 158n; performative, 4, 62, 143, 147; producing meaning, 4, 7, 14, 74, 140, 141, 144, 147, 151, 152; rhetorical, 3, 4, 5, 7, 61; as signifying practice, 2, 3, 4, 8, 139–142, 146, 147; as tradition of discourse, 6, 13, 138, 141, 142, 148, 151
Pollock, Griselda, 203n
Poovey, Mary, 132, 133, 193n, 194n, 197n, 201n
Price, Reverend Dr. Richard, 73, 74, 87, 90
property: and abyss, 8; and body, 14, 80, 84, 110; inequality, 55, 77, 99, 100; landed, 55, 61–62, 77–80, 91; monied, 77, 80; private, 100; semiotics of, 77; and wage labor, 99, 100, 112, 115, 134; women's, 112, 122, 134, 197n
public sphere: feminized, 34, 116, 129; masculinist, 1, 2, 6, 56, 57, 84, 128, 137, 140, 143, 152; as spectacle, 28, 37–38, 155n–157n; woman in, 37, 63, 82, 83, 98, 111, 122, 123, 137, 144

Riley, Denise, 124, 197n
Ring, Jennifer, 186n
Robson, John, 200n
Rose, H. J., 68, 81, 179n
Rousseau, Jean-Jacques, 2, 5, 7, 8, 13–59, 139, 142, 143, 148–152; abjection, 43, 44, 47, 57, 152; abyss, 7, 8, 19, 21, 22, 26, 32, 34, 43, 44, 51, 58, 165n; citizen-

ship, 18, 164n; class, 19, 46, 55, 150; Confessions, 45, 46, 50; Discourse on the Origin and Foundations of Inequality among Men (Second Discourse), 19–22, 27–29, 42, 50; Discourse on the Sciences and Arts (First Discourse), 20; disorderly woman, 16, 18–19, 148; Emile, 30–32, 39–50, 54, 170n, 171n, 172n, 173n, 174n; Essay on the Origin of Languages, 22–26, 30, 38, 52; exhibitionism, 28, 29, 46; female spectacle, 16, 34, 37; female voice, 30–31, 34, 39, 41; femininity, 16, 18, 21, 39, 45–47, 50, 58, 59; festival, 24–26, 167n; fetishism, 45, 47, 171n; gender inversion, 16, 17, 32, 35, 40, 48, 169n; Geneva manuscript, 50–53, 57, 58 (see also Rousseau, Jean-Jacques: Social Contract); Government of Poland, 53–56; Great Masculine Renunciation, 29–30, 45, 46, 56, 58; Hottentot, 19–20, 29; imagination, 17, 21, 32–33, 39, 42, 44, 47, 48, 170n; incest, 23–27, 167n; language, 20, 22–25, 31, 34, 42, 54; law, 18, 21, 25–27, 29, 36, 46, 50–54, 56; lawgiver, 51, 52–54; Letter to D'Alembert, 16, 30–38, 47, 147; luxury, 20, 31, 32, 36, 49, 56, 57; masculinity, 16–19, 27, 28, 31, 32, 37, 39, 42, 47, 54–55, 58, 177n; masochism, 17, 32, 35, 40, 48, 163n; masterful mistress, 17, 43, 50, 163n; maternal, 19–22, 24, 29, 38–40, 41, 43, 52–54; maternal voice, 19–25, 30, 41, 43, 52, 164n, 165n; money, 57–58; Moses, 53, 54; narcissism, 28, 29, 43, 45, 170n; nature, 16–18, 20–26, 33, 34, 42, 51–53, 57, 165n, 166n; perversion, 17, 18, 31–33, 44; salonnière, 31, 37, 165n; sartorial display, 18, 29–32, 36, 45–46, 48, 54–55, 58, 164n, 171n, 173n–174n; self-adornment, 28, 29, 36–38, 45, 46, 48, 54–56, 171n, 174n; sexual difference, 18, 23, 27; signified, 20, 23, 26, 27, 34, 39, 41; signifier, 23, 26, 27, 30, 31, 34, 36–37, 39, 41, 47; Signs, 22, 31, 175n; social contract, 19, 49; Social Contract, 50–53, 57, 58; Sophie, 42, 45–50, 150, 169n, 172n; spectacle, 16, 32, 34, 36–38, 48, 54–56; theater, 16–18, 25, 30–36, 38, 41, 56, 169n; Tribe of Benjamin, 175n–176n; Ulysses, 43, 44, 48, 51; veil, 21, 22, 24, 26, 33, 44, 47, 165n; wet-nursing, 40, 169n–170n